MW01120368

GONE FISHIN'

Mary & Donny
Merry Christmas 1999!

Heaps of love,
Sue Pete Tyler
and Mitchell

Dedication

For James

May The Ocean Of Life Provide Smooth Passage
And Safe Harbours

G

GONE FISHIN'

Graeme Sinclair

The Halcyon Press

Published by

The Halcyon Press.

A division of

Halcyon Publishing Ltd.

P.O. Box 360, Auckland, New Zealand.

Printed through
Colorcraft Ltd
Hong Kong
Typeset by
KLM Type
Cover by
Lorraine Still

No part of this publication may be reproduced, stored in a retrieval
system or transmitted in any form or by any means, electronic,
mechanical, photocopy, recording or otherwise without prior written
permission of the publisher.

ISBN 0-908685-74-2
Copyright © 1999 Graeme Sinclair
First Published 1999
Reprinted 1999
All Rights Reserved

Contents

Sponsor List

Special mention should go to our current list of sponsors.
Without them there would be no *Gone Fishin'*.

Exide Batteries
Air New Zealand
Black Magic & Wasabi Tackle
Club Marine
CRC
Furuno
Gulf Star Products
Holden New Zealand
Lion Breweries
Mercury Outboards
New Zealand Fishing News
Pro Dive
Rayglass Boats
R.F.D.
Thompson Walker Ltd (Penn Fishing Tackle)
Kawasaki

Introduction

Welcome to part of the *Gone Fishin'* story, the big game fishing, trout and salmon I have reserved for a future volume.

Many of the people who have been of major support are mentioned in the following pages and to you I just want to say thanks.

I have also included a page which lists the current sponsors and it is those people and associated products who assure that *Gone Fishin'* continues to evolve.

Please take note of who they are and if any products are relevant to you, please give the people who support your fishing show the loyalty they deserve.

Thanks also to the team at TV3 Network for having the wisdom to recognise that the worlds largest participation sport deserves television time.

To the people who so religiously watch *Gone Fishin'* and provide invaluable feedback – thanks a million, your dedication translates as ratings and ratings keep the show going.

Finally, as you read through these stories be aware that a few people mentioned are no longer with us.

Ray Tinsley – friend, explorer, author and character died from complications after a heart attack in the Fiordland bush. Kevin Anderson was drowned in a boating accident and Fiordland helicopter pilot, Trevor Green was killed in a crash near Lake Hauroko earlier this year.

None of us are immortal, battling a disease like Multiple Sclerosis has made me well aware of that but outdoor New Zealand has the ability to enrich your life.

Ray, Kevin and Trevor never took a day for granted or failed to appreciate the sheer beauty of our magnificent country.

If you have a dream, chase it, if you feel sorry for yourself, open your eyes and look around, it will lift your spirit.

Thanks for being part of *Gone Fishin'* and I hope you enjoy the yarn.

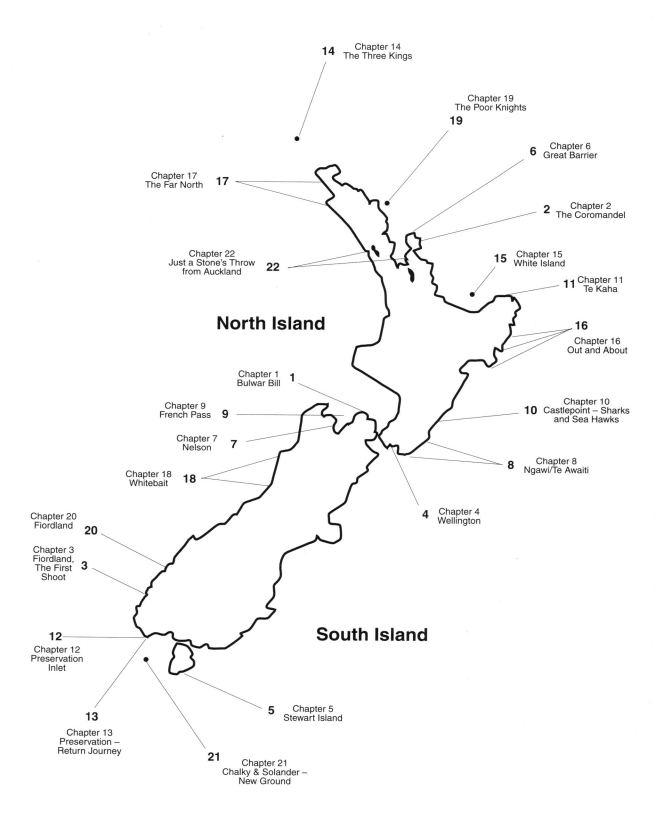

14 Chapter 14
The Three Kings

Chapter 19
The Poor Knights
19

6 Chapter 6
Great Barrier

Chapter 17 **17**
The Far North

2 Chapter 2
The Coromandel

Chapter 22
Just a Stone's Throw   **22**
from Auckland

15 Chapter 15
White Island

11 Chapter 11
Te Kaha

North Island

16
Chapter 16
Out and About

Chapter 1 **1**
Bulwar Bill

Chapter 9 **9**
French Pass

10 Chapter 10
Castlepoint – Sharks
and Sea Hawks

Chapter 7 **7**
Nelson

Chapter 18 **18**
Whitebait

8 Chapter 8
Ngawi/Te Awaiti

4 Chapter 4
Wellington

Chapter 20 **20**
Fiordland

Chapter 3 **3**
Fiordland,
The First
Shoot

South Island

12
Chapter 12
Preservation
Inlet

13
Chapter 13
Preservation –
Return Journey

5 Chapter 5
Stewart Island

21
Chapter 21
Chalky & Solander –
New Ground

1
Bulwer Bill

The first, the very first time we filmed *Gone Fishin'*, was in the Marlborough Sounds. It was a location chosen because as far as fishing goes, it's a dead cert. In the Sounds at the very least, you will catch blue cod and at best snapper, kingfish, groper, trumpeter and a host of other denizens that were very appropriate to a fishing television series.

I had visited Bulwer some years earlier when I was writing for *New Zealand Fishing News* and was overwhelmed by Bill and Audrey Fords' hospitality, the beauty of the location and the ease with which you could slip out to dive and fish places like the Chetwode Islands. We loaded our stuff into an old Beaver float plane.

"She's an old top dresser", said Garth the pilot. "Someone decided to stick floats under it. In Canada, Beaver float planes are a way of life, strong, reliable and even when loaded to the gunwales, she'll still take off. No worries."

Judging by the look on his face, pilots do indeed have a love affair with their flying machines. "She" was certainly one of Garth's favourite girls.

The forecast was NW 20 knots increasing to 45, the wind was clearly funneling through Cook Strait and the Beaver would become a roller coaster.

Several of the crew jammed themselves into a second plane and in the end director, producer, cameraman, sound man, dubious inexperienced "talent" and one of the sponsors began a flight from Porirua in the North Island to Bulwer in the South surrounded by a tonne of gear.

Once we bounced and thumped our way near the Sounds you could see the wind, because it left its signature in the white whirlwinds and plumes of water that peeled off the surface and screamed across the bays.

Glen Peek offers to help Tony Burrows (the sound man) with his sea sickness.

They are a beautiful sight, the Sounds on such a day, the green/blue of the bays, the white horses charging through Cook Strait and eddying around the bays. Those characteristic hills, occasional farmland and forestry surrounded by scrub and bush. Every shade of green and brown, yellow, blue and grey, topped with a threatening blanket of ominous dark cloud that spilled over the hills and filled the valleys. It was an exciting journey to begin our first shoot. The Beaver roared and lurched its way down towards the surface of Bulwer Bay, snuck beneath the turbulence and landed under the hills on the smooth surface of the sheltered bay. It was like an oasis in the storm and the first fish ever caught for *Gone Fishin'* was a blue cod landed while perched on the floats of the trusty Beaver. In fact the cod came in pretty thick and fast. Bill and Audrey greeted us like family, the planes set off on their roller coaster return home and we stowed our gear. The view from the Fords' home and accommodation is straight out over the bay and as we crowded in for dinner, darkness put a dimmer on the view and the weather started to scream and howl with true passion.

Even in our festive mood, playing pool, laughing and joking, smells of cooking filling the house, windows steaming, I could still hear the squalls barrelling down the valley. Isolated pockets of wind develop a mind of their own in a NW storm and shriek and roar through an otherwise sheltered bay, tearing and ripping at the scrub before slamming into the house. It is good to feel warm and safe and then particularly well fed. Audrey is one of those special people who can cook a banquet for an army in the blink of any eye.

Our first meal on a *Gone Fishin'* trek set the tone for future excursions − fresh blue cod, smoked salmon (from the farm out in the bay), paua and homemade apple pie. We slumped into bed, listened to the wind and contemplated the challenge of our first full day.

A day called tomorrow with a forecast of 50 knots NW.

We were up before daylight checking camera equipment and dive gear. The main camera was an old thing that should have been retired. Our budget wasn't quite big enough during series one, we had too many people on the payroll and learning was all about jumping in the deep end and having a go. This was seat of the pants television and the one thing we should never have compromised on was gear, especially the camera. No point in being in a great location if you can't record the images and sure enough, we had camera problems. Paul Richards and Mike Bhana found the right electronic band aid and we eventually piled into Bill's launch − at that time it was *Rico Rico* − and headed off through the squalls to the Chetwode Islands.

Bulwer is at the mouth of Pelorous Sound and the Chetwodes are a stone's throw out into Cook Strait. On that day, 5th October 1993, we were thankful of a large chunk of lee shore which usually means a bit of shelter somewhere no matter how hard the wind screams on an island, usually means a bit of shelter somewhere.

The Sound and the island's name were derived from *H M Brig Pelorous* under the command of Lieutenant Chetwode, which made a patrol of the Cook Strait whaling stations in 1838.

John Guard, the well known whaler at Port Underwood, reported to Chetwode the existence of a passage between Queen Charlotte

All that gear and one little itty bitty plane. Well it gave the pilot a laugh and necessitated two trips.

Sound and Admiralty Bay and piloted the warship through the Sound that bears its name.

"Not the best spot," said Bill when we tucked in behind the islands, "but at least your cameraman won't get blown over the side."

Bill's hands are those of a farmer, a man who has toughed it out on the land and sea for many years. His fingers are tough, gnarly and scarred and looked clumsy as he tied the long-shanked cod hooks to the line.

Blue cod are superb to eat and easy to catch. There are still good pockets to be caught in the Sounds but traditionally charters went out to take as much cod as the supposed anglers could catch. In New Zealand we are fortunately growing out of an attitude totally focused on meat hunting. I decided then and there that the attitude we would promote on *Gone Fishin'* would be one that translated as "take enough for a feed and put the rest back".

If we all did that then our children would be in a position to share a healthy fishery. Commercial restrictions through controls, such as the quota management and recreational guidelines apportioned in catch limits, are a very sensible management technique and while they are not perfect, they are a solid attempt to invest in the fisheries' future. You can do your bit by sticking to the limits.

Long-shanked hooks are very useful for cod. I have often dived and watched the voracious cod inhale the bait, it's as though every morsel is going to be their last feed. They suck it right down the hatch and as a consequence are usually hooked way down their throat. Long-shanked hooks make them easier to get off and mean less damage if you are dealing with undersize fish.

We hauled the cod in two at a time, generally two small fish that had to be released but every now and then something worthwhile for the larder. Bait took the form of barracuda or chunks of perch, good hardy bait that doesn't disintegrate too readily and invariably we landed three or four fish before needing to replace a bait.

The points and reefs near the islands were our target, the areas that traditionally hold fish, set up a food chain, have a bit of current whizzing by and send you home with dinner.

Mike and I dived on one of "Bill's spots", he has a very large number of wee spots that he never fishes or dives too hard and sure enough we had no trouble getting a few crays for the next banquet. After the underwater camera leaked and the wind picked up another 10 knots we decided to call it a day and head back for more equipment repairs.

The team had set off on the shoot imagining beautiful weather and no technical problems. The reality was a bloody storm and a procession of malfunctions. My diary entry read "Ho hum, tomorrow's another day".

During the evening we piled into Bill's Patrol and followed a goat track round the side of the hill and on to a saddle where we could look down towards D'Urville Island and French Pass. The Pass was sheet white, chunks of ocean swirling about and roaring up into the scrub. It looked spectacular as we sat on the exposed saddle, the Patrol rocking and shuddering against the wind, the tussock and scrub flattened against the hills.

We turned away from nature's little performance and threaded our way back to the homestead and the salmon, cod, paua steaks, crayfish and scallops – another notch slid off the belt buckle.

As we had consumed a fair amount of salmon, our first stop next morning was the salmon farm.

The pens are just nets, one holding the fish and a second outer net designed to keep predators, such as barracuda, at bay.

"Had a 'couda in the pen the other day," commented Dave, the farm spokesman. "Once he was in he didn't do anything, just sat there confused by the sheer numbers of salmon going round and round and round."

As Dave and I chatted, I noticed odd fish leaping in the air and splashing around. "They're happy fish," he said. "They're like dogs, when they feel frisky they start to play."

I came away from that one just a little sceptical – after all, I don't meet many happy fish. Maybe we'd have a better relationship if I stopped dropping·them in a frying pan.

The whole team transferred to Glen and Neil Peaks' charter vessel *Miss Akaroa*. After a dive in a pen loaded with 20,000 salmon, I could see why the hapless barracuda was confused. 20,000 circling salmon is an awesome sight.

We steamed out of the bay in conditions that were still pretty woolly, but the wind was down to 30 knots and we had a crayfish dive to film with the overhauled underwater unit.

Bill had a special spot and I have always prided myself on my ability to pluck a feed of crayfish.

"You boys better head off that way," said our host, "and I'll go and have a bit of a look back there. Not usually so good over there," he said, stabbing a gnarly finger in the direction of some interesting-looking country.

Mike and I were over the side in a flash, Mike to film and me to grab a few of the dozens of huge crays we expected to see lining the crevices.

We scoured the place, grabbed a couple of legal but not large crays and spent a bit of time in the very cold 12° water looking at a specimen about 4kg that was just out of reach.

It was great country, large boulders and guts to glide in and around, a blanket of kelp near the surface and hundreds of cod, spotties and perch following us around like a flock of sheep.

Mike and I arrived back on deck before Bill and filmed our return, complete with the limited dinner contribution.

The wind had buttoned back to about 20 knots and patches of blue squeezed their way between the scudding clouds. Gulls wheeled off the point and cruised in for a screeching inspection of *Miss Akaroa*'s deck. A dozen or so sooty shearwaters sat patiently on the ocean also waiting to pick up any discarded morsel. We had just changed out of our wet-suits when the local hunter returned. The catch bag was bulging, not with a large number of crays, but with a couple of real beauties. Bill's lopsided all knowing grin said it all.

There is no substitute for local knowledge.

We were home a couple of hours before dark and Mike, Tony (the soundman) and I decided to climb the hill behind the house in the hope of spotting one of the wild pigs that had been ripping in to a nearby gully. Pigs plough up a fair chunk of turf when they get going and this mob had churned up the ground in a fern-filled gully beside the track.

Bill had loaned me his 243 so we were in a great position to add some very flavoursome wild pork to the larder.

"We're still early," I said to the boys after glassing the pig rooting with binoculars. "Let's check out the view from the top and drop back in on them later."

"Why don't we just sit here," said Mike, but Tony and I managed to get him to waddle, heave and wheeze his way up the slope to take in the magnificent view of Cook Strait and Pelorous Sound.

The three of us sat on the hill-top that evening as the cloud peeled away and the blue turned to orange, red and gold. Nature was painting her canvas with warmth and promise, but in the morning we were due to leave. As the sunset lit the remaining cloud, we dropped back down to our meeting with the pigs and when still some distance away, the sound of grunting and squealing that means porkers in residence, drifted out of the gully.

Stalking in on all of that noise does wonders for the adrenalin and we were like three excited kids out on some great adventure.

The wind was still drawing patterns in the tussock and gusts swirled about, one gust the wrong way and the pigs would be gone, but luck was on our side as we stalked ever closer.

We sat on the edge of the track looking down at the ferns that shook and twitched as a couple of sizable pigs ploughed up dinner. Our vantage point was so close that we could hear them breathing and chewing, but apart from an occasional very fleeting glimpse, I couldn't get a shot.

The longer we sat there the less inclined I felt to disturb the scene. It was a beautiful evening and I felt privileged to be there, so why disturb it? That feeling of being in a position of privilege is one I have felt often on subsequent trips. After a while, just capturing the beauty of our country on camera is reward enough and quite often I choose to walk away from a deer, pig or fish that I have surprised going about its business.

With the last of the light and nothing to lose, we snuck down the track another 30 metres for a better look up the gully. Just as we were about to leave, I turned for one last look and a rather large pig shambled out and stood in the clear. I closed the bolt, took a bead and muttered "bang" to myself before ejecting the round and leaving everyone in the gully to go about their business.

We could smell Audrey's cooking before we got to the house and

The Bulwer and Miss Akaroa team pose for the camera. Hospitality at its best.

hear the laughter and clunk of pool balls. There was a chill in the air as the birds sang their late evening chorus and the wind had dropped to a faint whisper. What a day, beaten on the crayfish hunt, abused for not having any pork and thrashed on the pool table. I think that all of us knew that the real reward was in just being there and we were pleased to have almost completed the first *Gone Fishin'* "shoot".

Dinner was compliments of Audrey and Glen and for the record was made up of crayfish, cod, scallops, vegetables and pavlova (burp!).

Next morning a quick trip to the salmon farm for some takeaways and then a lesson from Bill on how to smoke salmon.

Here's his secret recipe for a hot smoke in one of those Kilwell smokers you can buy in a sports shop.

Split the fish and take out the backbone, salt it and let it sit for 12 hours. Then the secret ingredient, a very useful addition that should be in every angling chef's tucker box – lemon pepper. Bill adds it just before lighting up and 20 minutes later voila! Beautiful succulent smoked salmon. The recipe and secret ingredient works for almost all fish but it doesn't hurt to experiment and find your own magic touch.

The first series of *Gone Fishin'* was scheduled for 13 episodes and TVNZ was far from supportive of its future. Underfunded and inexperienced, we had still knocked off our first expedition. We felt pretty good about it but who would have guessed that this was only chapter one in a story that could now fill several volumes. If you have a dream the answer is to chase it, not listen to the critics but find like-minded supportive people and climb into it. Dreams can indeed become reality.

2

The Coromandel

Just one and a half hours' drive from Auckland you enter the wonderful playground of the Coromandel Peninsula. The township named Coromandel on the western side of the peninsula received its name on 12th June 1820. On 30th May, *HMS Coromandel*, then tender or storeship of *HMS Dromedary*, sailed into the Bay of Islands and left again on the 7th bound for "River Thames", as the whole of the Hauraki Gulf was then known. The visit was made for the purpose of taking aboard kauri spars which were in demand in the navy. The timber and mineral wealth has seen a number of 'booms' come and go, timber, gold, silver, rich strikes and large fortunes. Today much of the wealth is seen as the natural beauty of this idyllic part of our country and few people know the area as well as tour guide Doug Johannsen. We joined Doug on a day when the wind screamed and howled its way down the coast and put paid to any remote notion of heading off for a fish.

Our initial excursion was to the location of the Broken Ridge mine. Ten million dollars worth of gold was hauled out of the rugged scrub-covered hills at a time when $10,000,000 really meant something.

"The best Coromandel quartz was actually 30% gold," said Doug, "one of the best yields in the world."

His voice was an echo in the decayed-looking tunnel that we stooped our way into. The crew and I shuffled our way into the darkness, torches stabbing a beam against the walls that carried the pick marks of the miners. It was a chilly, eerie sort of place and when we switched the torches off at Doug's request, the darkness was so intense you could feel it like a weight on your shoulder. Doug's a bit of a practical joker and when the torches came on he lit up the roof.

"What do you think of these little beauties", he said, his beam illuminating a roof covered in wetas – hundreds of the darn things.

While our combined torches highlighted his unpleasant little mates, Paul tried to film the action.

It was then that Doug went to work with the little stick he carried, just to scare the living daylights out of some unsuspecting soul.

Tony, the soundman, was the target and as Tony stared intently at the wetas, Doug dragged his stick across the back of Tony's neck.

A blood curdling scream echoed through the tunnel and had us wondering what the hell was happening. Mr bloody comedian, the tour guide, had convinced Tony that a weta had shot right down his neck. Complete mayhem was the result but it was a great trick and as well as getting our share of history lessons, that day we learnt a couple of nasty little pranks. Doug is great company, well worth spending some time with when the ocean dances to a tempest, but beware of the tricks.

When *Gone Fishin'* first started we anticipated filming a serious sort of fishing show, but weather like that nasty brew on the Coromandel soon had us doing all sorts of things. You learn very quickly that you can't script the weather and you can't rely on the fish.

I decided that local characters, scenery and pieces of history were a real bonus, not everyone's cup of tea if you want to learn to tie knots and catch a steady procession of fish but much better than sitting on your bum hoping that the weather will improve enough to venture onto the briny.

Gone Fishin' soon became a lifestyle/entertainment fishing show with fishing being central to the theme, but all sorts of other things spinning off it. Maybe the variety is the reason why the show enjoys the popularity that it does.

Next day, 14th October, we loaded up the charter vessel *Whai*, skippered by Mick Ellwood.

It always makes me laugh when people first come to terms with all of the essential junk that a television crew carts around the country.

"We're only going out for the bloody day," said Mick, when we started transforming the *Whai* into a barge.

The *Whai* creaked and groaned her protest against the Whitianga wharf. What a beautiful place Whitianga is, a graceful, sweeping bay, an estuary that has become home to a marina for charter vessels and pleasure craft. The old game fishing club is one of those places that carries the stains, wear and faded photos that ooze fishing history.

People are friendly and why shouldn't they be, when a finger of farmland snakes its way down to the bay and on all sides are beautiful bush-covered hills with holiday homes and permanent residences peeking out on a view of bays and islands, diving and fishing. The air smells alternately of the land or sea depending on which way the wind blows, the gulls scream for a feed and the atmosphere is one of peace.

That is until you try and load Mick Ellwood's vessel up with too much camera gear.

She's an old cat, the *Whai*, twin steel hulls and enough power to call the pace sedate but she's seen more fish land on the deck than I'll view in my lifetime.

Anglers have a strong belief in luck, lucky hats, shirts, food, bait, lures, rods, reels, friends, boats, skippers – you name it – an angler has more excuses tucked away for bad days than you could ever imagine and more lucky answers for a good day than seems credible.

The old *Whai* was being put to the test and well out in the bay we cruised amongst a flock of diving, wheeling, magnificent gannets.

What superb birds and excellent anglers as they launch their aerial attack on balled-up, bait fish. So much of fishing success relates to a food chain where small fish are predated on by progressively larger beasties. The gannets and other seabirds hate to be left out of the equation and are classic indicators of where one might best target a feed. Those beautiful white and black birds with the painted yellow head and beady eyes, that even after free falling from great height into a frenzy of fish, never seem to have a feather out of place. They seem to be the perfect feathered angler and a great partner in the quest for superb fishing.

That day they led us straight in to the action. Out came the jigs, down in to the blue/green depths and wallop, instant hook up.

Pete Lamb with the sort of Kingfish to be secured around the Coromandel.

I never tire of the elation that comes with feeling the weight come on as you hook up and watch as the rod curves in to another fishing adventure. It is a great feeling. The tape rolled, camera and sound were set and we found ourselves filming the show's first barracuda frenzy. Barracuda, great bait, long silver tackle-eaters whose teeth make mincemeat of gear and turn monofilament line into dental floss. Jigs afford some protection because they are long and slender like a small bait fish with hooks at the bottom. The main body of the jig is chrome or painted lead so the 'couda hopefully bite the hooks or the metal body. They are voracious predators and if you hook other fish the 'couda are quick to identify a potential meal and usually zoom in and take everything except the head. Bang, thud, gone. You may as well pull your gear out of the water and go somewhere else.

That somewhere else turned out to be Cobra Reef near Red Mercury Island but our green/blue ocean was painted in streamers of white when we got there. Thirty knots had been the delightful, accommodating forecast and here it was screaming in as a procession of trevally and snapper hit the deck. One lone kingfish sacrificed itself to the cause, and the bait, the lucky bait of the day was sanma, a good oily bait fish cut into three and threaded on to a hook any old how. It pays to drag along a variety of bait and be prepared to experiment. My absolute favourite for snapper is the pilchard and it's one of the few dead baits that kingfish will take. There have been days when the target species turns its nose up at pilchards and you need to try something else such as sanma, bonito, mullet or another favourite, baby squid. Pilchards are also very soft so something a bit firmer is always handy to lug along. There were enough fish for a feed so we pulled the "pick" and with the ever increasing green and white seas rolling under our stern, headed for the sanctuary of Whitianga.

The old *Whai* rode the swells with dignity, the ocean just rolled on under the hull with an impatient hiss. Halfway home a pod of dolphins materialised out of the gloom, the scudding clouds and occasional showers had thrown a leaden sheen on the ocean, it was no longer a friendly place to be. The dolphins changed that, they are like companions that add comfort to any ocean journey and always possess a cheerful entertaining disposition. Swells had built up to about two metres and as the grey/green crest approached the hull, our friends darted along the face and nudged each other for a prime riding position on the bow. Dolphins are to me, ocean ambassadors, communicating all that is good and clean and fresh about a world that we have traditionally raped. No matter what we do, dolphins always seem to remain our friends, tolerant of our excesses and quick to show us how to enjoy a day on the ocean. I have dived with them in mid-ocean on days when it is so calm that spears of light stab their way into depths that are so clear as to make the ocean seem the colour of blue/black ink. At times the visibility must be 60 metres and I have been surrounded by hundreds of ducking, weaving, diving

Coromandel land based –
Prepare for the hard slog.

dolphins dancing their way into my memory. At other times we have leapt into 3-5 metres of clarity and only seen them at the last second when they race in out of the murk and suddenly appear within centimetres of my face. The great thing about being in the water with dolphins is that I have only ever felt completely comfortable, never ever threatened. A quick swim with our friends was a great way to finish a cruise on the *Whai*.

Next day, 15th October, the weather didn't let up and a hasty phone call had us changing plans and arranging to meet Kevin Darlow in Whangapoua for a land-based fish.

Whangapoua is fringed by one of the most beautiful beaches on the Coromandel but it is hard to choose when names like Hot Water Beach, Hahei, Cathedral Cove, Pauanui, Opito Bay and countless others on the east coast look like someone's dream beach in a glossy tourist magazine. Some of those beaches offer a walk in solitude along a vast strip of yellow sand, others the privacy of a small bay and all a place of real beauty.

In December and January, holidays mean more people but at all times, the Coromandel is an oasis away from hustle and bustle where the ocean playground is enhanced by clear rivers with deep swimming holes and walks in the bush or into mining or logging history such as that which is Doug's forte. Hills, bush, beaches, rivers, a friendly, small scattered population of people and a myriad of islands and bays make the Coromandel a wonderful place to get lost in.

On Whangapoua Beach the sand is so fine it squeaks between your toes, it is talcum powder and it drops away into a crystal clear bay.

I could still see the white water where the wind caught up with the ocean offshore but we were tucked under the shelter of the hills and it was the scudding, white fluffy clouds hurtling along in an otherwise blue sky that made us appreciate the strength of the offshore breeze. It was a spur of the moment call that changed our plans and dumped us into a great half day of fishing. As I say endlessly, there is no substitute for local knowledge.

We travelled a short distance from the Whangapoua bar in a tin boat, cruised across the face of a couple of idyllic secluded bays with their own private beaches and then landed on a rocky promontory.

"A good spot needs foul ground, current and a swell so you get a bit of surge and whitewater," said Kevin. "Big snapper love shallow, foul ground, the current carries your burley and brings the fish to you and the whitewater helps to stir things up and break down your burley." Kevin was offering critical advice to successful land-based fishing. Getting onto the rocks was an exercise in timing and with a couple of hundred thousand dollars' worth of television gear at risk, I came in for a fair bit of abuse, in fact almost my first mutiny.

At that time I think Paul, the cameraman, thought I was trying to drown him but we weren't really jelling as a team, Mike, Paul, Tony and I, partly because I am a very stubborn individual who still had a lot to learn and partly because the environment we were in necessitated doing things a little differently.

In the end the complete disgruntled group of us wound up on the rocks with fishing gear, television equipment and dry clothing.

The next exercise in frustration came when the director wanted to film all sorts of preliminary scene-setting stuff when the tide was perfect for our fishing. To put it politely, I refused, and we started rigging our gear. If it's prime time to fish, you chuck the traditional way of making television out the window and make it fit in with the best result. At that time we were still learning the lesson, and a few strong personalities all wanting their own way, added to the friction.

Fortunately we very quickly had fish to film. Kevin hooked up a John Dory that ate a blue cod that had eaten a pilchard. That is often the way. John Dory invariably grab live baits and of course the good old J.D is one of the best eating fish in the ocean. This was a Kevin success formula relying very heavily on burley. Burley is a distasteful mix of ground up ingredients like fish guts and frames, bread, barley, fish oil, pig pellets, anything you like, but not snapper. Snapper do not like the idea of cannibalizing their own kind.

Burley must be ground up nice and fine so that when it drifts down the current it serves to excite and set up a trail for fish to follow. They head upstream looking for sources of the tasty smelly rubbish and that's when they encounter your baits drifting down to meet them. The bait should be the first serious solid object the fish encounters and they are usually into it as if it's their last supper which, of course, it invariably is.

Burley is usually dumped into a sack or container with small holes in it. It can be used with equal success from shore or a boat and increases your returns tenfold.

Once you're in a good spot, with the right tide (I favour the last two hours of an outgoing tide off the rocks) and your burley trail drifts away down current, all that remains is to hang on and stand by for action. There have been days when it doesn't work but at those times you can just about guarantee that you would have been better off going to the fish shop. It was just one of those days. After Kevin's John Dory, things quietened down a little.

"I salt my pilchards for a week", said the guide. "Just layer them into a plastic container and sprinkle plain salt over each layer. It makes them tougher. They last three times as long, it doesn't make any difference to the fish."

If you're an angler you will know how soft (but effective) pilchards are and how frustrating it can be when the fish are a bit finicky and every bite means an empty hook.

"I recommend we try what I call a pilchard sandwich", said Kevin.

"A what?" I responded.

"Pilchard sandwich", he said. "Put two or three on instead of one".

Kevin and I used 10 kilo main line and 1.5 metres of 24 kilo trace. Two 6/0 black magic hooks did the damage, one tied to the end of the trace and the other sliding up the line and referred to as a keeper hook.

The hook tied to the end goes through the eyes of the pilchards, then the trace is wrapped tightly around both pilchards several times. The keeper hook is placed in the gut cavity of the bait, then several more wraps of trace continue a journey towards the tail, at which point a couple of half hitches finish the job. Both pilchards are held together with a hook protruding from the eyes and another from the gut area. It is a system I still use although I now fix my second (keeper) hook in position with a snell. Big snapper find it very hard to resist big baits and when I flicked that bait a short distance into the burley trail I was feeling pretty darn good.

Kevin's instruction was to fish your feet first, in other words don't try and cast over the horizon but trust your burley trail to have lured your target pretty close. Don't use any weight and spool out line so that the bait can drift down the trail and appear as natural as possible. Big snapper don't get to be big by being totally stupid.

If you fish off a boat and there's plenty of tide, then a ball sinker may be necessary to get your bait down to where the fish are. The answer is to experiment.

Fishing off the shore is often seriously underrated. I would stick my neck out and say that more big snapper and kingfish are caught by the land-based team than by boat fishermen.

There is no chance you will get sea sick, admittedly you have to be careful around the swell but it is a very exciting way to secure a feed.

At this point our filming had been a wee bit ordinary. In one of these early shows we needed a 9 kilo (20lb) snapper to hook our viewers and almost on cue something very large picked up my bait and headed off for Cuvier Island.

"Let it run, let it run", screamed a very excited Kevin.

The reel was in free spool so the fish could pick up the bait and swim away with it. Free spool means that no resistance is required to pull line off the reel. If a big fish feels resistance before it swallows the bait it will spit it out and leave you with nothing but disappointment.

If is very exciting as the fish usually roar off for ten or 20 metres, stop, then swallow the bait and then finally head for the hills.

That's when you tighten up the drag on the reel, lean back and set the hook.

The drag provides a system of variable resistance making it harder for the fish to pull line and therefore tiring it out.

We set our drags to a third or a half of line breaking strain so that on 10 kilo line the fish was having to exert 5 kilos of pressure before line flew from the reel.

This fish did it very easily and it seemed like an eternity before it slowed down and I started to get line back.

When we started filming, all of us wanted good big fish desperately and here was the first, way out over the weed-covered rocks and snags.

The best land-based fishing country is also the worst for bust-offs and breakages and this guy showed its pedigree by heading straight in to the rocks and snagging the line.

This fish had the characteristic head shakes of a big snapper. You can feel it and see the rod thump down − bang, bang, bang − in a heavy, solid rhythm.

Line screams off the reel and you lean back hard against the weight, waiting for a chance to retrieve line, and then wind down the bend before completing the process again and again.

When that fish went into the rocks it became a stalemate.

"Just lean back, keep the pressure on and hope for the best", said Kevin.

"Shouldn't I give it slack line and see if it swims out?" I replied.

"No, just tighten up, lean back and hang on. If you're lucky he'll thread his way back up the line and come free!"

I did, I tightened up the drag as much as I dared and just leant back with a huge bend in the 13 foot surfcaster.

Nothing happened. If I was really well snagged the fish could have broken, gone and left me leaning back into a piece of line wrapped around the rocks.

Everyone was edgy, we wanted that fish. I remember leaning back and then, probably for the first time, noticing where I was. I stood on a point of rock with a sheer black cliff at my back. Scrub grew in fingers down the less precipitous sections of hillside and gulls rode the thermals that eddied around the valleys in unseen currents.

In front of me a ribbon of white laced the edge of the surge as it rose up against our jagged rock plateau and then fell away, spilling out of a hundred rock pools.

Three or four gulls sat on a rock a few feet away and one bolder, brave bird pecked away at a discarded pilchard, all the while fixing that cold predatory stare on the humans that it didn't trust.

The white lace ribbon was backed by kelp and other brown weed. Beyond it the clear Coromandel water showed the outline of the rocks that were causing me all the trouble and a cloud of burley snaked away in the current until the deeper water took over and coloured everything in rich deep blue.

Occasional wind gusts rode in across the bay rippling the surface and left a crisp clean smell in the air. Suddenly the most important thing seemed to be just enjoying where I was for the sake of it.

From that moment on I came to understand what a privilege it is to travel the country, share fantastic adventures, taste the air and appreciate nature at its best. Filming *Gone Fishin'* became an immediate privilege. My thoughts were interrupted by a slight give in the line. I had kept the pressure on until my arms started to ache and suddenly I had a little line back and then a little more until the fish did what Kevin had predicted and worked its way free. Quite suddenly everything changed and nine kilos of very welcome snapper emerged from the depths and yielded to the gaff.

The prize was ours, it was on camera and we were absolutely elated. It was fantastic and if it hadn't been for that fish getting all fouled up, a lot more time would have passed before I really learnt what it means to get out and revel in our fantastic country.

The frustrations that came with learning to film and compromise and getting the best result paled behind the need to appreciate a place for its beauty first and worry about the fish second. After all I had already learnt that it takes more than a few fish to tell a good story and when it comes to luck, it is amazing how good anglers like Kevin Darlow create their own luck. They know their area, the habits of the fish, the appropriate techniques and when to head out and do battle. Once again we had come across a local who knew his way around.

3

Fiordland, The First Shoot

I have spent weeks, even months of my life, hunting, diving, fishing, exploring and gazing in awe at the sheer beauty of Fiordland.

More than any other natural high, Fiordland has always had the ability to inspire, humble and surprise me.

So many people that I meet have no idea of what lies in the bottom west corner of the South Island of New Zealand, one of the most amazing adventure playgrounds in the world.

The region is a cocktail of inspiring geography, vicious weather cycles, endless forests, snow-covered peaks, glaciers, rivers and of course the whole area is seamed with valleys and fiords.

I have only ever written about the area in the frustrated manner of someone who could never find the right words to convey the heart and soul of this place.

Filming *Gone Fishin'* has enabled me to take cameras in to record the beauty, both above and below the water. It oozes out of every square centimetre and I will never forget our first "full on" Fiordland shoot. It was a beauty.

Helicopters save a day's travel down the coast from Milford Sound by boat. They accomplish in half an hour what 24 hours of heaving and pitching on a storm-tossed ocean would achieve and when time is important and getting your backside kicked on the briny is not, then choosing a chopper rates as no contest.

This was my first serious opportunity to direct a shoot, to take on responsibility for coming out at the end with all of the shots that would tell a really good Fiordland yarn.

Paul Richards, Tony Burrows, Janey Hayes, Richard "Hannibal" Hayes (the pilot) and myself plus 700 kgs of gear jammed ourselves into a Squirrel helicopter at the tail end of a pretty solid Fiordland storm.

Hannibal's base is the beautiful lakeside town of Te Anau. On the

Paul Richards (camera) and
Tony Burrows (sound)
learning all about Fiordland's
weather and sandflies.

south eastern side of the lake the plains, foothills and farms reach to
the outskirts of Te Anau township and the lake.

Fiordland's mountains rear up on the Western Shore and roll
around the northern end, although on 3rd May 1994 only a narrow
strip of green indicated that there was bush above the lake.
Everything else was as black as the inside of a cow and thunder and
lightning flashed and echoed round the hills.

Several times we dived into the hangar to shelter from a torrential
downpour that was alternately rain and hail. A very good friend of
mine who I used to hunt Fiordland with, the late Ray Tinsley, always
said that thunder and lightning meant a change of weather and most
of the time it did.

"What are our chances of getting in?" I yelled at Hannibal above
the din that saw hail bouncing off the hangar's tin roof.

"Supposed to clear, we'll go and have a look when this lot blows
through", he said.

We were on our way to Supper Cove at the head of Dusky Sound,
where I could picture the charter vessel *Pembroke* cruising back and
forth at the mouth of the Seaforth River, dwarfed by snow-covered
peaks, a brew on the stove and a warm cabin in which to plan the

next 3½ days.

Owner, Kathy Jameson, skipper Dick Moore and commercial fisherman Mark Harris were already on board. All we needed was a break in the storm, an open pass through the mountains and a little bit of luck. We headed off into 35 knots of SW, bucking and lurching our way across Lake Te Anau and Lake Manapouri. Rain showers hung like dark curtains against the bush and mountains and an occasional break revealed fresh snow dusting the tops.

The cloud grudgingly peeled back a little as we headed for the pass that opened the way to the Seaforth River and Supper Cove. I have never seen so many shades of green as those that paint the Fiordland forest.

The machine was warm, the Pass was not. Snow flurries came hurtling through horizontally but there were lulls and little pieces of shelter so we got the shots and reunited ourselves with the ride. From the pass we dropped down between the peaks and in much calmer conditions roared our way closer to Dusky Sound.

Hannibal has thousands of hours flying on venison recovery and as soon as he pulled an evasive manoeuvre that had us slowing and spinning in midair I knew that he had spotted a deer.

"She's a bit sluggish with all of this weight but there's a deer standing in the middle of a slip back there", and sure enough there she was, a large red hind standing in the clear away from the sodden dripping jungle.

"Too much weight to hold the machine at this altitude", said the pilot so we slid back down the ravine and into the open valley of the Seaforth.

Suddenly there it was, the red-hulled *Pembroke*, waiting patiently amid some of the most spectacular geography in the world. It didn't take long before crew and gear were on board, brew of coffee was in hand and the last whine of the departing chopper remained only a faint echo above the valley.

"What do you want to do first?" said Kathy.

"You could tempt me with a bit of a fish right here", was my response.

On several occasions I have caught good blue cod and tasty school groper at the mouth of the Seaforth. After the chopper ride I just wanted everything to settle down. I wanted to stand on the deck and appreciate this fantastic place, slow down and let it soak in.

What an entirely different scene it was from Auckland 24 hours earlier. Hustle, bustle, traffic, houses, airplanes, noise, smoke, people and now this; a small boat in the vast wilderness of Fiordland where even the air tastes clean and the water is crisp and pure.

When you've flown in rather than rolled your way down the coast, it takes time to absorb it all.

We filmed our first fish while jigging some nice blue cod and dozens of perch which the locals call jock stewarts. The perch are very tasty but few people in the region eat them, probably because they are prolific, don't fight, have spines all around their oversized

Survivors (i.e. everybody) from the wreck of the steamer Waikare – Dusky Sound – Jan 1910.

heads and look a shade on the ugly side. Jigs, baits, bait flies, cod and perch are not choosy – they just scoff their way through anything real or artificial.

"The moose were released just over there", I said to Mark.

"Don't know much about them, don't think there are any left these days anyway."

I last had a look for them in 1985 and saw footprints and high browsing that could only belong to moose.

Four bulls and six cows were bundled off the oyster boat *Dispatch* and put ashore. It was 6th April 1910 and this was the second attempt to establish moose in New Zealand, as the first near Hokitika had failed.

On 19th March 1909, Sir Joseph Ward, then Premier of New Zealand, made application to the Hon. A.E. Forget, then Lieutenant Governor of Saskatchewan, for three male and seven female moose. The application was turned over to Mr Howard Douglas, then Dominion Parks Commissioner. It was assumed that the animals were for propagating purposes in the forests of New Zealand. The moose were collected from two parks – Elk Island and Rocky Mountain.

Very few moose were to be found around Banff in those days, and therefore, to make a fair shipment it was necessary to catch some at Elk Island and convey them to the mountain park to augment the small number there. Old-timers, who today have forgotten details of the shipment, remember their anger at the Government for taking away the few moose then found near Banff. Seventeen animals were shipped in November 1909, but there is no record of the numbers of each sex, the actual point of destination, or the ages of the animals.

A copy of the letter was sent to Mr Howard Sibbald, Superintendent of Kootenay Park, and he in reply stated, "1909 was the year I started with the Parks branch and helped catch and ship the moose. I cannot remember who was in charge of the moose on the train journey to Vancouver, but I remember that they were all young animals and that we gave them plenty of young willow to eat for the trip."

The animals did breed and some semblance of a herd has existed in Dusky ever since. With a life expectancy in excess of 20 years it takes only a very few animals to mate successfully for the herd to linger in the dark recesses of Fiordland and linger they do.

When you consider the North American habitat with its swamps and rolling grassland and compare it with Dusky Sound, the fact that the moose held on at all is a tribute to their hardy disposition. Swamps exist and initially food was plentiful but by the mid-1930s red deer were starting to breed out of control in many parts of New Zealand, including Fiordland. Their numbers became so great that they ate out all of the most desirable food plants and started on the least palatable. That left the moose with those morsels that grew out of reach of the red deer and that advantage meant survival, although of course young moose would have had a difficult first year.

In 1934 protection was removed from deer and moose although at that point only one bull moose had been shot under licence by Eddie Herrick in 1929. Much of the early hunting in New Zealand was controlled by licence and animal liberations were an attempt to turn the colony into a hunting preserve for the wealthy. From the 1860s to early 1900s there were dozens of successful deer liberations but, unlike many European and American situations where control was a product of policy linked to population and geography, in New Zealand the bush threw a blanket over the attempt and by the time people woke up, the animals were out of control. That situation was not rectified until the helicopter recovery operations of the late 1960s and 1970s.

In 1938, government deer cullers entered Fiordland and were paid a retainer plus commission. The commission was sixpence per tail or one shilling and sixpence for a full skin. The meat had no commercial value other than as a supplement to the cullers' larder. It was left to rot.

In spite of extensive culling in the moose area and a wounded and lost chance to Bill Chisholm in 1938, the animals remained elusive ghosts in the bush and throughout their history there wouldn't have been more than a dozen shot. Eddie Herrick secured the second legitimate bull in 1934 and Percy Lyes from Hokitika shot the third and last (to date) in 1952.

Ray Tinsley and I had several conversations with chopper pilots who flew the area for years on venison recovery and all of the chat went one way.

"You're bloody mad! If there is a moose in that area how come with all of our flying we haven't seen any. They're long gone."

The choppers hunted the areas that would allow them a shot, i.e., the river flats, the slips and the open tussock tops. Everything else in Fiordland is either water or trees, tall trees and underlying scrub that becomes an endless mosaic of green blur at 80 to 100 knots. A handful of animals hanging tenaciously to survival make pretty poor odds for a sighting, especially when they have no reason to advertise their presence.

On the ground the search seems almost hopeless and then after several days there is a hoof print or high browsing that is way beyond the full extension of red deer. Your heart beats faster, the adrenalin flows and behind the next tree could be one of the last of New Zealand's moose.

It is enough to make you want to go back and chase this history on the hoof and all the other jewels that flow from the Dusky Sound treasure chest.

Late in the afternoon we steamed away from our moose history and tried to track down groper at the mouth of Fanny Bay. The surface of the Fiord was a dark blackish brown because the huge freshwater runoff lies as a layer on the very clear salt water. It is a wonderful environment in which to dive, dropping through a layer of fresh water murk and into a truly unique marine environment. There were no dives that afternoon because once away from the shelter of Supper Cove, squalls sought us out, blowing rain and hail across the decks. A short sharp chop developed near Fanny Bay and white streamers of spray peeled off the bow and thudded into the wheelhouse screen. The groper were not on the bite so we headed further out into this vast expanse of islands, bays, mountains and waterways, anchoring for the night in a haven called Cascade Cove. Our Fiordland adventure was under way.

Next morning we "pulled the pick" and moved a short distance out into Cascade to catch a feed. *Pembroke* drifted adjacent to a flat area with a stoney beach and in several areas the stones had been cleared away to leave a smooth passage from the water right up to the bush.

They were sealers, boat runs built during the early 1800s to enable sealing gangs to haul their craft out of reach of storms and into an area above the highest tide. The sealing gangs had done their best to wipe out the fur seals, it just wasn't economic to slaughter the last for a few skins so they were left alone, ultimately protected and now flourish along many areas of the Fiordland coast. There are large colonies around the Five Fingers Peninsula and on the Northern end of Resolution Island.

They, like my friends the dolphins, are fantastic to dive with, being inquisitive, playful and incredibly graceful in the water.

We managed a feed of cod but were plagued by spiney dogfish. They drove us away so a course was set for Pickersgill Harbour where Captain Cook spent a month in 1773. Cook moored the *Resolution* in a tiny cove and his ship's artist painted a prominent branch that grew horizontally out into the bay alongside the ship. It's still there, as too are some of the old tree stumps on Astronomers Point beside the harbour. We spent a wonderful couple of hours filming these pieces of history. Cook's men brewed the first beer in NZ at this camp, they called it spruce beer. The team also scoffed all sorts of interesting tucker and one of Cook's favourite little morsels was supposed to be a pie made with the poi bird, which just happens to be the tui. Cook and the crew waded in to the abundant bird life, dining on a variety of delicacies that, thanks largely to stoats, weasels, ferrets and rats, have been virtually wiped out. Takahe and kakapo were the major casualties, but as we stood on Astronomers Point, tuis, bellbirds and fantails sang their song, perhaps knowing full well they were not heading for the pot.

The scurge of shore-based activities is the sandfly. That minute black bundle of trouble with a bite like an alligator and millions of mates is a pain in the backside. Without them and the occasional waterlogged mosquito, Fiordland would be the perfect paradise. Maybe their purpose is to scare a few people off, and when combined with violent weather, they have the ability to turn back a few would-be adventurers.

I would have loved to have been a "fly on the wall" and watched

Janey Hayes – Miss NZ, international model on the Pembroke *catwalk showing off the latest in hunting gear. Look out Bambi.*

Cook and the boys as they stepped ashore in Fiordland for the first time. How long would it have taken before the little black scurge started sinking their fangs into the unsuspecting Englishmen? Maybe after months at sea they stank too much to worry about.

Cook had first sighted what he named Dusky Bay from the *Endeavour* on 14th March 1770, but due to unfavourable weather he was unable to make landfall. I guess he was bitten by the Fiordland bug because there he was playing around for a month in 1773 eating tui pie.

Next stop was the wreck of the steamer *Waikare* which struck an uncharted rock in January 1910, and with the last remaining steam, was driven into Stop Island.

The *Waikare* is a great dive, 10-20 metres deep, 30 metres visibility, plenty of marine life and still enough intact wreckage to identify parts of the ship. By this time one of my real passions was filming the underwater footage for the show and I love the fact that people can now see what I used to rant and rave about. Fishing and diving are, to me, perfect partners, as dives are relatively short and you need time on the surface if the objective is to have more than one splash in a day. So what do you do while you're sitting around? Grab a fishing rod, of course, and add a few fillets to the crayfish that you intend to "dive into" that very evening.

Kathy and I splashed down onto the *Waikare*'s grave. No-one lost their lives when she sank, but 3000 tonnes of steel rolled over and died.

I have been a frequent visitor over the years and find this artificial reef full of surprises. The water temperature was 11 degrees and the *Pembroke*'s hot shower was the post-dive target. Just to the side of the ship a favourite little crevice had yielded a few crays for tea and as Paul and Tony stowed camera gear, Kathy and I underwater equipment, a pot full of crays boiled on the stoves.

Fresh crays steaming hot and succulent waiting for a few cod fillets to sizzle in the pan and then combining in a heck of a feast.

I love stepping into the cabin at the end of a great day, grabbing a hot "cuppa" and sitting back to review the sights, sounds, catch and in this case, look back at what we had filmed that day. What Paul had filmed was just great, the underwater footage did justice to the old ship and everyone was in great humour.

A tiny speck that was the *Pembroke* threaded her way between forested mountains and islands through a labyrinth of darkening waterways and sought out the anchorage at Luncheon Cove. We were heading towards one of those regular Fiordland surprises. When we arrived, another vessel was at anchor and as *Pembroke* cruised past there was what looked like a dog sitting on the aft deck.

It was quite dark by this time but the animal could be quite plainly seen under the deck lights then I realised what I was looking at. It was a baby seal. We pulled alongside for a look.

"There are a whole mob of baby seals in here", said one of the crew. "They keep jumping up on the duck board so I just climbed

Bulwer — The Marlborough Sounds — Bill and Audrey Ford's retreat for lucky anglers.

Bill and Audrey Ford pose with spoils from the chase.

The Coromandel can produce some outstanding scallops. Here's one that is XXXOS − more like a Stewart Island model.

Surprise, surprise, another healthy Bay of Plenty snapper. Graeme Cook is justifiably chirpy.

Joining the charter vessel
Pembroke *in Supper Cove, Dusky
Sound, and so began a fantastic
trip.*

*Pickersgill Harbour in Dusky
where the Resolution was moored
for a month in 1773. The place
just oozes history.*

Off to frolic with the seals in Luncheon Cove. The first European house in New Zealand was built here and so was the first ship.

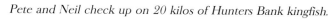

Pete and Neil check up on 20 kilos of Hunters Bank kingfish.

Pete (Lambo) Lamb and Blue Nose offerings from the Wellington trenches.

Dawn – Halfmoon Bay, Stewart Island – red sky in the morning, sailors' warning. It blew its socks off.

A commercial fishing boat makes hard work of the run back to Half Moon Bay in a rising NW gale.

Crayfish get to be pretty big in these parts, any bigger and the divers would have to wear body armour. This one tips the scales at about 5 kilos.

Bit of a Stewart Island feed compliments of the Anderson's and including the ever-present crayfish, salmon, oysters and mussels. The paua were still cooking.

Heli-fishing on Great Barrier Island – from left: Rod McKenzie, GS and Lance Donelly (with friends).

The sheer beauty of Great Barrier Island is something you could not capture in a single shot. It is rugged, wild and unspoilt.

Great land based fishing spot on the northern side of Great Barrier. Nothing like the last two hours of an outgoing tide.

down, picked it up and put it on the deck. He just sat in my arms, had a look around, and then headed into the wheelhouse. I'm just putting him back in the tide." And with that the baby seal was deposited back in the cool dark water which, even to a seal, would have seemed pretty second rate after a warm wheelhouse. I don't recommend you go picking up baby seals, it's not something we would even attempt, but it was captivating to see how much trust that little fella placed in his human companions. He barked, which sounded like a bit of a complaint as he swam out of the arc of the deck lights to join his friends on the rocks at the foot of a dark cold forest. If that was the way they were (so incredibly friendly) when the sealers clubbed them to death in their tens of thousands, it is easy to see why it would have been absolute carnage.

As soon as it was light, Paul, Tony, Janey, Kathy and I paddled in to film the seals.

Luncheon Cove is an oasis, a superb anchorage surrounded by hills. You have to weave your way in through a couple of channels so that once anchored you feel totally landlocked.

I have ridden out a couple of howling, screaming Fiordland tempests in this anchorage, it is a beauty. Luncheon is also the place where the first European house in New Zealand was built and where the first ship was completed. The whole of Dusky has a fantastic history associated with it.

Our objective, however, was to film the seals and what a great time we had with these inquisitive little guardians of the cove. Because of all the rain the first 60cms of water was the usual stained brown murk so the underwater camera was next to useless, but Paul recorded some great stuff on the nearby rocks. Four babies occupied one little vantage point and they were very curious about the rubber-suited humans that followed them around the bay.

I don't know what the temperature of that surface layer was but it felt freezing and if I had been a warm-blooded seal pup and someone offered a nice warm boat to nest in, I would have been out of that water like a bullet.

It took 20 minutes in the shower to stop shaking and get the blood flowing again but that's a small price to pay when nature offers to share one of her gifts.

As we wound our way among the channels and sought the open sound, the heavy layer of cloud broke apart, revealing precipitous mountains and the rich blue of a sky washed clean.

The only sound was the *Pembroke*'s diesel, the only scar on an ocean as smooth as silk was the ever widening ripples that spread from *Pembroke*'s stern. Fiordland had woken up in very good humour and her mood was infectious.

I stood at the cabin door, looking, and feeling a faint sweet-tasting breeze caress my face.

A conversation started up in the cabin as Kathy threw some bacon in a pan and the sizzle and smell drifted past on the faint breeze created by our passage. Janey wandered out. "Breakfast Sinker", she said "and then Mark wants to try another groper hole. Reckons we'll get right on the spot in this weather."

Janey was Miss New Zealand once and an international model and here she was quite at home in Fiordland, clad in sea boots, long johns and a bush shirt. Janey can hunt and fish with the best of them but never loses that something special that set her apart on the catwalk.

After breakfast we drifted slowly across a section of bay near Cascade and caught groper, just three small ones, enough for a feed and then continued on our journey. By now all of the camera and underwater gear had found a space and we had relaxed a little. Believe it or not, filming is not quite the holiday that it may seem and each day we start with a set of objectives, material that we need to shoot. It requires skill on the part of camera and sound, co-operation from the weather, the fish, the people we are with. Filming a show like *Gone Fishin'* is at times very challenging but the people we meet, the characters, really make a difference and when all else fails there is a piece of magic called New Zealand and here we were in a place that would occupy a starring role anywhere in the world.

It would take weeks of exploring to trace all of Dusky's coastline, Captain Cook made a start but his work was only the beginning.

The Acheron Passage links Dusky Sound with Breaksea Sound to the north and the Acheron's western shore is the eastern side of Resolution Island.

It was to the Acheron Passage that *Pembroke* steamed late on the afternoon of 5th May.

I sat wedged in the wheelhouse, chatting with Dick.

"Had a great dive up here last week", he said "huge gardens of black coral trees and crayfish literally covering the walls. Don't know if the crays are still there but it will be worth a look."

Just on dark, Dick, Kathy and I sat geared up on the aft deck. Mark nosed *Pembroke* under the sheer walls of Resolution Island. The forest grew down almost to the water's edge and the Fiord was dark and cold looking but absolutely calm. I gave an involuntary shiver as I checked the underwater camera and lights one more time. The water here is a couple of hundred metres deep so you dive a cliff that plunges down into nothing but blackness.

"Okay," said Mark, "make the most of it."

Three divers cleared the deck and splashed into a typically unique Fiordland dive. The first thing that happens is a fight for breath as ice cold fresh water leaks into your wetsuit and literally takes your breath away. You know what it's like when you are about to jump into a cold pool at the end of summer. Pluck up courage, hurl yourself in and after the initial shock, things don't seem so bad.

Paul and Tony thought it was a great joke as we huffed and puffed our way through the early chill. I had 200 watts of camera light, enough to turn night into day and the others had powerful torches, but during the first part of the dive it was surprisingly light.

As I descended the fresh brown blanket there was little to see, but then at about three metres, I broke out into a gloomy world where the visibility seemed only limited by the distant darkness. It was like floating in space. The walls of the island continued vertically downward and Dick's black coral trees grew all over the wall. Black coral trees are actually white, pure rich, almost fluorescent white, as it is the internal dead core of the coral trees which is black. They stand out like fruit trees, stark and white and beautiful, only infinitely more intricate and delicate. Black coral always seems to have coloured snake stars wrapped around its stem. They come in black, orange, yellow and brown looking for all the world like a snake coiled around the branch of a tree. The ends of the trees, the delicate white filaments, wave in the current as though in some permanent graceful dance. A beautiful friendly little fish called the butterfly perch lives around the trees schooling in groups of between ten and 20. Soft corals grow too and anemones and other plants, several types of fish, a world like no other, absolutely unique to Fiordland. I dropped down to 30 metres where it was green and gloomy, adjusted my buoyancy and filmed Kathy and Dick gliding past 15 metres above. Something bumped against my leg, a small school shark that rose out of the depths with the gathering gloom.

As I looked down I saw more and more making their way up into the lighter gloom of late evening near the surface. Suddenly it was quite eerie and I remembered the seal colonies and great whites that live in these waters. On those cliffs there is no protection, you just remind yourself that you have a greater chance of being struck by lightning than being eaten by a shark.

I sidled up to 20 metres and edged along the cliff behind my companions. Suddenly the wall of rock changed, instead of plants and fish, the whole face was covered in crayfish, dozens and dozens of them. It was almost pitch black and the camera lights were losing their sting, but I filmed that wall of crayfish. Many people have since commented on it. The cliff moved as they sought to escape my lights or Dick's grabbing hand. We ran out of time and surfaced, all jabbering like a bunch of excited kids. I looked up through the trees, floating in that crisp surface layer, cold but elated after a fantastic dive. The sky was clear and between the mountains, stars were trying to fill the gap. Millions of them and if you looked hard enough it seemed as though they joined up way off in the distance light years away. The *Pembroke* slid towards us along the ink black water of the Fiord, engine chugging, Tony and Paul laughing in the cabin, frosted windows inviting us back for another feed. There is more to this trip as we set off next day in search of blue fin tuna but the game fishing stories will live in another volume. At some point you must visit Fiordland but beware it gets into your blood and continually beckons you to return.

Fiordland was once again living up to its reputation, a beautiful pristine playground always prepared to share a secret or two and always unpredictable.

Mark Harris – showing how stressful fishing in Fiordland can be.

4
Wellington

During series one we found ourselves in Wellington with esteemed land-based expert, Pete Lamb.

"Lambo", as I have called him ever since, is a tall, woolly, Swanndri-wearing example of the staunch wind-blown angler. Lambo will trudge miles to a favourite spot at Cape Brett or Cape Runaway, having driven all night from Wellington just to get there. Locally he knows every nook and cranny, fissure and reef and we were on a quest for the elusive blue moki.

Wellington is perhaps the most maligned of our major cities, everyone talks about "Windy Wellington", but when you check out the location from an angler's perspective, the province and the city have much in their favour.

Cook Strait is on the doorstep, rugged cliffs and reefs surround the harbour and extend up and down the various coasts. There is great fishing and diving to be found by anyone based in Wellington and, of course, the Marlborough Sounds are only a short cruise away across "the Strait".

Wellington, our capital city, was named in 1840. A letter from J. Word, Secretary of the New Zealand Company, to W. Wakefield on 29th May, explains the circumstances.

"The Directors, understanding from your dispatches that the locality of the principal Settlement has been definitely fixed by you at Lambton Harbour Port Nicholson, have considered it essential for purposes of publicity to adopt a name without any delay for the First town. Considering the probability of that settlement becoming at no distant period the centre of British power and influence in those distant regions, it is the opinion of the Court of Directors that the name 'Wellington' is peculiarly appropriate, and will connect the most honourable national association of the Mother Country with the future town. It is therefore the wish of the Directors that the first

Town should be called 'Wellington' accordingly."

The name, of course, came from the Duke of Wellington who has supported Wakefield in his colonizing schemes. Sir Arthur Wellesley, when raised to the peerage, took his title from the town of Wellington in Somerset. The Strait became fringed with the names of heroes, for Nelson followed and then Marlborough.

On a wind-whipped Friday morning we set off with Pete in his beaten up Nissan 4x4 that had clocked up more kilometres than a self-respecting taxi. The crew tagged along in a new Pathfinder. What a procession, Peter's beast with rods bristling like the quills of a porcupine, gnarly paint job merging into rust, bait, bags and bits balanced on the background. We were followed by a shiny new Nissan and headed down the Wellington motorway as early traffic fought its way into the tall office buildings that dominate the Wellington city skyline. Fortunately all of those commuter cars were heading in the opposite direction.

If you are one of them you should try taking a mid-week break and head off for a fish against the flow of traffic. It's like being set free, having been imprisoned in some repetitive drudgery. Even a day will recharge your soul. It should be compulsory.

The moki man – Pete "Lambo" Lamb with one of the most elusive fish we have set out to target. We tried everything – paua guts, crayfish and mussels. Very frustrating. "See", he said, "moki do exist."
Photo Pete Lamb

"We're on our way to the Makara coast", said Lambo in his deadpan way that always suggests that he may be pulling your leg. "I used to bike out here when I was a kid. Took all day and usually camped overnight but we caught some great fish. Have you ever tried to bike home with a 50lb kingfish, bloody awkward."

About the time I started to get a good whiff of sea air we turned off the rutted shingle road and into a paddock. For the next 30 minutes the four wheel drives earnt their keep as we clawed our way around farm tracks, always heading for the coast.

It was a beautiful day made more so by green pastures and steep, scrub-filled gullies. The clay track snaked away into the distance, sheep fixed us with a mindless gaze, bleating occasionally or just standing there gawking and chewing in the way of stock that have long ago learnt that running away is pointless.

We started getting short of land and on a steep, scrub-covered coastal hill, Pete's old wagon employed the last of its brakes and stopped us on the edge of the much steeper cliff. The view was spectacular, clear across Cook Strait to the South Island. A light swell pushed a ribbon of white water against the heavily indented rocks. Black slabs pushed out from the base of the hill, ideal to stand on and flick a pilchard into the burley. Bull kelp, that rugged coastal plant, secured itself to tidal rocks with a vast brown foot. After a severe storm, a fair chunk of kelp gets thrown onto beaches but I am amazed at how that singular foot anchors the plant to the coast. Watching the broad leaves of kelp, some five metres long, ebb and flow in the tide, it looked like nature's little finishing touch to a spectacular seascape. The ever present seagulls rode in on their thermal highway as we loaded packs and camera gear, rods and reels, bait and burley, two truck loads of gear spread out among four humans and a land-based mountain man. We were on our way downhill and every step down was one we had to claw our way back up. At times I had to turn and face the cliff, edge carefully down a vertical chute to a flatter ledge where all manner of things would be passed down. But what a view, hills green and brown, giving way to black cliffs that plunged into the ocean. Birds wheeling and screeching, ducking and diving, a light breeze laden with ocean smells, the rocks, the waves and that kelp fringe. It was great to be alive.

At the end of the journey a burley bag was hurled into the wash zone and soon spread its foul-smelling mix out into the current and beyond the waves.

"Plenty of burley's the answer", said Lambo. "I've got my favourite paua, kina mix in one bag and ground up fish frames and guts in the other. Soon find out if there's anything around."

Our greatest hope was for a kingfish, a hard-fighting, sleek, fast yellowtail kingfish, but when filming, anything will do for a start. The heroics can wait for after.

"Got to get to know your spot", said the guide. "Things like time of tide, bite times, because fish don't necessarily feed all day and the moon phase all make a difference, so it's worth doing some homework. We've got the last couple of hours of the outgoing tide, the bite time's about an hour away and pilchards are my number one bait, in this spot anyway."

We rigged a single hook and to help keep the very soft pilchards in place, Pete wraps cotton around them.

"Last much longer", he said, "otherwise you spend all day pulling in an empty hook."

Once the pilchard is threaded, start winding cotton round and round and round, binding the pilchard initially to the hook and then up the line.

It looks like the fish equivalent of an Egyptian mummy that has partly unravelled. Bits of pilchard protrude between the string ready to ambush whatever storms past.

We used 13 foot surfcasters because the length helps to fight a fish clear of the kelp and guide it to a place where a landing is feasible. It means using the terrain and the swell to your advantage, especially when 80lb of yellowtail kingfish is battling for its freedom.

The thing that saved our bacon in that spot was the good old kahawai, the most underrated fish in NZ, both for sport and culinary applications.

All over NZ you hear the echo "it's only a kahawai" but if tackle is matched to the fish, in other words use lighter line weights, you are in for some fantastic sport. Kahawai are one of my favourites, especially when the camera's rolling and no one else wants to be a star.

The kingfish were absent, the kahawai were not and I got to another beautiful part of our coast that Lambo tells me fishes as well as it looks.

"We're past the best of the tide but I've got another spot we can fish till dark", said Lambo, unwrapping himself from the rock ledge that had served as a release point for yet another kahawai.

"I'm not climbing another mountain today", Paul the cameraman said, with a mutinous look.

"Don't worry", responded Lambo with that look that didn't seem to be quite telling the truth. "You can drive right to the next spot, fish out of the Pathfinder if you want to."

That helped to prepare Paul for the slog back up the cliff.

All was accomplished without mishap, just the loss of a lot of sweat, and we retraced our path through farmland and shingle roads before looking at a late afternoon panorama of Cook Strait. By the time we drove down into Oteranga Bay the wind had dropped out and the Strait looked like orange glass. It reflected orange light from a lowering sun and in the distance the black mountains of the seaward Kaikouras were fringed in red. If nothing else, it was a beautiful place to be.

In the bay, wavelets hissed their way onto a fine shingle beach, the gulls moved in to scavenge a late evening feed and Pete and I cast mussels wrapped in cotton to the unsuspecting blue moki. It was a beautiful spot, "fishes as well as it looks" came the echo but someone

Pete and Cook Strait Bass –
an "average" beast for
Wellington.

had sent advance warning to the moki and the best we could do was a couple of banded parrotfish.

The search for the elusive moki continued next day when the same procession drove through Wainuiomata and ran out of road somewhere along the spectacular coast. Four wheel drive came into its own along the beach and I had the pleasure of towing a bogged down Land-Rover out of some shingle that the Pathfinder ate up.

Lambo's brakes were holding up and we squeaked to a halt beside a group of guys who had been diving.

As well as a sack of paua (abalone) that they were frantically shelling, one of them had speared a couple of moki.

"Any left out there?" I asked.

"Yeah, plenty, some pretty good ones too," he said.

Rocks and reefs stick out of the ocean here and there. It was nearing low tide and we would fish the incoming. Hardly any swell rose to meet the coast and the bull kelp rolled lazily with the ebb and flow. It was another beautiful day.

"Try some crayfish for bait tonight, the moki can't resist it and this place fishes as good as it looks", said a confident Lambo.

We sat on the shingle, yarning, rods stood in the holders, the tips

41

dropping to the occasional bite.

Banded parrotfish and a very small moki slid up the beach on the end of a hook. They were released, sent back to their laughing mates. As anglers we were mere spectators on a beautiful warm Wellington evening. Lambo dragged out his blues guitar and mouth organ and as the sun set and spread its orange glow across the bay, he composed a song "The Moki Blues".

"You should stay another day", was his parting shot. "I've got a couple of spots that are prime, they fish even better than they look."

That was the end of October 1993 and I didn't get a chance to put Lambo to the test again until February 1995. In between times he sent me a procession of large, probably computer-enhanced, moki photos, with invitations to return because at the time of mailing we were in prime moki season.

When I went back, the Swanndri-clad moki man had partially traded in his ropes and crampons and had teamed up with a couple of chaps who ran charter boats.

"Could never give up land-based", proclaimed a defensive Lambo, "but we get to some great spots . . ."

"Yeah, yeah!" I said, "that fish as good as they look."

They also land some mean tarakihi near Wellington – here are a couple of beauties.
Photo Pete Lamb

"How did you know?" came the deadpan response.

It is amazing how trips to similar locations can vary, how seasonality and weather and good fortune can combine to create a winning combination.

Whatever it was, we were embarking on a couple of angling days that were unbeatable.

Lambo, his boat owning buddy, Neil Pilfreyman, Grant Atkinson, the cameraman, Mike McCree, soundman and I found ourselves on an ocean of glass watching the sun come up. We were heading to a place called Hunters Bank off the West Coast, north of Wellington and under the shadow of Kapiti Island.

Another of Pete's great spots was about to be put to the test.

The first challenge on the agenda was to take the underwater camera for a dive and film some of the inhabitants of this fishy looking reef system.

We dropped onto a pinnacle that peaked 15 metres under the surface and dropped away into a series of ravines that flashed crayfish, crayfish, in a large neon sign. It is magnificent country and as I rolled down the side of the peak and looked up, a school of kingfish glided up out of the early morning gloom. Kingis are very inquisitive, and in my old spearfishing days we used to have a bicycle bell on our spear guns. The soggy-sounding ring, ring was often enough to get a kingfish close enough to spear.

On that beautiful day I chose to film the 30 or 40 that milled around, fish up to 25 kilos, white-bellied, dark green topsides, prominent yellow strip, tail and fins, and as sleek and fast as a torpedo.

Kingfish were our angling target and suddenly the day was filled with promise.

There were crayfish in the crevices, schools of butterfly perch, wrasse and of course the odd very large blue moki stooging around. The rock itself is covered in soft corals, anemones, sponges, shellfish, blennies, crabs and all sorts of beautiful multi-coloured ocean window dressing. It takes light to reveal colour underwater as the primary colours virtually disappear in the first 10 metres. As the light diminishes, so to does colour and that is why many divers see a world of blue and grey. Dive in exceptionally clear water or take a torch and suddenly the ocean world is as splendidly hued and rich in colour as anything on land.

What a dive, the water temperature was 20°C and the visibility 20 metres.

As soon as I hit the surface there was an unleashing of excited babble that translated to kingfish smashing through bait schools all round us.

"Hurry up, hurry up," screeched the moki man and one quick glance at the boiling ocean was all I needed. No further encouragement was required.

It is such a good feeling, knowing that the fishing is going to be great. I get so darned excited that my hands shake and fixing hooks or jigs to line is a major challenge. My heart thumps away, I leap around and can't wait until I hook up and the rod completes a graceful arc and "loads" up. It is then that I am in angling heaven. I never get bored waiting for that moment, hours, even days, slide by in the quest for great fishing.

The kingis were thrashing through schools of what looked like pilchards. Terrified bait fish moved in a frenzy across the surface, a silver shower of kingi tucker that fought for life under the rich blue sunny canvas of a perfect day.

"They usually take a jig if you cast it and retrieve as fast as possible across the surface", said Lambo.

Whizz, splash went the cast; crash, splash, wallop went the kingfish and Pete was hooked up. The camera rolled, the action was hot.

The odd gannet cruised lazily in and dived into the frenzy of predator and predated. More gannets, more gulls, whoosh, splash, screech – even the birds were having a ball.

Our jigs were tied on to a doubled main line, the knot used being a spider hitch, a very easy knot to learn and a very useful addition to your angling armoury. Any tackle store owner worth their salt should be able to show you how to tie a spider hitch. The idea of using a knot that doubles the main line is to add strength and durability to the challenge. A single strand of 10 kg monofilament line is virtually invisible and even doubled up doesn't put off kingfish in a frenzy.

If you are having trouble getting into the action, sometimes it pays to use lighter, less visible trace, or even tie straight on to the main line.

Whizz, splash went the cast; crash, splash, wallop went the kingfish and I was hooked up.

A silver, 200gm chrome-plated jig on a fast retrieve had done the trick.

This place was as good as it looked.

Kingfish instinctively dive for the rock bottom when you hook them, so you really need to put maximum pressure on early in the fight or you are history. Drag pressure is only one part of the equation. A high speed, free spool reel like a Penn 555 casts like a dream and is designed in such a way as to enable you to apply extra pressure by using your thumbs.

Thumbs on the reel or a thumb forcing line against the rubber cushion in front of the reel adds resistance but increases strain on the line.

It is a technique that, when mastered, can be very useful but you need to know how much pressure your gear will stand before a bust-off.

That knowledge comes with time.

Some kingis beat us to the punch and earnt their freedom by dragging line across the rocks of Hunters Bank. We kept two of about 20 kilos and let the rest go. The frenzy was over in an hour of total excitement and we had to be back in by lunchtime.

That half day was another spur of the moment filming decision that paid off and next morning we embarked on another one.

Daylight on 10th February saw us on Brian Delaney's launch displacing a gently rolling Cook Strait swell. Lambo and his friend Ginger (another Brian) were determined to show us how good the fishing was just out of the harbour.

Paul Webley, a friend, came along for the outing as did Bill Hohepa.

Our target was a spot called "The Trenches", a section on the charts that looks like a bit of a canyon and is supposedly a dead cert.

Once again we needed to be back by lunchtime and once again the day started with a sparkling ocean and blue sky.

Fishing deep water requires a different approach and line such as thin diameter non stretch dynabraid has made a huge difference to the challenge of hooking and hauling fish in 200 metres of water.

Monofilament line is very elastic and when fishing in 200 metres you are on the end of something that feels like a big rubber band.

When a fish bites you feel nothing, it is a fishing lottery and you are left hoping that a fish will hook itself.

With dynabraid, even at that depth, you can feel every little nibble, you can strike and act as soon as a fish is hooked.

The best hook to use is a commercial hook called a circle tuna hook or variation on the theme. These hooks describe an almost complete circle, but boy do they hook fish by themselves.

This deep water fishing nets some huge beasts but is really meat hunting rather than sport.

Fish come out of the depths with their swim bladders blown up and blue nose, hapuka and bass generally float up the last 20 metres totally incapacitated.

Still, if you are after a feed and want to see some pretty interesting critters, then a deep water drift can serve up all sorts of surprises.

We hauled in a dozen blue nose, a ling and a bunch of hoki before the wind got up and pushed us back into Wellington Harbour.

From a filming perspective there were fish everywhere and naturally enough Lambo's parting shot was "Great spot eh mate, it fishes as good as it looks", delivered in that same deadpan way that suggested a wry sense of humour.

Kim Dobchuk with two very large moki. As the size would suggest, they are great battlers. One day moki!

5

Stewart Island

Before we had sufficient money to film *Gone Fishin'*, a group of us wound up investing in Mike Bhana's company, Wild Film & Television. Mike had some great ideas but was short on funding, but in spite of a skeletal budget, Mike, Grant Atkinson (Attie), Anthony Nevison (soundman) and I wound up in Dunedin during December 1992, chasing a rather large great white shark called KZ7.

When the movie Jaws was filmed, the fictitious beast was supposedly 25 feet long, a length which most definitely stretched the imagination. Before too long, a couple of great whites appeared off our coast that turned fiction into fact. Brutus was the great white legend of the Three Kings and KZ7, Dunedin's equivalent. Both were reported to be tipping the mythical 25 feet.

We were all full of brash and bravado when it came to getting in the water with KZ7 and if we had ever crossed paths, I have no doubt that we would have done it. Whatever it took to get the shots.

Unfortunately, or perhaps fortunately, the weather intervened and a huge roll and screaming southerly kept us off the ocean. Living on fish and chips, crammed into a motel, nothing to film.

"How about we head off to Stewart Island", I suggested to the team. "The whole northern side will be sheltered in this weather."

After much debate we loaded up, checked out and headed south in the quest for something to build a story around.

That evening, 14th December, found us steaming out of Half Moon Bay, Stewart Island and heading off to drop a bunch of hunters in Port William. The weather was calm and clear as we hauled in a feed of blue cod off Bobs Point.

Stewart Island is breathtaking, rolling hills, vast expanses of beautiful deserted beaches, bays and inlets, bush to the water's edge or tussock sandhills and scrub. From the air the island looks as though it would be at home in the tropics, instead bearing the brunt

Salmon farming in Paterson Inlet – yes, we did get to sample the merchandise.

of storms that scream out of the furious fifties and march unchecked through the Southern Ocean.

In spite of the chance of crisp weather, Stewart Island is an adventurer's playground – tramping, hunting, diving, fishing, bird watching, exploring, taking a breather, whatever your bent, you will find a suitable outlet in this pristine paradise.

The first printed reference to Stewart Island in the 1816 edition of the Oriental Navigator is as follows; "Stewart Island: This is the southern-most of the isles called New Zealand. It was discovered but not examined by Captain Cook in 1770, who has exhibited it as connected with the Island T'Avai Poenamo; but it proves to be a distinct island, being separated from the former by a straight containing a number of small isles, and called Foveaux Strait. The coasts of Stewart Island were explored by the ship *Pegasus*, Captain S. Chase, in 1809 . . . The plate annexed exhibits the fine harbour of Southern Port . . . on the south-east side of the island, as surveyed by Mr. William Stewart, first officer of the *Pegasus,* and since commander of the ship *James Hay*, to whom the public are now indebted for this communication."

At 8.30 that evening I jumped in for a snorkel off Horseshoe Point and after splashing around in 20°C water up north, my thin wetsuit was no match for the 13°C of Stewart Island. It was invigorating, to say the least, but beautiful kelp gardens, clear water and prolific fish life combined with the ease with which I was able to snorkel a feed of paua and crays, meant that the cold was soon forgotten. Sometime after 9.00 I was back on *Moana*'s deck talking to skipper Tom Sawyer and deckhand Kathy Marshall. Kathy was filleting blue cod like a seasoned pro as I stood there advancing my filleting education with both hands wrapped around a steaming cup of coffee.

"They're easier to fillet when they've been left to set for a while", she said.

"These ones are a bit fresh."

There are plenty of shows we have filmed with a filleting lesson attached. Bill Ford does a superb job in the Marlborough Sounds and the late Kevin Anderson on Stewart Island. Learning to fillet can save you a lot of heartache, not to mention save time and ensure that you're having something more substantial than a few lumps of flesh to throw in the pan.

Darkness does not fall on Stewart Island during the summer, it kind of gradually blends in. It's so gradual and the twilight so extensive that when we tied up at 10.15pm, it was only just dark.

We camped in the South Seas Hotel in Half Moon Bay and woke to a SW of 30 knots with occasional rain.

The beautiful sweeping bays and places like Paterson Inlet mean you have an adventure haven in most storms. There is always somewhere to go and something to do, but be prepared to wrap up warm.

The locals in the pub had been a bit 'standoffish', perhaps a little uncertain about the pedigree of the visitors. Mike had decided that partying with the local team was the way to develop a good relationship and it was a very haggard-looking specimen that stepped onto *Moana* next morning.

We had a series of three dives planned and post party trauma is not a diver's best friend. Mike was the underwater cameraman at that stage and the performance was not up to the usual high standard.

First stop, Paterson Inlet salmon farm, much bigger than that which had caught our attention in Marlborough Sounds. 20 acres of pens returning $60,000,000 per annum at that time. There were between 10,000 and 50,000 salmon in a pen, which they entered at six months old and were harvested two years later.

When we turned up, some of Mike's party animal mates, complete with glazed eyes, were processing 17 tonnes of fish. They told us that at times they process up to 40 tonnes. It was great to see and our first dive was a splash in the pens, thousands of salmon swimming round and round.

The splash with the salmon made us hungry so we cruised across the Inlet and under the shadow of the forest, decided on a feed of scallops.

"One of the good things about this place", said Tom, "is that you don't have to be fussy about where to dive. Jump in here, it's about 12 metres deep, start swimming and in five minutes you'll have all the scallops you're allowed."

That was the prediction and that was the reality and we weren't talking about just legal size, we were talking huge. The scallops that legends are made of. Two lightly crumbed and equally lightly pan fried scallops to a plate. That's the way they were served back in the pub, fresh, huge and succulent, the way scallops should be. If you are a sashimi fan (raw seafood), as I most certainly am, can I recommend freshly shelled scallops dunked in soya sauce and wasabi followed by a cold beer chaser? Absolutely beautiful and if a cold beer is not forthcoming, try a crisp clean chardonnay.

We were in our wetsuits for a good chunk of the day, leaping in and out of little adventures as we explored the wonderland of Paterson Inlet.

To keep the chill out I usually slip a survival suit over the top of my wetsuit. When it's cold and the breeze whips over a wet wetsuit, it sucks out body heat in no time. A survival suit and a warm hat make all the difference because even in summer a SW on Stewart Island means a large drop in the temperature.

Our last dive of the day was on the wreck of the full rigged whaling ship, *Pacific*, that dragged anchor and foundered in 1864. The *Pacific* is rotting away beneath the sediment of Paterson Inlet. Large copper bolts, timbers and cladding lie protruding from the mud, and with a growth of weed, the old ship is home to a variety of fortunate plants and animals.

Sealing and whaling attracted many such ships to the rich waters of Stewart Island and Fiordland. Some returned with riches and stories, others, like the *Pacific,* had purchased a one way ticket.

After that third splash we decided to head back to the warmth of the South Seas and have a breather. When it's not dark till after 10.30pm and light again very early, it's easy to forget about sleep, but a few dives is a great sleeping pill, besides, Attie and Anto deserved a break.

The salmon farmers were in the bar when we arrived and they were much more friendly than the night before. A couple of pints of Speights invited close inspection.

"Game of pool", said one of the locals.

"Don't mind if I do", I responded. Never been one to turn down a game of pool and a bit of a chat with the locals. Occasionally I manage to play reasonably well, every now and then I don't.

Crack went the white against the racked up balls on the break and that was all we got to see of the game. He sank the lot − down trou!!

I'm sure many of you know of the great Kiwi custom that accompanies a loss on the table without sinking a ball. Yep! It's the 'down trou'. The very embarrassing dropping of pants in front of the locals but when in Rome, do as the Romans do.

When on Stewart Island if the dropping ceremony wasn't voluntary a few of the local lads would give you a hand. Down they went and from that point on we were accepted without reservation. What an invitation. A great night of banter, yarns and pool was enjoyed by all and sundry and early morning found us back on *Moana* and heading off for a dive on Whio Rock.

The target was a feed of crays and several specimens notable for their colossal size wound up in the catch bag and ultimately in the pot.

Flat calm, sunny conditions and genuine warmth radiated from the sun by the time we surfaced.

It was a perfect day.

We cruised back to the pub for another feed of giant scallops and met a pilot who was flying his family around NZ in an old WWII Devon.

"Want to come for a spin around the island?" he said.

On a perfect Stewart Island day we could not resist the temptation to go and film some of the incredibly valuable aerial shots that help make a show come alive. We took the back door off and roped Attie into a place that would enable the camera to do its work. What a flight. If you ever get to Stewart Island, which you must, then grab the chance of a scenic flight on a good day. It is a graphic indication of how the bush, bays, inlets, mountains, hills, plains, scrub, tussock, beaches and cliffs combine into something stupendous.

Stewart Island is indeed a wild beautiful spot.

Back on earth we teamed up with Phillip Smith, initially to grab a last feed of scallops, and then during late evening to head off along Ocean Beach to film kiwis. The Stewart Island kiwi is the largest of these quaint flightless symbols of our nation. The birds we illuminated in the spotlight were about 65cm high and apparently weigh up to 3.6kgs. They eat sand hoppers and kelp flies, which live among the rotting heap, just above the high tide line. Phillip Smith guides parties on a number of similar excursions and it is absolutely captivating.

So there we were with all sorts of beautiful pictures, still no fishing show, definitely no great white sharks and a realisation that if this television lark was ever going to pay, someone was going to have to find some money.

John Angus and I began a search that netted enough to get the first series into financial difficulty but at least we had a place to use the film we had gathered on Stewart Island, but it was the next trip during the second series that really consolidated the story. It was mid-April 1994 when Paul Richards, Tony Burrows, Tom Davis and I flew to Invercargill, "grabbed" the Foveaux Express and headed across the strait, returning to Stewart Island. Foveaux Strait was flat calm and friendly, the forecast boisterous and vindictive. It was a "shoot" I won't forget in a hurry. Mike Bhana and some of the other people involved in series one, Larry Keating and John Angus, together with Ken and Anna Lucas, had decided to pursue other interests, as there didn't appear to be any value in continuing making television at a loss. I decided to take on the roles of several people, trim the budget and give the whole thing one good go. Series two was the result and series three, four, five and six have followed.

Anyway it was the lean, mean television machine that visited Stewart Island to join the late Kevin Anderson and wife Dot aboard *Moana*.

Kevin and Dot treated us like kings, we had a ball. Kevin was tragically drowned in a boating accident on Great Barrier Island in

1997. I will never forget his enthusiasm and hospitality. I learnt a great deal from Kevin.

On Tuesday 12th April we spent the morning filming some scenic shots around Half Moon Bay and then some introductions "Welcome to *Gone Fishin'*".

It was 1.30pm before we clambered aboard *Moana* with a "ring in" dive buddy named Paul Webb dragged in, so I wouldn't drown or get carried away on the end of the new underwater camera.

We headed for a reef a few miles NE of Half Moon Bay, the sky was the colour of lead and looked as heavy. The wind came in gusts and hinted that it was out to commit premeditated murder. Nature was restless, brooding, out for blood. I stood on the deck gearing up and an involuntary shiver raced up my spine and lifted the hairs on the back of my neck.

For some reason certain dives don't feel right and this meteorological unrest didn't leave me with a good feeling about what was to follow.

The wind hadn't 'come away' in a full blown storm – it was biding its time – and I didn't want to make it difficult for the skipper by being 25 metres under the drink when all hell broke loose.

"Should be OK", said Kevin, "if it turns to custard I'll be on top of your bubbles revving the engine. Come straight up, you'll be right."

So Paul and I splashed into a world that moved to a different drum beat. The rocks were covered in a coarse, red, stumpy kelp-like weed. In shallower depths, bull kelp danced gracefully to the rhythm of the swells. Butterfish, wrasse and moki glided through the ravines. It was too deep for paua but crevices held promise of a big crayfish. Paul wanted to catch one and I wanted to film one. We cruised through the canyons, brushed by the weed jungle, a relaxed fossick totally oblivious to anything that might be happening on the surface in that other world. I love to dive; to cruise and look, film and learn, is captivating. Paul was just ahead of me buried under the kelp when suddenly a shower of bubbles erupted, a head popped up and two very round eyes conveyed that the diver had been face to face with something of major interest.

Paul pointed frantically under the weed and I needed no further encouragement. Under the weed was a crevice and in it was a crayfish a shade over 4 kilos. I looked up but Paul kept gesticulating as if to say grab it. The challenge of communicating underwater was immediately apparent. In the end I swam out of the way and left the gap open for him. On land I would have said "I've got the underwater camera, you grab dinner". Underwater it was a bit more complicated and those big round eyes disappeared under the rock. Immediately there was a shower of mud and debris, arms, legs, feelers, everything shrouded in a snowball of gloom.

Suddenly the round smiling eyes rose above the murk, crayfish in hand, and we headed for the surface.

Back to the world of leaden sky but still only a breeze. Kevin had *Moana* shadowing our every move and very quickly we were winched

aboard. The water that had been 13°C in December was 9°C in April. The breeze sucked body heat out of the wetsuit.

It was time for a hasty change into warm gear.

"Biggest cray I've caught", said Paul. "I didn't want to muck it up, that's why I thought you'd better grab it", he said. It was a very friendly gesture.

"Can't film and grab at the same time", I replied but I must admit the old trigger finger was a bit itchy.

Paul, the cameraman, can't help himself when there's a fishing rod about and while we changed, he and Tony had lines over the side catching a procession of cod, some of them real beauties. The timing was great as it coincided with the first serious squall bearing down on us.

I could hear the wind screaming long before it hit and a line of white water snaked across the bay before crashing and slamming into the hull.

Moana groaned and heeled slightly as if yielding to the tempest. As is often the case, the wind eased slightly after that initial buffeting and the shower blew through, leaving us time to get cleaned up.

Paul Richards was having a ball. "This one feels like a beauty", he said, and sure enough a huge blue cod, 4 or 5 kilos, sailed over the side.

"Got to get that on camera, put it back over the side, Tony can shoot it."

So Tony became camera, Kevin got a lesson in directional microphones and Paul happily filled the role of chief angler and pulled in a beauty.

An albatross skimming the waves, beautiful birds and great companions.

"Forecast says 45 knots of westerly and I think this is the start of it", yelled Kevin in competition with wind, waves and gloating cameraman. "Better head back and hope it drops down in the morning."

With that, the nose came round and our down sea run became a punch into the gathering storm.

Moana drove straight into it and that heaving sea broke clean over the bow, showering spray 10 metres in the air. We had a glimpse of how we must have looked as a nearby fishing boat was running a parallel course and heading for home. All we had was occasional looks but it was enough to see the vessel completely disappear. Everything was heaving, spray filled the air and a great dive ended in an exhilarating run home.

Paul took the wheel and Kevin started filleting cod. Even in that storm the birds arrived in numbers to feast on the bits that were hurled off the stern. Sooty shearwaters or muttonbirds ducked and dived and seabird royalty turned up in the form of albatrosses and mollyhawks. Beautiful big birds that glide rather than fly and possess a wonderful majestic presence. They are a thrilling sight at any time but to see them so at home in a storm was a real thrill. For the

Paul Richards, the cameraman, until I went for a dive, then he became the fisherman. Always on the look out for a cappuccino machine.

albatross this was business as usual.

That night we joined Kevin and Dot for a typical Stewart Island home-cooked meal comprising crayfish, seafood chowder, corned beef and vegies. It was to fortify us against the storm and boy, were we going to need it.

My diary says SW 50 knots gusting 70 and as we completed a left hand turn out of Half Moon Bay next morning the weather was really warming up. It was cold and miserable, the spray was bitter enough to feel as though it was stabbing holes in my cheeks. If yesterday's little effort was in second gear, suddenly the storm had found overdrive. The rain drove in horizontally also trying to rip the skin off your face. Water, cloud and rain merged and tore at each other's throats. *Moana* ran into the grey breaking swells and sought the shelter of Port William. A lee shore created by bush-covered hills provided an oasis in which to fish and dive. At this time there was a virus attacking the famous Bluff oysters but there was nothing stopping divers from picking up a feed. When Paul and I leapt into the partially sheltered briny the 9°C water actually felt warm. Topside it was cold enough to snow and felt as if it wanted to.

Those beautiful big succulent Bluff oysters lay on the bottom in their solid, little shells, so in 20 metres of water and after a ten minute dive, we had all we could eat. In those conditions we dived with the catch bag attached to 50 metres of rope and a large orange buoy. It shows the skipper where his divers are, even when squalls are blowing the tops off the bay and of course you surface right under it. Thus reunited you no longer have to worry about being driven across Foveaux Strait and off to South America. That safety line is an umbilical cord that can save lives.

Once on deck, the shaking started, serious tremors that started with toes and finished somewhere near the chattering teeth. I even shiver as I write this. Once reunited with thermal underwear and half a dozen layers of clothes topped with a full set of wet weather gear and sea boots, I started to feel better.

"Wrap your laughing gear around this", said a smiling Kevin who had just prised out of its shell, the biggest fattest oyster I have ever seen.

Down the hatch. "Absolutely beautiful and yes I'll have another", I replied. By the end of the day my oyster love affair was at an end.

I had a good feed and decided to film the close of the show by saying "and that's all for this episode of *Gone Fishin'*" after swallowing an oyster and making all sorts of appreciative noises. Unfortunately I kept mucking it up and so we had to do it again and again and again. My oyster tank was full to overflowing and I was ready to throw up, which I would have done if there had been one more take.

Before the oyster eatathon we set a few cod pots.

"You want to see some blue cod, this is the way to catch them", bellowed our host, as he attached a smelly bait bag he called a snifter to the inside of the pot. A cod pot looks like a crayfish pot with four entrances that funnel down into the interior. Over the side goes the baited pot, and hey presto, an hour later, it's a blue cod summit conference. I jumped over the side and filmed the hapless cod swimming around on death row.

This time I started shaking before I hit the bottom. A wet wetsuit is refreshing in the tropics but not on Stewart Island during an April storm but the shots on the underwater camera were worth it.

We had proved to ourselves that even when the weather conspires against you there are opportunities. I love to film the ocean in good moods and bad and I will not forget what it took to make those Stewart Island stories. A good friend is one who never loses his sense of humour when the chips are down. Kevin Anderson was such a man. All through that storm we had a great laugh and enjoyed the spectacle.

Stewart Island was another reminder that the ocean is something you never beat and should never take for granted. Be thankful for the good days and very wary of those that are not.

6
Great Barrier

Great Barrier Island is on Auckland's doorstep and yet it feels a world away. The island is a beautiful oasis characterised by an undulating, sometimes steep, often bush-covered landscape. The population is sparse, mostly clustered around Tryphena or Claris near the southern airfield.

The two grass airfields reflect the character of Great Barrier, they are synonymous with rutted shingle roads, 'laid back' people who have opted for an alternative lifestyle and a natural quaint appeal. Most stunning of all is the geography, endless bays, untouched valleys, superb beaches, clusters of islands and a rich blue ocean knocking constantly on the door.

My trips to Great Barrier have always been an adventure. On every trip there is something to discover, experience and enjoy – it is an exceptional place.

Our first attempt to film 'Barrier' was on a heli-fish organised by John Farr, the well known land-based guide, who has a knack of sleuthing out big fish.

Pilot Tim Briggs was working for North Shore Helicopters at the time and had collected just enough hours to make landing on the rocks near Miners Head a very interesting event.

The versatility of the helicopter is never better demonstrated than when they land anglers on narrow ledges of almost inaccessible rock and set up a few hours of great fishing. We were tackling the last couple of hours of the outgoing tide, the best time to fish and the largest area of flat rock to land on. By the time we left, waves were washing up between the skids.

Our helicopter flight was in two hops, our first stop being the lawn of a rustic but very appropriate hut that John uses to house his fishing parties.

At night you can walk across the stream to Claris Beach and catch

snapper or kahawai while gentle waves hiss and suck under your feet.

We dumped a tonne of gear and organised to ferry camera crew, equipment, anglers, burley etc. etc. to Miners Head. The greater part of our flight was low level, weaving in and out of bays, swooping through saddles and generating the sort of adrenalin that is useful when targeting a 20lb snapper.

In ten minutes the first load was spilling out onto the rocks and burley was heading for the briney. The machine peeled off the rock and roared out over the ocean to gain height, before banking round and disappearing over the rim of the cliffs that formed our backdrop. The turbine screamed, blades clattered but as soon as the Jet Ranger was behind the cliff, the only sound was ocean talk and the chatter of birds that had beat a hasty departure from their rookery when we appeared. They set up their picket line on the rocks, protesting that we had interrupted their day and should therefore share our bait and burley.

Land-based fishing on Great Barrier can be exceptionally good, plus you always think that no one has set foot anywhere near your spot, ever. It is wild, isolated and very beautiful but these cliffs were not always so well regarded because it was here that the steamer *Wairarapa* foundered in 1894 with the loss of 121 lives. At 8 minutes past midnight on October 29, 1894, the *Wairarapa* steamed into the 250 metre cliffs that surrounded our tranquil fishing platform. No one was aware of the fact that the ship was off course and she ran headlong into the cliffs. It was sufficiently rough for waves to break over the ship as she settled and pluck passengers from the decks. Our survival on the ocean is so often at the whim of weather and waves, strike the wrong combination and pleasure can turn to tragedy.

Smashed steel plates and a jumble of superstructure mark the *Wairarapa*'s grave. The ocean's inhabitants now call the ship home and as a dive site her underwater garden is a real picture, but whenever I glide through the wreckage I imagine the absolute terror, the complete horror, that must have accompanied the disaster.

The return of Tim, blasting over the cliff, banking heavily and dropping like some large noisy, very ungainly bird onto the rocks, interrupted my reverie and that of the seagull picket line. They scattered in a squawking, complaining cluster of ruffled feathers.

With the machine shut down, the birds were back, a pilchard was quickly threaded onto a hook and flicked into the burley trail.

"No sinkers", said John, "just let it drift out into the trail, doesn't matter if it falls to the bottom, a big snapper will have no trouble tracking it down."

One of the challenges in these situations is that of balancing the loss of bait with loss of gear.

Very often in the rocky, broken, weed-covered ground, you get snagged on the retrieval, so you try and judge when smaller fish are likely to have taken the bait and only then, when the hook is empty, do you try to get it back.

Firmer baits, such as the very successful baby squid, ensure that you stay baited for longer.

I prefer to cast and retrieve quickly in those situations because often a lengthy stay on the bottom means moray eels or stingrays, neither of which are welcome visitors.

It wasn't long before we started pulling in a procession of kahawai, then an odd snapper, and finally my rod loaded up on something very solid.

The tide had turned and was fighting its way up the sides of our plateau towards the helicopter. Waves were building up and bursting over the black wall of rock.

This fish did all of the snapper things, it pulled plenty of line, shook its head and fought like a champ.

I leant back with as much pressure as I dared and finally a large orange/red shape materialised out of the deeper blue and was dragged near Tim's waiting gaff. With a few flicks of the tail, 20lb of snapper disappeared back into deeper water. My heart was in my throat, Paul the cameraman was winding me up and Tim tried to improve his precarious gaffing position on rocks that spent half their time underwater.

"Just about", said John as the snapper arrived on the surface and rolled over. I leant back, wound in a few turns, Tim reached with the gaff and a larger than normal wave chose that moment to smash onto the rocks. Tim lunged, missed, reached again but the wave had spoilt his aim and the gaff went through the line. He almost jumped in and grabbed the fish but checked his dive and the snapper recovered enough to fin back into its home.

It was one of those days, but after the chopper flight around the coast, catching a good feed and sharing the beauty of the Barrier, it was a loss that fell short of tragedy.

That was our last flurry and with the ocean at our feet, we beat a hasty retreat, leaving the seagulls with a feed of pilchards and a brief end to their protests.

During May the Island can get a little crisp but when eight people cram into camp, a fire is lit and the smell of cooking filters through the room, everything seems very cosy.

I love the banter that develops after a day's fishing, the times when everyone picks on your mistakes or congratulates a particular success. It is also a time to plan the next day and talk tackle and strategy, how to get the jump on huge Barrier denizens.

"I'll send my mate along the rocks an hour ahead of us tomorrow", said John. "He can get all the burley working, so by the time we arrive in the chopper, everything should be humming."

That, we all decided, was a fine plan and bound to give us the edge on the snapper.

I awoke before daylight to the sound of snapper fillets sizzling in the pan. John was firing up breakfast, as his buddy shot out the door to deliver a 24 kilo mountain of burley to the snapper population.

Paul, the cameraman, dragged himself out of bed and gave me that "beyond the call of duty look" that reminds you that he isn't a morning person.

"We're in for a nice day", said the cook, wiping his hand across a steamed-up window to show us that the stars were being hunted by the gathering dawn. The day would be clear and calm, perfect.

"Won't be long before that burley goes to work and then hang on, it's going to be a big snapper day."

Kingfish are also regular visitors off the rocks and we were hopeful of connecting with something in the 30 kilo bracket.

We crunched through frosted grass, leaving a row of white footprints from the hut to the helicopter. Tim had to be back by lunchtime and the tide was perfect for an early fish.

The spot, when we landed, enabled us to fish all of the outgoing tide. It was a vast expanse of sloping brown and black rock that dropped steeply at the water's edge into a rugged bay that was perfect for a big mooching snapper. The rock was punctured and split with numerous channels and fissures but weathered and smooth above high water. Barnacles and limpets, weed and anemones emerged as the tide receded. Crabs scuffled and scurried as we walked to the water's edge and flicked our baits to the foe. The stage was set, bring on the fish, the camera was rolling.

Auckland angler, John Eichelhiem, joined John and I as the fishing trio and half our number had walked to the spot while the chopper carried the film crew and cameras. Believe it or not, I chose to walk the invigorating couple of kilometres that took us through grassy glades and trees, along the beach and around the rugged cliffs of the point we stood on. Almost immediately John and I landed school

snapper, it seemed as though the "early burley" trick was working. Then it went quiet, dead quiet, not even a kahawai.

"Can't understand it", said John Farr, "I've left this spot alone for the last couple of months. The snapper should be nudging each other out of the way to get at the baits."

The sun climbed, the tide receded, the pilot looked at his watch.

"Sorry boys, I'm going to have to go", came the call.

Something had happened to our perfect fishing day, all of that early burley, all of that hope, a good tide, what could possibly be wrong?

"I'm sorry", said John Farr, "I just can't believe it. Every time I burley this spot, we get good fish, plenty of them. It doesn't seem possible."

With heavy hearts and plenty of unused film, we started to load the heavy gear into the chopper. Several of us were going to walk back through the valley above the cliff, it would act like a tonic to wipe away our frustrations. The pohutukawas grew in a fringe around the cliff and down into the valley. The hillsides were covered in trees and grass, the deeper gullies choked with scrub. But as we cleaned up, even the beauty of our location couldn't shake John out of his disappointment.

"Don't worry", I said, "we can have another go, it's still been a great day."

"I'm sorry", he repeated, as he walked down to pull in the empty burley bags that had been fastened to lengths of rope and hurled into the weed at the edge of the wash zone.

John pulled on the first rope, in came the burley bag.

"What the hell", he screeched, "the bag's still full, in fact my mate

Big snapper are what it's all about and these are all big Barrier snapper. The largest 12 kilos.

didn't take the burley out of the plastic bags."

All morning the big snapper had probably been window shopping, swimming past our burley bags, staring at the contents and heading for greener pastures.

The language became very colourful when we realised that the entire burley supply was still safely wrapped in its plastic coating and had done absolutely nothing to attract the fish.

"Last time I get someone to do the job", said our guide, as the rest of us rolled about laughing our heads off. In the end even John could laugh, but when you have a television crew on hand and you want to promote your business, you are entitled to a good innings. This had not been what John expected because he is one of the best, most successful land-based guides in the business.

To make matters worse we had caught a number of moray eels and in typical fashion I had been stirring John up. "Looks like you have a new nickname", I teased, "Moray John, the eel catcher."

"Don't be a bastard", he hissed, "the day's been bad enough without that."

Next morning, 25th May, we set off with Adrian Van Doreen to dive the wreck of the *Wiltshire*. We had run out of snapper time and I wanted to film the wreck. Black ominous-looking cloud scudded overhead and an evil breeze whipped up the bay – it suddenly looked and felt like winter.

Adrian runs the dive shop and Great Barrier Dive Charters from a base in Tryphena Harbour and his back door is a diverse paradise. He is a long way from the *Wairarapa* wreck but that of the *Wiltshire* is almost on his doorstep.

On 31st May, 1922, the passenger/cargo liner inward bound for Auckland, ran onto the rocks at Rosalie Bay. It was a bad mood night on the ocean and in appalling conditions, the crew sheltered in the saloon as heavy seas pounded the ship.

The hull broke in two at 11.30 next morning and the situation began to look desperate. Other ships appeared but could do little in the wild, heaving seas.

Shore-based rescuers tried to fire a line to the *Wiltshire* but their attempts failed and it wasn't until 2nd June when crew floated a line ashore on a hatch cover, that the 103 exhausted officers and crew were rescued.

When 10,000 tonnes of ship breaks up and spreads itself over the ocean floor there is quite a jumble.

The *Wiltshire* has been blasted as salvagers sought to recover large amounts of copper wire but as a dive she is fascinating.

Serious wreckage starts in 10 metres and disperses down the rocks into deeper water. It is a fascinating place to scratch around or film and while conditions became decidedly gloomy topside, 25 metres visibility made our cruise around the wreckage absolutely delightful.

Adrian plucked a sizable cray from under a slab of steel and deposited it in his catch bag. After over 60 years, the *Wiltshire* has attracted the plants and animals that the ocean feels should "pretty her up".

The wrecks of the Barrier represent only a small fraction of the amazing dive experiences to be found on cliffs, boulders, kelp forests and gardens. For the fisherman/diver, Great Barrier Island is a very exciting place to visit.

A short time after that trip I had a call from Lion Breweries who were running a competition, the winners of which they wanted to send fishing on the Barrier with me.

I suggested that with the number of people they wanted looking after, Moray John and I should do the job.

The weekend duly arrived, there were no cameras to be seen, which turned out to be a real pity, and two plane loads of eager anglers flew out and landed on the Claris strip. We were blessed with perfect weather and Friday night saw us camped at the legendary Tipi & Bobs, an angler's haven with bar, restaurant and accommodation nestled on the edge of Tryphena Harbour. Our anglers were very definitely in a party mood but John and I left them to it. It was going to be a big day and I for one, was not going to waste a second of it. If you are looking for a great fishing base it would be hard to go past Tipi & Bobs. People who fish always make good hosts and Bob Whitmore knows a thing or two about catching snapper.

The day started with a hearty breakfast and then we headed off by boat to a transfer point where we crowded onto a ledge of rock. Our ferry departed, the burley went in the water, and after the removal of plastic bags, a trail drifted out into the current and we were set.

Pilchards, tied two at a time, sanma and baby squid were the preferred bait and within 20 minutes one of the guys screamed a scream of pure elation.

"I'm hooked up to a train", he yelled, his voice electric with the thrill that came from watching something very large head for the horizon.

The day had dawned overcast but calm and I have a good feeling about fishing the overcast, it seems to prolong the morning bite.

Our angler thrilled to the challenge, John and I headed along the ledge armed with gaffs.

"Keep the pressure on", said Moray John.

"Shall I wind up the drag?" replied the angler.

"No, don't touch it, all you'll do is cut the fish off, be patient."

It is excellent advice, you should always know how much pressure to apply relevant to the breaking strain of the line. People often feel that if they are not winning a battle early then the answer is more pressure.

The result is usually a broken line and a trophy fish swimming away a little smarter for the experience.

Our angler started to tire but so did the fish and the classic head shakes transmitted their intensity to the rod. With each shake, the heavily loaded rod dipped towards the water, thump, thump, thump, it went. John and I looked at each other knowing that it was a beauty.

"I wish we were filming this", I whispered.

Great view of the approach to Great Barrier Island from the Claris side.

The angler's elation had changed and he looked all purpose. Concentration and determination had replaced elation as this fight was far from over.

Blue cracks appeared in the cloud and the dark water changed to a rich blue. There was a flash of white but a couple of sweeps from a mighty tail and the beast was lost from view.

We were crowded around, the other guys holding rods but paying more attention to the scrap, when suddenly there was a yell. I spun around, expecting to see a thrashing body flailing away in the tide, someone, I thought, had fallen in. I was wrong, someone else leant back, rod bent halfway to the water and reel screaming, howling as line snaked away into the blue.

"Yahoo", yelled angler number two, "I've never caught a snapper bigger than 5lb – yippee. It feels as big as a horse." The rod settled into a rhythmic dip, dip, dip, and we knew the angler, if he could just hang on, was going to smash that 5lb record.

"Quick", screeched angler one, "I can see it", and see it we all did. A huge snapper, an angler's dream, rose up and rolled onto its side.

"Guide it towards me", said John, already earning a reprieve from the name Moray John.

Smack went the gaff and 27lb of superb snapper was safe.

The angler danced, he sang, he yelled, he laughed, he was in heaven.

"I've never caught a 20 pounder before", he grinned. "I don't care if I catch nothing else all weekend, that fish just makes my trip."

Angler two puffed and heaved and he too worked a beautiful fish to the rocks. It tipped the scales at 23lb.

64

That weekend, everyone caught their dream fish, you couldn't have written a better script and of course, there was no camera.

John Farr was re-crowned King of the Great Barrier snapper guides and a smile lit his face.

"You know we're going to have to try again and film a day like this", said Snapper John.

"Yes", I agreed looking out over the beautiful angling paradise called Great Barrier Island.

*Great Barrier Land-Based
fishing sometimes means a
bit of a stroll. John Farr leads
the way.*

7
Nelson

It always seems to be fine in Nelson. Every time I take "the crew" there, the sun shines, the fish bite and we come away with an action-packed show.

Our first *Gone Fishin'* shoot was in March 1994 and some of the action was exceptional, but off camera a few things went astray.

Daryl Crimp, well known cartoonist, some time restaurateur and always an angler, was to be my buddy and did we pick a perfect day. When we finally got Crimpy's boat in the water way after daylight, the wind was still in bed, not even a puff.

I find Nelson to be a delightful city, a place that has the feel of a country town but the restaurants, crafts and culture of the city that it purports to be.

Nestled on the edge of the vast sweep of Tasman Bay, Nelson is a stone's throw from places like D'Urville Island, Abel Tasman National Park, Golden Bay, Nelson Lakes, National Park and of course there is great fishing to be found just out of the harbour.

"You'd better get over here", an animated Crimpy had said at the start of a late night, well-lubricated phone call.

"Where are you?" I queried.

"Nelson, you stupid bugger, and I want to see some snapper on that half hour of scenery you call a fishing show. The snapper are jumping into the boat down here!"

"How much have you had to drink" , I asked wondering what the motivation was for this good-humoured attack.

"Nuff."

"Well, when is the prime season?", I responded hoping for a courteous response. "Now you ass, why do you think I phoned, you'd be too late to pick fruit."

Unfortunately it takes a bit of time and organisation to get a film crew together and plan a shoot that has things like weather contingencies built in. The fluke in this case was that the following week we were filming French Pass and D'Urville Island, Nelson's neighbours.

"I tell you what", I said, "if you guarantee that we'll catch fish, I'll be there next Thursday on the 31st."

Silence. "Are you there Crimpy?" I said.

"Yep", he answered, "but that puts me on the spot."

"Well, you're the bloke who reckons they jump in the boat. Have they changed their minds?"

"Nope, you just make sure you're here with plenty of tape, I'll do the rest."

Click went the line, but I wasn't sure if alcohol had lubed the tonsils or whether he had genuinely warmed to the challenge. There was only one way to find out and one day to film in.

We drove from French Pass to Nelson on the 30th and checked in to the Tahuna Beach Motels.

Paul, the cameraman, was excited because it was almost Easter weekend, we had been away for a while and his wife was flying in on Thursday night. Tony and I were flying back to Auckland while Paul and Felicity were taking the Pathfinder for a spin around the South Island.

We were a happy crew and Crimpy told us the forecast was perfect and there were one or two fish about.

It was amazing how the closer we got to Nelson the less positive became the fishing stories.

"Yeah, one or two around but you know what fishing's like, can't guarantee anything."

"That's not what you said when you called me", I said defensively.

"When did I call you?" he said indignantly, then added, "just teasing, we'll get you a fishing programme, trust your old mate."

The day started slowly but we eventually got Crimpy's car fixed, found the key to the boat, worked out who borrowed the outboard's gas tank, found some bait, purchased some burley and found out where the boat ramp was.

We spluttered our way down a mirror smooth harbour towards the entrance, meeting a slight roll as we cleared the boulder bank and turned right.

It was a crisp morning and we seemed to have the ocean to ourselves.

"Great", said the cartoonist/angler, "I don't want anyone else to know about this spot."

He was sincere but I pointed out that putting a day's fishing about his secret spot on national television was likely to guarantee that he got some company on future outings.

This place was so close to Nelson city that it was virtually impossible to film without landmarks.

We slowed, Crimpy looked about him furtively, still hoping to keep our outing a secret, then reached for the anchor and biffed it over the side.

The anchor hit the bottom at nine metres and the burley job began.

"Most people drop burley over the side and forget about it", said the now serious angler. "I drop a bag to the bottom, put one in mid-water and have a third just under the surface. It may sound like overkill but I'll pull fish up this trail from a mile away."

Crimpy added to the surface burley by scraping mullet frames and sending flakes of fish drifting down and away in the tide. I have always found that tide and snapper go together and of course it's self-evident that you need current to carry your burley and set up a trail.

We used a floating keeper hook on 24 kilo trace with a main fixed hook tied to one end. A pilchard was the preferred bait and the first snapper arrived within five minutes. I caught four in the next ten minutes before Crimpy pulled in two, one on the main hook and one on the keeper.

"Bit slow today", he said with a supercilious grin. Within 20 minutes we had snapper swimming up the burley trail and splashing around the back of the boat. It was great, superb, everything that was promised and then Crimpy hooked a beauty.

Nod, nod, nod went the rod, the reel shed an exciting amount of line and the camera rolled.

A light breeze lay a pattern of ripples on the surface, distant mountains proudly displayed their early winter snow and the very pretty city of Nelson was bathed in sunshine.

"Yeah, that'll do, way bigger than anything you've caught", said the angler, as I gaffed his fish aboard. It was a 7 kilo beauty, star of the show. A few kingfish turned up, smashing into the bait fish that milled around on the surface. We were ill-prepared and I lost my surface popper in an instant.

By 11.00am we were back at the boat ramp and nothing more than faint ripples danced across the bay. It was beautiful and a great show had been filmed in record time.

"We're heading over the hill to Takaka this afternoon, I'm going to film Pupu Springs and then float down to the Takaka River. Why not come along?" I suggested to the cartoon expert who now called himself a fisherman.

"Don't even know if my wetsuit still fits", said a version of Crimpy a little more portly than the "model" I had known a few years earlier. "Yeah, I'll come along for a laugh."

We scoffed a quick lunch and set off, Paul and Tony in the Pathfinder, Crimpy and I in his old Holden.

Pupu Springs is just out of Takaka township and is famous for its spectacular purity and clarity. As a dive, there is a unique beauty to the springs with dancing stones and pebbles rising above the escaping flow. Weed beds surround the six metre deep spring and fresh water crayfish and occasional trout add a little interest. It is so clear that the feeling is one of floating in space.

The drive from Nelson to the Springs takes about an hour and a half, passing through Motueka and then climbing over the winding

Takaka Hill and down into the untouched beauty of Golden Bay. You skim the edge of Abel Tasman National Park near the summit and gaze across a landscape of limestone pillars, rocks and buttresses. The Abel Tasman area at sea level is a procession of beautiful bays, beaches and islands. You could explore the Nelson region for weeks and never cut the same trail twice.

At the Springs I changed quickly into a wetsuit and organised the underwater camera. After filming Crimpy and the bouncing stones, the plan was to drift the Pupu outflow until it met up with the Takaka River. I had done it a few years before for a laugh and remembered a large number of trout in very filmable locations.

Paul, Tony and I got to the edge of the Spring and were set to record our introduction. From behind the bushes came a lot of swearing and cursing. Crimpy was having some problems.

"Darn wetsuit's shrunk", he said, trying to tuck a few of the more conspicuous bulges in to a suit that was now a couple of sizes too small.

"I'm sure it fitted me last Christmas, hmmm, maybe it was the one before."

We eventually packaged him up, pushed everything together and forced the zip up under his neck. It was so tight he couldn't hold his arms by his side and his head and unruly mop stuck out the top, cheeks and forehead the colour of beetroot.

"Think I'll flop in the tide, the suit will give a little in the water", said a faint and very high pitched voice.

We filmed a quick introduction and the "whale of Pupu Springs" and I made our way into the cool gin-clear outflow. The visibility was indeed seemingly limitless and the afternoon sun illuminated every bouncing, bubbling pebble, piece of shingle, and the weed that surrounded the pool and flowed downstream forever dancing to the whim of the river. Within 20 minutes I had my underwater shots of the Springs, so Crimpy and I headed off on our hour long floating journey. The volume of water picks up, the banks crowd in and small rapids add to the excitement between the pools. Within a very short distance I realised that I had made a mistake and should have left my weight belt behind. I was just positively buoyant in the pool but in the aerated water of the rapids, I started getting knocked around.

The weight helps to control the underwater camera during such a drift but a smack on the housing soon turned the underwater camera into another unnecessary burden.

There were large sleek trout under logs, in the bottom of pools and sheltering under the bank. All I could do was look.

I was thinking of ditching the belt, when at the bottom of a piece of white water, the arm holding the camera shot under a log, while the rest of me draped itself over the top. The impact took the air out of my lungs but I thought that if I let go, that would be the last time I would see the underwater camera.

Eventually I tore the camera free and cartwheeled off downstream and into another log. This time there was no air to remove from my lungs and the ribs did their best to cushion the blow. My float down the quiet stream was losing its appeal.

Crimpy, the cork, bobbed along ahead of me having a ball, I bounced along like the loser in a demolition derby. In the next quiet section I regained my dignity and stayed attached to weight belt and camera.

"Great fun", yelled the buoyant cork.

"I'm sure it is", I said trying to work out which ribs were broken.

"What's wrong with you?" he enquired, eager to find another chance to line up a barrage of abuse.

"Nothing, just admiring those fish, but camera's gone down."

"Ha, call yourself a cameraman, try the on button", he laughed and finned away down the avenue of trees that almost shielded the late afternoon sun from view.

I lay on my back at that point and watched tuis, bellbirds and fantails flit through the trees, their delightful melodies ringing in my ears. Tuis and bellbirds are the songsters of the bush, their melodious bell-like calls sound almost as though the tui is competing with the bellbird for sheer beauty of call. It was one of those delightful moments that fixes a place in your memory.

Soon the motion changed and the smooth flow formed into wavelets and then tumbled and broke again over logs and small boulders. I smashed over another log and into another boulder, all the while maintaining a vice-like grip on the camera. As a white water rafting guide, I knew how to read the river, but even so, my lack of buoyancy and control made a simple float a fair sort of battering.

Another quiet section of sheer beauty and then we were out into the broad expanse of the Takaka River. At the junction, trout were lined up like spectators at a football match. What a sight, I looked up to get Crimpy to fin over and have a look, but he was 50 metres downstream.

Although the scenery and fish were everything I had hoped for, lack of footage was a real disappointment.

Paul and Tony had driven the vehicles to a point 150 metres downstream and filmed our arrival at their feet.

Crimpy pounded out, full of the joys of spring. I felt as though I had been through a mincer.

"You're not fit, that's your problem", exclaimed my ever-supportive mate. There was no point in telling him what happened, I would never have lived it down.

Needless to say, it was a good week before the bruises faded and everything was on the mend. The answer, of course, is that you never take any body of water for granted, not the ocean, a river, a lake, a stream or a puddle, they are just waiting to bite you back. It was funny that I received a reminder in that delightful, clear joyride down from Pupu Springs. Try it, you'll wonder what the fuss was about, but don't wear a weight belt with an underwater camera.

I thought that was enough adventure for one day, but I was mistaken.

Paul and Tony loaded all of the camera cases back in the Pathfinder and headed back over the hill so Paul could pick up Felicity. It was the end of a prolonged spell of filming. Crimpy and I bounced along behind them in the old Holden.

It was dark by the time we groaned our way to the summit of the Takaka Hill and started to meander our way down the twists and turns that lead to the plains and hence to Nelson.

About halfway down the hill we came round a bend and there was a mortally wounded, almost new, Pathfinder smashed into the bank.

Crimpy and I pulled off to the side as a wide-eyed Paul came dancing up to the window.

"I skidded on that patch of shingle and lost control", came the verdict. Tony was standing off to the side with a relieved sort of grin hanging on his face.

"Everyone OK?" I asked.

"Yeah, everyone except the wagon, it's taken a bit of a knock."

"Just as well you didn't slide the other way", said Crimpy, "no one would be smiling if you went over the bank."

All we could see of 'the bank' was a black void dominating the darkness. The boys were lucky, the Pathfinder was not and Paul had to rent a car for his journey around the South Island.

In spite of the mishap we had thoroughly enjoyed our 24 hour Nelson adventure with Daryl Crimp, cartoonist, angler, part time restaurateur and whale of Pupu Springs.

Nelson produces its share of great snapper especially now the fishery seems to be in recovery mode.

8
Ngawi/Te Awaiti

The Wairarapa Coast is one of New Zealand's best kept secrets and places like the fishing village of Ngawi cling to a coast that is as rugged as it is beautiful. I hadn't even heard of Ngawi until a very good friend of mine and retired commercial fisherman, Daryl Sykes, drew my attention to it.

"Most beautiful place on the coast", he said, "the fishermen use trailers with long booms to launch their boats through the surf. More bulldozers per head of population than anywhere else in the country plus you've got the lighthouse, seal colony and great fishing."

The great fishing bit had me in an instant and we made plans to film Ngawi. A couple of days before we left home on the Wairarapa shoot, Aaron, the soundman who replaced Tony, phoned up. "Sorry", he said, "I've put my back out and won't be able to make it, but don't worry, I've found an experienced replacement for you."

"Does he get sea sick?", came the logical response, "this is a rugged coast and if the lad gets sea sick, we'll all have a miserable time."

"No", said Aaron, "he's got a cast iron gut."

I phoned Johnathon with the cast iron gut and organised for him and I to drive from Auckland to Ngawi, a fair sort of hike. The cameraman was Grant Atkinson from Wellington, by then Attie was a veteran of many *Gone Fishin'* shoots.

We stayed in a farm stay a few kilometres along the coast from the township and hoed into a procession of beautiful home-cooked meals.

The coastline is spectacular, a thin strip of land bordered on one side by cliffs and on the other by a restless, heaving Pacific Ocean. There are a couple of semi beaches where surfers think the break is just Christmas but the greater percentage of the coast is a jagged line of rock that the ocean has beaten up for countless centuries. The only shelter for fishermen is on the beach and a few have wound up there when their intention was to stay afloat.

Larger ships have also been lost on this coast and no one treats it lightly. Every commercial fisherman from Ngawi has stories to tell of the times they "got the wind up".

As has happened with seal colonies all over New Zealand, the Cape Palliser colony is experiencing a baby boom.

They are beside the road and draped over a large chunk of rugged real estate. If you are coming at them from a downwind position, one thing you will find easily is the seal colony.

Along this magnificent windswept section of the coast, one thing stands out, Cape Palliser lighthouse. It sits high on a prominent headland and looms over the bay. The headland is, of course, Cape Palliser, from which the light derives its name.

Many a ship succumbed to the notorious gales that scream out of the south and in days before steam, several ships were driven onto the rocks of the 'Bay'.

The first was the barque *David,* in 1841, with the loss of 3 out of a crew of 29. The same year the American ship, *Elbe,* made an unintended stop.

In 1844, between April and July, three schooners were lost. Three more ships, one of them unidentified, were lost the following year. The toll continued and in 1869, the full rigged ship, *St. Vincent,* was wrecked, with the loss of 20 lives. The notorious Cook Strait gales were responsible, so in 1893, moves were made to establish a lighthouse on the Cape.

With the commissioning of the light in 1897, wrecks decreased dramatically, although the area still claimed the unwary or imprudent ship and crew. Six months before the light was first illuminated, another full rigged ship was wrecked within four miles of the lighthouse and 12 of her crew of 21 were drowned.

The Cape Palliser light stands 258 feet up on the southeastern tip of the North Island. From its 58 foot tower the light flashes twice every 30 seconds and is visible for 22 miles. The once manned lighthouse is now functioning on automatic, as are all of our critically appointed safety sentinels.

Why did I need a replacement sound man with a cast iron gut? Well it gets a little rough off the coast and there aren't many spots to put someone ashore. We fished day one on the crayfishing vessel *Mirvon,* owned by Dave and Raewyn Sinclair.

"Come and help pull a few pots", said Dave, "and we'll stop and have a bottom fish."

At daylight we all loaded gear aboard, then ourselves, and stood there as the bulldozer slowly backed the massive trailer into the surf.

A couple of big V8s and twin jet units saw *Mirvon* off the trailer, spun around and heading off for a day's work in the blink of an eye.

The crew prepared baits and Attie, Johnathon and I wedged ourselves in a corner out of the way.

Raewyn came along for a fish and a very keen angler she is. She is also a very successful one. We had about 80 cray pots to pull before

What does a great hunting area look like? Well, actually it looks like this – Te Awaiti hunting block.
Photo Chris Jolly

Dave would stop and fish, it wasn't long before the work started in earnest.

"The coast is loaded with crays", said David. "They've introduced a system called quota management where we are each allocated a tonnage that can be fished each year. When the quota's up, the gear comes out of the water. We used to fish for 12 months and hammer the coast but now my season is over in 3 or 4 months. The fishery has improved dramatically and the divers tell us there are crays all over the bottom. It's good for everyone."

For my money the quota management system, as applied to rock lobsters (crayfish) in particular, has been a resounding success. Everyone can find a feed of this delectable delicacy.

Other regulations applying to crays include a tail width of 54mm for males and 60mm for females. Females can't be snatched when they have eggs under the tail and no fish can be pulled when the shells are soft. Fisheries regulations vary around the coast and the onus is on the angler to become familiar with local idiosyncrasies.

We ripped through the pots, pulling out and measuring crays, flicking "shorts" and females in egg or "berry" back over the side. The sky was blue, the hills stood out stark and barren and a heavy surge thumped in hard against the nearby coast. Crays move from deeper water to shallow as the season progresses and much of our work was in about 20 fathoms. We fished the edge of reefs and pinnacles that Dave had marked on his G.P.S., or global positioning system.

The G.P.S. enables you to identify a spot and drive back to it any time you like. When used in conjunction with a good colour sounder, these "tools of the trade" improve efficiency no end, for both commercial fishermen and recreational anglers. For reliable electronics, one name stands at the top of the heap, Furuno, ask any commercial fisherman.

In 20 fathoms and less we were riding quite a swell. Once those big lazy Pacific swells roll in across shallower, broken ground they rear up and the closer to shore they move, the more bad tempered they get.

"Ok", said the skipper, at last, "let's catch a feed."

Dave threw over an anchor and we baited hooks with the same mackerel that was used to bait the cray pots.

Straight to the bottom and bang, blue cod, two at a time. The usual tackle tied in a ledger rig with a heavy sinker on the bottom of a 1.5 metre trace, swivel at the top and two hooks in between. I've mentioned that techniques for blue cod don't need to be too scientific and off the coast of Ngawi there is no shortage.

They also catch good groper with the prime season being mid-November till the end of February.

Add in a few tarakihi, occasional kingfish and snapper, albacore, skip jack tuna in the summer, big sharks and offshore trenches that hold broadbill, blue nose and bass and you are looking at an exciting fishery.

We filmed away quite happily until I realised that Johnathon had been very quiet. A glance in his direction showed that being at anchor was not agreeing with him. As I began the next chat to camera, a whole series of heaving noises began, complete with retches, and then Johnathon's breakfast went sailing over the side. A dreadful waste of bacon and eggs.

"Sorry folks", said the soundman, winning an academy award for the most polite "technicolour yawn" delivered up to the ocean.

From there it was all downhill. Johnathon tried desperately to do his job but he was battling the dreaded "mal de mer" and old mal wasn't settling for second place. He got so bad that he finished up wrapped around the winch frame. It was time to go home and nobody has ever been more pleased to see "terra firma" than "Mr. Cast Iron Gut". Seasickness takes no prisoners, if you are afflicted it can be a terrible thing and on a fishing show that spends a great deal of time on the ocean, it is a distinct disadvantage.

Many cures are bandied around, all are worth a go because many of them work, but try and choose something that doesn't make you drowsy, or all you do is sleep the day away. Many people who believed there was no hope have been cured, shop around if you are a sufferer, you could be pleasantly surprised. It's just putting the remedy to the test that may be unpleasant.

That was the end of our ocean-going Ngawi experience, but that night we were all invited to the annual party, where I had to dress up as Father Christmas and give presents to kids that ranged in age from 1-75.

One thing I'll say for the team at Ngawi is they sure know how to party.

While I was on the coast I found out that the hunting was

exceptionally good and Chris Jolly had invited us down for a diving/hunting excursion not too far up the coast from Ngawi. We had one day to film the impossible and it turned out to be a beauty.

On 5th February 1997, Rhys Duncan (camera), Tarx Morrison (sound) and myself joined Chris Jolly and Colin Jones for a diving/hunting day. Chris' son Simon assisted in the dive and a couple of Chris' friends waded out to pluck a feed of paua.

I thought I would get away with my 3mm tropical dive suit but someone forgot to tell the Wairarapa Coast that, in February, the water should be tropical.

It was very crisp but the prolific seafood took my mind off any thoughts of being cold.

There was a fair old sea running, large swells picked themselves up and rolled over a few prominent offshore rock and pinnacles. The heavy surf bore down relentlessly on the outer rim of rocks but inside was a large pool of waist-deep water filled with weed-covered boulders. It was dead low water and the surf kept at sufficient distance to enable us to chase a feed of paua and crayfish. Lunch for eight with enough left over for the next day. That was the target and when I waded in and looked under the first rock, I realised that

Colin Jones with a good Te Awaiti stag. Jonesy is a guide that few can match – Well done lad. Photo Chris Jolly

getting a feed would not be a problem. The underside of that boulder was packed with large paua and with the help of a dive knife I started flicking them off the rock and into a catch bag. Paua are subject to limits, the length of shell needing to be 125mm, but everything we looked at was over 150. You can take 10 per diver per day and only on snorkel, but on this coast at low tide, you hardly even need to get your feet wet.

What a wild, rugged chunk of geography this coast is and what a sportsperson's paradise. There are places like the Kaikoura Coast where I did a lot of my early diving, that always served up a feed of paua and crays or where I could always spear butterfish and moki. If you know where to go you can still achieve the same objective along that equally beautiful Kaikoura coastline.

What makes large chunks of the Wairarapa different is that you don't need a compass or secret spot, the population of pauas and crays is pretty darn healthy.

I love that feeling of energetic isolation many parts of our coast possess – sheer beauty that is enhanced by a crackling energy as if nature's elements are all competing. Towering hills and bush-filled valleys rear up above the coast. Pigs and a good population of red deer browse the gullies, clearings, scrub and tall timber. There is no one else around, you feel as though the whole thing has been laid on just for you and I started getting excited the instant I caught a glimpse of the coast.

"What a beautiful sight", I said to Rhys and Tarx once the vehicles pulled up alongside the "Jolly team".

"Do you reckon we'll get a feed?" said Tarx, who at 6'4" and 135 kgs, needs a fair bit of "topping up".

"Mate", said Chris Jolly, "we'll have you looking like a blimp before the day's over. No one leaves this coast hungry."

Our dive lasted 20 minutes with Chris and Simon going out into the deeper water for a serious sortie on crays. Colin and I, assisted by a couple of other lads, were responsible for the paua. I had to stay within reasonable camera range, but standing up to my knees, I pulled out paua and crays and waved them in front of the lens.

The show motto is particularly applicable to places like this "take enough for a feed and leave the rest alone". Every now and then you hear of poachers wading in to this coast trying to steal our birthright. If the locals catch them, chances are justice will be pretty swift. I, for one, want to know that my kids and their's can enjoy the same experience. It'll only happen if people adhere to limits or take less than the daily quota. Chris and Colin take just enough for a good feed and that's what we were about to organise.

The boys have a base for their hunting and diving activities they call the "Blowhard Hut". It is an outdoor home away from home and it is straight behind the coast, several kilometres up a twisted metal and clay track. Ideal 4 wheel drive country.

After the dive, our little procession wound its way up the "road", filming the Pathfinder's journey and the expanding vista of ocean,

Daryl Crimp laughing because he fluked a bigger snapper than me. You have to get luck sometimes Crimpy.

Rhys Duncan filming a pot full of steaming succulent, mouth watering crays "Get the picture". Part of an awesome feast compliments of Chris Jolly & Colin Jones – Te Awaiti Station – Wairarapa Coast.

Did I say seafood? – Te Awaiti again and mincing the paua to go with the crays.

French Pass – another of those little havens offering superb fishing, diving and hospitality. The Marlborough Sounds just begs to be explored.

Paua – beat the living daylights out of them especially the large white muscular foot. (Make sure you remove them from the shell and take off the gut first.) Throw them in a hot pan for a brief sizzle on each side. Beautiful.

Dave "Tui Dundee" Burkhart with a Castle Point kingfish. Dave is a commercial fisherman with a wealth of knowledge that is well worth tapping into.

A fine trumpeter compliments of Dave Burkhart and Sea Hawk. When the coast near Castle Point is calm, the fishing can be mind-blowing.

Paul O'Brian and James Sinclair smiling their way into another immaculate Te Kaha day.

Rob Cochrane and Cindy Lucas celebrate the arrival of dinner compliments of Te Kaha's pub reef.

An average Te Kaha snapper caught at the end of a hard day's filming. That was the one and only snapper that co-operated. Phew!

At the head of Long Sound the chopper deposited Ray Tinsley, Graham McGeogh and I plus a tonne of gear. Thank God the weather was co-operating.

Making friends with old fisherman/explorer George Burnby after telling him we were park board rangers and there to arrest him. Glad you've got a sense of humour, George.

Graham and Ray in the cave where the Maori chief Tarewai was laid to rest.

How rough can it get in Fiordland?? – Very!!

The Cindy Hardy, *quite the ship to explore Fiordland. A place to relax and soak up the scenery.*

The late Trevor Green, a hell of a pilot, pausing on the tops so that we could film the view.

hills and coast.

"Breathtaking", I said to Chris as we stood on the last vantage point before the road tucked in behind the coastal hills, entered the bush and scrub and wound its way along the ridges to the hut.

"Don't like the look of these clouds", said Colin, "think it's going to bucket down."

The cloud hung black and bloated over the distant hills, slowly and steadily gnawing its way along the skyline towards us. A gust of wind picked up the sweet smell of impending rain and threw it in our faces.

"Yeah, it's going to rain", I added, "nothing surer."

We tumbled back into the vehicles, I engaged 4 wheel drive, low ratio, and the Pathfinder ate up the remaining mud, broken ground and bogs before we swung round a bend and came face to face with the Blowhard Hut.

What a spot, high on a ridge, surrounded on three sides by bush or hillside and a superb view out over a valley that just had to be a great spot to hunt.

This was not the first time "the boys" had organised lunch "Blowhard style". A fire was lit outside and a huge pot full of water readied to receive the crays.

Colin and Chris organised the batter to whip up a feed of pancakes while we waited for the main course; crayfish and paua fritters.

As the crays boiled away another gust of moisture-laden air whipped through the trees around the hut and roared off down the gully. The kanuka danced and the first glob of moisture hit the tin roof, splat.

The black wall of cloud rolled over the ridge and as the temperature slid, the warm fleece jackets went on and with a steaming pot of crays in hand, we dived under the verandah.

Rain did its best to hold back, just the odd drop, still that contained half a cup of moisture.

"We use the crayfish water to tenderise the paua", said Chris. "Just drop the paua in the water that's come off the boil, leave them for a couple of minutes and hey presto, the paua almost fall out of the shell. From there pull the guts off, cut out the mouth and throw the rest of it through the mincer. In no time mate, we'll have a serious sort of a feast."

We hooked into the pancakes, then replaced them on the hot plate with paua, prepared the crays and as the heavens opened up, sat back and enjoyed a feast that put a huge smile on Tarx Morrison's face.

"Not bad, not bad at all", he said, through a huge grin, all the while nursing the remnants of a 1.5 kilo cray.

Rain played its tune on the tin roof and gusts of wind shook the now very appropriately named "Blowhard Hut".

"Not looking good for a hunt", I made the mistake of saying.

"What's wrong with you, getting soft, Sinclair, too much time in the city?" queried Jolly, obviously wanting me to make a decision that would keep him dry. A very good lad with the reverse psychology is our Chris.

"No", I said. "If you can hack it, so can I."

Jones just laughed. "No one's going anywhere at the moment", he said, as a clap of thunder chased the lightning that seemed to land on top of the hut.

We just grinned at each other and scoffed more paua fritters.

We got changed, just in case, a few layers of camouflage fleece, a cover to keep the rain off the rifle scope and a piece of insulation tape over the barrel to stop it turning into a river.

"The bush will be quiet when this blows through and the deer will be all over the clearings", said Colin who is a retired culler turned hunting guide.

Twenty minutes later, the storm had all but passed and we were running out of excuses to stay in the warm, dry hut. Tarx, the soundman, stayed behind to nurse another couple of crays while Colin, Chris, Rhys (the cameraman) and I grabbed our gear and headed out the door. We pushed through the kanuka and were sodden within ten minutes but the breeze blew up the gully and into our faces. I love hunting after the rain, when anything noisy in the bush has been turned to sponge and a sweet clean breeze blows in your face. You can feel that the time is right and in a place like this it is only a matter of time before you run into a deer.

We slid down towards the first clearing and something crashed off into the scrub.

"Deer", whispered Chris "don't worry, there's plenty more".

I love to hunt on my own, to stalk the bush and sneak around as quietly as possible and here were four of us trying to film a sneak attack on the local deer population. The feeling that you get when conditions are right is hard to describe. Every sense you possess works overtime trying to see, smell, hear, taste and sense something that puts you in a position for a successful hunt. It is a great feeling, every ounce of your being is totally alive.

The gully opened up and suddenly we moved from the stunted, tight kanuka to the open majesty of superb native forest. Mixed podocarp with everything from tall rimus to intriguing little lancewoods. This was a stunning stand of natives and here and there were clearings covered in rain-soaked grass, the sort of tucker that deer cannot resist.

Colin and Chris just looked at me, waiting for a reaction. My smile must have conveyed the right message, we grinned at each other and moved on. This was a hunting paradise. Even Rhys, who had never hunted, picked up our excitement and kept the camera ready to "shoot".

We edged through the trees looking for anything out of the ordinary, the flick of an ear, a movement, a patch of rump, anything different from the forest growth.

Suddenly Chris held a hand up, we stopped. His finger pointed off to the left and about 80 metres away down through the trees a bush shook when there was no breeze. An ear flicked and out of the greens and browns, the head of a deer materialised. I eased to the right and placed a huge tree between me and the quarry. I indicated that Rhys should ease in behind and we snuck ever closer, silently edging ahead over the sodden ground. Rain drops fell out of the trees in a constant drip, drip and I was filled with a feeling of anticipation. When I stuck my head out from behind that tree, would the deer still be feeding?

The answer was yes, Rhys set up the camera, I lined up the cross hairs, right between the eyes and squeezed the trigger. Blamm. The shot echoed around the gully, the deer spun around and was gone.

"Damn", I muttered. The boys looked at me as if to say what are you mucking around for. When someone else is watching and you miss, nothing you say or do seems like a worthwhile excuse.

"I had a good bead, the rest was steady", I mumbled in apology.

"Sure", said Chris as he headed off in disgust.

Within 50 metres he stopped and lifted a hand.

I eased forward and another deer stood smack in the middle of a clearing, eating afternoon tea. Rhys fired up the camera, I took a bead on the neck, squeezed the trigger and thud, down went the deer. It must have heard the previous shot, but because of the thunderstorm, chose to disregard it. Fatal error.

"About time", said Chris, "glad you finally got your act together."

When you see it on television, I cut out the miss. Very convenient, the editing process.

The shot hit about 150mm higher than where I aimed, the scope had had a knock. I was partly redeemed.

After shooting something comes a responsibility and that is to carry out the meat. Indiscriminate shooting is absolutely criminal. It is very rare that you meet someone who doesn't abide by the law of the bush and "lugs" out what they shoot. Anyone who doesn't take on that responsibility doesn't belong in the hills.

"I'll carry it out", said Chris.

"No", I protested, "no one has ever carried a deer for me and I don't expect them to start now."

I loaded up the meat and we trudged off for the hut. For some reason, the further we went, the more like lead my legs became. It got to a point where I couldn't carry the meat another step.

I was disgusted, thought my fitness had hit an all-time low. Chris carried it the rest of the way.

It was a short time later that I found out I had multiple sclerosis. What a shock. Within 10 months my backside was in a wheelchair and I had taken on the greatest challenge of my life.

I refuse to let this disease take away my love of the bush, the mountains, the oceans, rivers and lakes and already I am spending more time out of that chair and planning a host of expeditions.

I don't care if I wind up being lowered onto my boat by block and tackle, "the show will go on".

*Another Te Awaiti stag –
compliments of Chris Jolly
and crew. No wonder the
hunter looks pleased.*

It is friends like Chris Jolly and Colin Jones who keep in touch and make sure you still get to fish and hunt, that make it much easier to fight a disease like M.S.

Next roar I will be back at the Blowhard Hut, eating another lunch, breathing and tasting that magnificent air, and lining up another feed of venison.

The answer is, never ever give up!

9

French Pass

Although I had fished and dived around French Pass and D'Urville Island many times, I had never driven the road from Rai Valley to the Pass, until we set off to film the area.

Danny and Lyn Boulten run a business called French Pass Sea Safaris and they had invited us to participate in something they reckoned was pretty unique. It lived up to everything they had promised and more.

There is something special about the labyrinth of shingle roads that wind their way into our 'back country'. These dusty, rutted highways keep the less inquisitive folk away from some of our real scenic attractions. When you turn off at Rai Valley, a portion of the journey is sealed and the road twists and turns through bays, ridges and around a great many hillsides, each affording more spectacular views. Scrub- and bush-covered hills plunge down into the bays and valleys slicing the landscape into humps and lumps, offering great hunting for pigs and deer.

Larger settlements like Okiwi Bay nestle in their chunk of paradise and hardy souls from past generations have turned scrub and bush into farmland. The further you travel, the more a feeling of remoteness takes over and the more inviting the view looks to an old hunter/diver/fisherman.

By the time we pulled into the Boulten drive on a perfect late March day, I had a real hankering to go and catch a fish, and with only an hour of daylight remaining, the crew and I jumped in Danny's boat and set off for the whirlpools and awesome tidal flows of the nearby Pass.

Dumont D'Urville discovered French Pass in 1823. "To preserve the recollection of the passage of the Astrolabe", wrote D'Urville, "I name that dangerous strait 'Passe des Francois' but unless in any case of emergency I would not recommend anyone to try it and then only with a strong breeze well established and nearly aft."

My first trip through had been many years before when we set off in search of the *Gazelle* and *Koranui*, two ships that found the Pass something short of benevolent. As well as the wrecks, we hunted large crayfish, but I remember being in awe of the place, whether in the safety of a launch or scurrying around on a slackwater dive.

Danny gunned the runabout out of the bay, the same blend of hills, scrub and bush that I have described before, but this time one side of the channel flowed along the coast of D'Urville Island.

"Hunting still good on the island?" I said to Danny.

"Sure", he responded, "when you get permission and know where to go, a few deer but good numbers of pigs."

He turned his attention to the Pass and the spillway through which the ocean was sucked.

"Only place in the world where you can see two ocean levels at the same time", said the skipper, spinning the wheel and applying more power to counter the whirlpool that appeared out of nowhere and sucked hungrily at the hull. *St. Christopher* was dragged through the rocky gap and spat out onto the swirl at the lower downcurrent side of the Pass.

"Always get a wee adrenalin rush sneaking through there, even though I've done it hundreds of times before. You get the feeling that if you ever got smug this place would set a trap for you."

I am most comfortable with those skippers who treat the ocean with the greatest respect and Danny's words had a meaning that was loud and clear.

The only thing that took the sheen off the surface were the stretch marks of current beating up on a vast expanse of restless water. Out of the main stream the flow was lazy, although a lot of water eddied backwards, but around the gap in the Pass, whirlpools were born, struggled and died, dragging the surface water into their grave before spitting it out and being reborn further along the downstream flow.

"Anyone had a boat sucked under in here?" I asked Danny.

"Someone in a tin dinghy could get themselves in trouble, but we're quite safe", he replied, as yet another whirlpool spun us around trying with all of its considerable strength to wrestle us below.

In this unique environment we started to fish.

"Been some great snapper in here recently, always get a feed. Lyn's getting everything ready for a meal of fresh snapper. That's how confident we are."

Off the side of the main flow that can scorch along at up to eight knots, we threaded either barracuda or pilchards and hurled them over the side.

I stop labelling days as representative of the best fishing I have had because I'm spoilt rotten and many occasions become very special. This was one of them. Before the first pilchard hit the bottom, something picked up the bait and swam away. I locked up the drag and hit it hard. The rod curved in that wonderful exciting arc that said hook up and my first French Pass snapper pulled line from the reel in a bid to escape. Danny just smiled that 'I told you so' grin as he too fought to wrestle a snapper to the boat. Paul Richards happened to be filming the action and Tony Burrows was the soundman, both had that very satisfied look on their faces that translated as 'of course I'm happy, we're having fresh snapper for tea'.

Danny and I waded in to the snapper, it was fantastic fishing, drifting along the edge of the main flow as both pilchards and barracuda were taken with equal zeal.

As darkness approached, an orange glow settled on the water and the temperature took a dive, but real garnish on the main course arrived when the moon nosed above the horizon and spread its beautiful glow through the Pass. A frenzy of fishing finished off with another of nature's exquisite paintings. What a backdrop. By the time it was completely moonlit we had long passed the keeping stage and our fish were released but it was such a beautiful night that none of us wanted to go home until the last minute.

Our biggest fish were about 7kg, very respectable and very tasty.

"Better head home", said a reluctant skipper, "Lyn will be having kittens."

So that was it, a fantastic full moon entrée but that was by no means the end of our day.

After a feed of snapper, fresh vegetables and with a few mussels thrown in, it was off to check the film and prepare for day two.

I think people get a bit of a surprise when they join us on a shoot. The expectation is that we swan around, have a good time and that everything falls into place. Not so, when we finish filming we check to make sure that we have the images I need for an edit and the audio is OK and then the team ensure that everything works efficiently and pack it away. We usually start at daylight or before and finish way after dark but you know what, no one seems to mind very much because we are usually in a fantastic place with great people. Travelling around New Zealand is a privilege and every place is friendly, it's just occasional individuals who are not.

The morning dawned crisp, clean and inviting, so we filmed around the bay and then recorded the arrival of a float plane with a friend of mine, Chuck Shearer, on board. At that time Chucky was fronting a segment of the TV3 sport programme, *Mobil Sport*, so he was in for a couple of days of adventure.

Lyn, Chucky, Danny, Paul, Tony and I went out and hauled in a feed of cod.

"We're having a BBQ on the beach", said Lyn, "these cod will be fine but we could do with a few paua."

I've never been slow to put a wetsuit on and neither has Danny. On a likely looking chunk of coast we shot over the side and grabbed a dozen of the many paua that were jammed in the crevices. The kelp rolled lazily in the surge, the sun sparkled its way through the cracks in the weed and butterfish cruised through the channels and crevices.

Danny and Lyn know their backyard very well and take delight in adhering to the old "Take enough for a feed" philosophy.

"You know", said Lyn, "a lot of people seem to want to take home all that they catch. It's as though they want to cover the cost of the day in an equivalent value of fish."

At some point most people start to understand the real value of the experience, even reformed burglars like me.

Sure, I'm now in a privileged position, but I no longer have to catch the biggest or the most, just enough for a feed. In fact, happiness is being on the ocean with a rod in my hand. We wound up in a rocky little bay typical of D'Urville Island and it was there that we partook of a mid-day feast.

There are a number of ways to tenderise paua, the most common being to beat the living daylights out of them.

To shell them you push your thumb between the shell and the muscle until you encounter the resistance of the foot which attaches muscle to shell and then just force your thumb hard against the shell and push.

The attachment breaks and you are left with a beautiful shell in one hand and the meat in the other. After removing the gut bag and cutting out the mouth, the rest is delicious. Many people scrub off the black coating on the meat with a plastic brush but I don't bother. On or off it still tastes the same. Danny beat our catch with a lump of wood before throwing them in a pan. One of my favourite recipes is to beat them, slice them and then place the "chip" like chunks in a plastic bag with flour. Give it all a shake so the paua pieces get a coating of flour on them and then a quick sizzle in a hot pan. Hey presto, the result is not only delicious but so tender you can cut it with your lips. Just the thought of it makes my mouth water and on a beautiful beach on D'Urville Island our lunch sizzled and Lyn dragged out all sorts of extra things like salt, pepper and soya sauce. It is the little extras that make a big difference.

In 1770 Captain Cook had stopped here in this bay to replenish the *Endeavour*. It is fair to assume the crew didn't go hungry.

It was a quick scoff because fishing was on our mind and a light layer of cloud had drifted in to produce the sort of overcast that gets me very excited. When the sun is too intense, the fish seem less inclined to activity, especially on the surface, but this cloud took away a big chunk of glare.

"Now I don't want you to film landmarks in this next spot", said Danny. "It's a beauty and I want to keep it that way. Too much fishing pressure will wipe it out."

We decided to target kingfish and snapper, the seasonal visitors that are much in demand.

The spot was near a point where tide swirled and backwaters on the edge of the current held immense promise.

When jigging, it is important to keep the jig as close to vertical as possible, so in tide that means drifting. If you try to fish at anchor the tide lifts the jig off the bottom and the line angle increases to about 45°.

Rule of thumb for the ideal weight of jig to line is something like 100 gm jig, 10 kg line, 150gm jig, 15 kg line and so on.

I use heavier weights than that indicated on many occasions but that is a good start.

In addition, get rid of treble hooks and go for singles, preferably Black Magic chemically-sharpened hooks. Single hooks do much less damage than treble hooks and are much easier to remove.

If you are releasing fish, this makes life for everyone much easier and you can always test your skill by flattening the barb off the hook. It takes a good angler to apply constant pressure to big snapper and kingfish. With no barb, one mistake and the fish is on its bike. To make the jig move like a wounded fish, just lift and then drop the rod tip, lift and drop, lift and drop and so on.

Our first hook ups were barracouda and usually that means pack up and go somewhere else.

They are good bait but steal jigs in an endless expensive procession. If you want to target them, add 30cms of wire or cable trace above your jig. Chances are they won't cut through that and you can wind up with some great sport on light tackle, but I'm afraid 'couda are not for me.

"Time to shift eh Danny?" I asked.

"No, stick it out for a while."

"This feels better", said Lyn, as line disappeared from the reel at a pleasing rate, "might be a kingfish", she added.

It sure looked like it as the fish ran off line at will, a testimony to great power.

"Hmmm", said Danny, "get your lines in guys. I'm going to try and lead this fish away from the rocks."

Kingfish have an instinct for foul ground, that's why scraps with kingis in rocky territory are often very short. Whizz, bang, thank you, I'm out of here is the usual kingfish script.

Driving the boat out into deep water as soon as you can sometimes turns potential disaster into success and Danny's little ploy was working.

"I'm getting more line back now", said the angler, and looking down, a large white shape turned and rolled back into the depths.

When you start to see that white belly you are definitely winning.

"It's only a matter of time", said Danny.

"Just as well", said Lyn, "my arms are killing me." One tough customer to another and an angler with an extra ounce of determination.

The shape reappeared and rolled on its side on the surface, beaten.

What a beauty, 25 kilos of perfectly proportioned angling thrill.

"I'd like to let it go", suggested Lyn.

"Fine by me", I said looking at Danny for confirmation. "We've still got cod for tea and more snapper from last night, we don't need it", and with that the hook came out and a subdued-looking kingi swam away to sulk in the depths.

"There's a lot of splashing out there", said Chucky, pointing to what initially appeared to be a work up, but turned out to be a pod of dolphins making their way out of the Pass and along the coast.

"They come through the Pass every day, bit like old friends", said Danny.

"Do you mind if I jump in with the underwater camera?"

"No, not at all, they'll let you know if they mind and leave you to it."

Danny and I both went for a splash with a large group of common dolphins. They were playful enough to make several passes at distances as little as two metres before deciding that we weren't worth the effort and continued the daily patrol.

I have enjoyed dozens, even hundreds, of such encounters and never tire of these wonderful ambassadors of the deep. Every swim with dolphins is special and this family have a particularly famous ancestor.

Pelorous Jack was the first dolphin in history to be protected by proclamation.

In the 24 years from 1888-1912 he met and escorted ships through the Pass, across Admiralty Bay and on to Pelorous Sound.

It is said that he never missed a steamer traversing the route.

Back on 'the point' we resumed our jigging and had another visit from the dolphins.

We also had a heap of fun popper fishing. Casting and retrieving surface poppers can be a visually spectacular way to fish. A popper is a wooden or plastic plug designed to skip erratically across the surface. You cast them and retrieve them, creating the appearance of a wounded fish but this wounded fish is armed with a couple of treble hooks. They don't work as well with singles, unlike the jigs, but flattened barbs make catch and release a realistic option.

The poppers caught plenty of kahawai and a ton of voracious barracouda. 'Couda hurled themselves out of the water and pounced on a mouthful of hooks, what a surprise.

"I'm going back to jigs", said Danny, spooling a chrome Lethal lure into the depths. It bounced to the bottom and wallop − hook up.

"Feels like another kingfish", said the angler, bending to the task.

What a battle, the fish didn't run too far away, it chose to fight on the spot, which should have been a clue to its identity.

After ten minutes, a heaving, determined angler reeled in 6 kilos of fat snapper.

"Fantastic", I said, "bet you're not going to let that go!" But he did. "Got enough to eat", said Danny, "someone else can have the pleasure of catching that little beauty", and a very happy snapper slid back into its late afternoon home.

It was flat calm as we cruised home, the ocean was like a millpond, the dolphins could still be seen in the distance and the hills of the Sounds and D'Urville Island were standing up stark and dark blue as the dimmer switch arrived on the day.

There was hardly a sound other than the roar of the outboard and the hissing of the sea as it parted on the bow and peeled off the hull.

We all just smiled as we cruised back to a feed of cod, snapper and crayfish.

We had one more day left in paradise and it started with a sea kayak around part of D'Urville Island.

It was quickly followed by a dive with a bunch of inquisitive seals and finished with a cruise home in an exhilarating sea. At the tip of the island the swells shouldered each other out of the way in a very untidy fashion and I was thankful for my wetsuit. The camera equipment was stowed and with the sea getting angrier by the minute and the wind starting to howl, we roared our way "downhill" on the roller coaster ride home.

There is so much to see and do from the Boulten's French Pass base, it is easy to run out of time. We didn't get to go mountain biking, or see some of the bird colonies, but we learnt enough to know we will pay Danny and Lyn Boulten another visit. As I've indicated, this place is like a large slice of paradise.

Grant (Chucky) Shearer preparing for a little sea kayaking, one of the 'other' activities supplied by Lyn and Danny Boulten of French Pass Sea Safaris.

10

Castlepoint - Sharks and Sea Hawks

Not so long ago the big annual Wairarapa Club tournament was called the Sharkarama and so great was the carnage that they used to drag dead sharks away from the weigh station by the truckload. With a change in name to the Wairarapa Superfish, came a change in philosophy and today very few sharks are actually killed.

Indiscriminate killing of fish is hopefully history but the Superfish still delivers the best prize to the biggest dead shark with makos singled out as the most desirable species.

The venue for this tournament is the beautiful coastal village of Castlepoint. The name was bestowed by Captain Cook because of its distinctive natural features, a massive rock sentinel that rears up above the beach and natural harbour.

Castlepoint is on the coast not so very far from Masterton in the Wairarapa and is one of several beautiful, rugged, windswept, almost idyllic spots to be found along the coast. As well as the lighthouse dominating bastion of rock, the bay is garnished with a large sweeping beach that develops into sandhills and then rolling farmland. The village is an absolute picture and when the weather lets you get out and fish, the results can be mind blowing.

We turned up to film the 1997 Superfish. For Rhys, Tarx and I, this was our first visit to Castlepoint. It was so good that we filmed again in 1998.

Dave Burkhart is a commercial fisherman who has worked the coast for many of his 35 years, as too, did his father. Knowledge passed from father to son and honed through experience, means that Dave knows his stuff. *Sea Hawk* is an alloy cat, a shade over 10 metres and pushed along by twin 225 hp outboards. Needless to say, she is quick, nimble and ideal for getting on and off the coast in a real hurry. No one takes the risk of trying to moor a boat, everything right up to 15 metres is pulled out of the water on a daily basis. The

Gone Fishin'

commercial boys know the treacherous and foul moods common to this coast and don't take risks. They are, therefore, the ideal blokes to fish with.

Dave is a real lad, in fact borders on being a larrikin, always trying to pull your leg, always trying to outfish you and always tracking down superb spots.

As the sun tried to rise on day one of the 1997 tournament, we loaded the last of the camera equipment aboard *Sea Hawk* and with Dave muttering about the 'office hours' we kept, set off for a three day adventure.

The red strip to the east showed that the sun was at least trying but the sky and ocean were the colour of lead and a rising southerly whipped streamers of white off the top of a sluggish swell. We headed east, straight off the coast, the deck covered with several hundred kilos of the foulest smelling burley it has ever been my displeasure to be associated with.

"Good brew", said Dave, "we'll try for a big shark today, head out to about 200 metres and drift. Sharks won't be able to resist this stuff."

A couple of miles off the coast we started passing huge work ups of kahawai. Massive balled up schools that were thrashing the water to foam.

Hapuka – 53.5 kgs. Caught middle of February 1997. Green as hell when caught!
Photo Dave Burkhart

"Mind if we stop?" I said to Dave.

"What for?" came the retort, "we're not fishing the kids' section."

"I'd love to flick a couple of kahawai out with my fly rod", I said, "won't take a minute and the world record is only 3kgs on 10kg tippet."

At that time I had just discovered the joys of saltwater fly fishing, one of the most exciting sport fishing options around and with the weather looking ugly, I didn't want to miss an opportunity like this.

A grumbling Dave pulled the throttles back and a happy G. Sinclair flicked a fly that looked like a whitebait imitation (grey rabbit) into the middle of a kahawai frenzy. Instant hook up and on a fly rod, instant fun. There are very strict rules governing game fishing, but none more pedantic than those applying to saltwater fly.

Everything from length of trace to shock tippet are regulated, the boat must be in neutral when you cast to the fish and hook up, you can only used fixed handle gaffs, not flying gaffs, which makes life interesting on big fish. And so on and so forth. After 20 minutes I had three kahawai to the boat, the third looking very much like a world record, so in the bin it went and off in pursuit of sharks we headed.

Out off the coast a number of miles we slid to a halt and Johnny, Trevor and Dave Anderson rigged traces for sharks and started shovelling ladle fulls of burley over the side.

'Splat, splat' went the foul-smelling ooze as it hit the surface. A film of oil spread across the ocean and the heavier pieces of minced fish frames drifted off downcurrent. The burley trail was on its way.

"How big will the shark be that wins?" I asked the skipper. "The biggest mako over 400kgs wins a new Nissan Navara 4 x 4 so that's what we're after and makos that size and bigger can be found along this coast. You can guarantee that the winner will be over 300kgs anyway", said Dave.

Hmm, I thought, that is a serious piece of work and it made some of the small trailerboats I'd seen heading out, look pretty small. I wouldn't know where to start when it came to getting 300 or 400 kilos of very upset mako in my 6.5 metre Ramco. It didn't sound like a clever thing to do but on 10 metres of *Sea Hawk* the boys were looking forward to the challenge.

Our first shark arrived within 15 minutes, a 2.5 metre blue shark made lazy progress as it looked for the source of the burley and a more substantial feed.

"There's a second one back out there about 50 metres", said Trevor, and sure enough a dorsal fin carved an erratic track across the oily surface.

Rhys is the most dedicated cameraman I know and among the smell and with a rising southerly rolling the tops off the swells, Rhys's stomach was turning cartwheels.

"You're as white as a sheet", I said in my usual sympathetic way. "You look as though you're about to throw up, must have been that cup of cold fat you had for breakfast."

Trumpeter. 22kgs. Caught January 1998 – FV Seahawk. We seem to have a good stock of trumpeter on the grounds now!

That was it, over the side went breakfast and when Rhys's face reappeared from an inspection of his burley contribution, he looked as though his health was improving.

"Needed that", he said with a grin, picked up the camera, went to work and never missed another beat. As an observer of sea sickness rather than a sufferer, it is amazing how often one good 'throw' solves the problem and turns misery into an instant recovery.

However, sensitive spectators who are also fighting a severe bout of nausea usually follow the leader and sure enough Tarx, the soundman, soon added his heavy duty breakfast to the trail.

Still, it seemed to work for the sharks and within an hour, half a dozen blues cruised around the back of the boat trying to chew the props, burley bins and anything else that was covered in the smell of fish.

As for the target makos, no sign, but I couldn't believe how quickly sharks arrived once the burley went in the water.

I have filmed a lot of shark footage with the underwater camera and had thought about jumping in but I've seen big stroppy makos arrive and drive away blue sharks in much less of a burley trail than this. That, combined with a rising sea, changed the focus back to the fly rod.

I lay over the stern of *Sea Hawk* and recorded some nice shots of sharks inspecting the stern of the boat and then suggested to Dave that we have a bit of sport.

"Wouldn't mind trying to hook one on the fly rod", I suggested.

"You've got to be joking, Sinclair", he replied, with his top lip curled into something like a snarl.

"Not a show of holding one of those on that trout tackle", he scoffed.

"World record's only 67 kgs and any one of these is bigger than that. Besides, I've got my big rig, a 14 weight rod and Penn 4GAR."

"Mate, I don't know what a 14 weight is or a GAR but you can't tell me you'll hold fish like that on a fly rod."

Dave is good at showing his disapproval and he looked at me like something smelly and unpleasant stuck to the bottom of his shoe and trampled all over the lounge carpet.

With great ceremony I rigged my pride and joy, and ten minutes later was hooked to 80 kilos of blue shark. Blue sharks to me should never have been classified as game fish. They are generally pathetic sport and no good to eat, but on a fly rod this fish elevated his kind to a level deserving real respect. He roared off for greener pastures with us in hot pursuit and if it wasn't for the wind and deteriorating sea conditions, I reckon we would have had him but after one and a half hours and almost in reach, he busted off.

"That was pretty impressive", said a much less sceptical skipper, "might try it again if we get another chance." But there would be no more chances that day and we beat a retreat to the beach and a break from a heaving, disturbed ocean and some respite for the crew's heaving, disturbed stomachs.

On the beach was a gantry and hanging off the gantry was the day's biggest shark, a 287 kilo mako, just the start the organisers had wanted.

Among a great deal of ridicule, I weighed in my humble kahawai, which turned out to be a new world record. Saltwater fly fishing is yet to take off in New Zealand, but we have so many species well suited to this sport, that it is only a matter of time.

At 6.00am next morning we were on the ocean — a beautiful calm day on a sparkling ocean and a swell that had dropped to a gentle roll.

The kahawai schools seethed all the way along the coast, we caught a few albacore tuna. I lost a nice mako after 30 minutes on the fly rod.

We weighed nothing but caught a feed of blue cod that Dave cooked on *Sea Hawk's* BBQ. What a lunch, drifting on an ocean like glass, sun beating down and a menu that included blue cod fillets and venison steaks. Not bad.

Our last day dawned crisp and clear but the weather gods were plotting mayhem.

At 5.30am we were on the ocean heading south.

"I'm taking you to a spot my dad used to fish for big groper and trumpeter, great place", said the skipper, above the hum of the outboards and slapping of the hull. What a stunning morning, the sun took a peek above the horizon and then threw itself boots and all into a glorious day. We stopped for a look at Kahu rocks because a diver had talked about a close encounter with a great white and the boys talked half-heartedly about trying to catch it.

Our objective however, was bottom fishing for several tasty species, so it didn't take long to prise Dave off the Kahu rocks and on to the secret spot. This time we anchored in about 45 metres of water. The rolling hills and steep, scrub-covered country reared up out of the ocean. Much of the rolling country had been beaten into submission and turned into farmland, the properties being large and the country pock-marked with steep gullies filled with kanuka and occasional mixed podocarp forest.

Standing out to sea, the effect was stunning, a landscape of earthy tones and bright bands of green, gullies full of the promise of great hunting and an ocean equally as wild, rugged and productive.

There was not a ripple on the surface, not a puff of wind to take the sheen off the mirror and the fishing was red hot. All Dave could say was "I told you the fishing was good down here".

The ice bin rapidly filled with cod up to 3.5 kilos, groper to 25 and a sole trumpeter of 14 kilos. At one point dolphins cruised in for a look, gave us a very unhurried inspection and headed off for a conference with the Kahu rocks. It was idyllic.

Late in the morning Dave decided on a quick burley for the great white before racing the weather back to Castlepoint. A bank of cloud over the land meant trouble but it looked as though it would hold off for a while.

We burleyed up and in no time at all a blue of about 100 kilos swam up the trail.

"I think I'll jump in and film this guy", I said, looking at the lazy patrol the shark had set up on the stern. I was just rigging the underwater unit when Trev said that something was bothering the blue.

"I'd wait a while if I were you", he said, "there's only one thing that puts these guys on edge and that's a bigger shark."

I stared down into the ink blue sparkling depths and out of nowhere a mako came hurtling in. All aggression, the mako decided the blue was unwelcome and drove it away. The mako returned, looking very agitated and very hungry. I decided that discretion was definitely the better part of valour and packed away the underwater camera. This 150 kilo mako was not a shark to swim with.

He was also not a competition winner so the boys left him alone.

It was time to "make tracks". All of our fish were caught using large baits on a ledger rig. A sinker on the bottom, a couple of hooks attached to a lengthy piece of heavy trace and away you go. For sharks, the boys had 8 metres of 600lb 49 strand cable and a single 14/0 shark hook. A whole tuna or mackerel was used for bait and a chunk of the hook and trace was covered in plastic shrinkwrap, the idea being that sharks are sensitive to too much exposed metal especially when embedded in a bait. It makes them suspicious and less likely to hook up. The shrinkwrap is the answer. Personally, I hate catching things that don't get eaten, like large sharks, but I was very happy with a bin full of tasty species that could still win prizes and then be put to good use on the dinner table.

Superfish. Over the last few years the club has landed a lot of fish (sharks) about this size, the latest was about 430kg. (Jan '99).
Photo – Dave Burkhart

As we headed home, the wind came away almost without warning, a northwesterly straight off the land. It roared off the hills and turned the ocean to foam. We thumped our way north, hugging the coast to make the most of the shelter, but it was a hard ride.

Back on the beach, sand blew in clouds and swirled its way into everything, vehicles, boats, hair, clothing, a tenacious nuisance that was making things very unpleasant.

The 287 kilo mako proved to be the winner, but the huge marquee in which the prizegiving was to be held was battling to hold its ground against the northwester.

We all piled in that evening for the prizegiving, the huge area of canvas flapping and lurching like a wild thing.

I wound up challenging Dave to a wrestle in some sumo suits. It was great fun, both of us in massive padded outfits but I was thrashed and christened Dave with a new name – Tui Dundee was born not because he wrestled me but because he had grabbed the tail of a blue shark and wrestled it aboard, much to Rhys's surprise. He had leapt out of the path of the snapping jaws before Tui got it under control and threw it back over the side.

It was that and Dave's liking for a shocking beer called Tui that ensured that the new name would stick.

The wind picked the evening to climb into top gear and suddenly the pitching flapping marquee became a dangerous place to be. A couple of hundred anglers with a party on their mind were suddenly out in blinding gusts of wind and sand. Enthusiasm for a party deteriorated considerably and the prizegiving took place at the clubrooms next day.

I had seen enough of the fishing to really look forward to a return match and Tui Dundee was good enough to invite us back in 1998 to fish on *Sea Hawk.*

The local club put up a prize of a new Nissan Pathfinder for the heaviest shark. No minimum weight, someone was going to drive away in a new vehicle. The fish that won it turned out to be a blue around 130 kilos. Someone had told the makos to go on holiday and they took the advice. We spent a day drifting around, catching and releasing a couple of blues, but our real quest was to head south again and try another of Tui's secret spots.

On another beautiful day, just like the year before, daylight found us just shy of Kahu rocks, roaring along, thinking how good it was to be alive. Multiple sclerosis was making me unsteady on my pins and the boys had dumped an armchair on *Sea Hawk* so I could take the weight off.

"Feel like some crays for breakfast?" asked Tui.

It was a silly question because fresh cray tails split and sizzling on a hot plate are hard to beat. As well as Tui, John and I, the 1998 team included Tarx, camera assistant Becky Smith, Andre Newlands and cameraman Ben Johnson. We wanted to win the champion team prize, which meant heaviest average over a wide range of species and we reckoned one of Tui's secret spots would do the trick.

But first things first and breakfast was on the skipper's mind. He and Johno work pots right through this part of the coast and a couple of lifts had us with enough crays to satisfy the heartiest appetite.

You can imagine the scene – a perfect morning, over goes the anchor in a spot where the fish nudge each other out of the way to get at the bait. The ocean is so flat that when you look towards the sun the surface erupts in stars like bursts of light that flicker on the surface and send shafts off into the rich blue depths. The hot plate on the BBQ hisses as a dab of butter skates across its surface and within a minute, half a dozen cray tails cook noisily under a cloud of steam. Lemon juice is squeezed over the fish and the noise of the sizzling plate lifts a notch or two.

"Only take a couple of minutes to cook," says Tui, "I like to grate a bit of cheese just before I take them off. Nice with a bit of fried tomato, salt and pepper or even a little soya sauce."

So we all stood around gorging ourselves on fresh, ultra fresh crayfish and preparing for action.

One of my favourite rod/reel combinations for bottom fishing in under 100 metres of water is the Penn 555 on a Jigmaster rod. The combination, loaded with 10kg line, means you can handle a fair chunk of fish, although I was asking for trouble if one of the 50kg groper took a liking to my bait.

We started off with huge cod nudging 4 kilos and then happened on a few groper around 20 kilos.

"Well Sinclair, what do you reckon about this spot?" asked Dave.

I just smiled at him, I was hooked up and had my hands seriously full with what turned out to be a beautiful big trumpeter.

In the 12 months since our first outing, Dave had decided to charter *Sea Hawk* during the commercial fishing offseason. He and Johno had been getting clients some huge fish and I knew he would be trying for us. Filming superb angling does wonders for a new charter business and this one serves up more than just great fishing. We had a day better than our outstanding effort of the year before and although we didn't drive away in a new Pathfinder, we did win the champion team prize. Becky was a breath away from taking out champion woman angler and we were a very chirpy crew at the prize giving.

Dave takes notice of things like moon phase, time of tide, bite times, drift, bait and tackle selections and a host of other factors that take the luck out of angling.

There is no substitute for experience and it was "Tui Dundee" who set us up for our winning performance.

What you learn on a charter with the *Sea Hawk* team will help you with your casual fishing. The most successful anglers have a habit of leaving a reasonable percentage of luck in their wake. It still plays a part but study and experience certainly improve the odds.

Snapper. Caught February
1998. 50 metres of water.
You do not catch very many
snapper on this part of the
coast, but they are all about
this size!

11
Te Kaha

It is amazing how often a phone call is the kick start to a serious round of adventures and when Steve Sneddon phoned and suggested a trip to Te Kaha, I could never have imagined what it would lead to. Steve and I wound up fishing on Paul and Reg O'Brian's Te Kaha Cat and it was the first of many trips to this wonderful coast.

"Gidday Moitee," said Paul, as Steve and I ambled up onto the O'Brian verandah, went through the introductions and sat down to lunch.

The O'Brian verandah is the social centre of Te Kaha. There are more meals, fishing stories and beers shared there than on any other part of the coast. One of the reasons is the legendary O'Brian hospitality. Paul, Tracey, Reg and Fran love meeting people, filling them full of food and liquid refreshment and listening to them relive a great day of fishing for snapper. The other reason for the verandah's popularity is the location. The ocean's noise is the music that accompanies the banter and the murmur of the breeze in the old, gnarly pohutukawas and blows away the cobwebs after a long drive. Lawn slopes away from the house to the fringe of beautiful old trees and beneath the trees a rugged fringe of coast and that beautiful stretch of water Captain Cook named the Bay of Plenty.

Yes, the O'Brian verandah is a special place and lunch didn't last long at all. The reefs of Te Kaha are very fishy.

We anchored on a spot affectionately called Queen Street, an offshore reef that produces some huge snapper. Almost before the burley went over the side, Steve hooked up, and within an hour we had a bin full of snapper up to 7 kilos.

Hmm, I thought, I've got to come back and film a couple of shows in this place, so on 1st February 1995, the *Gone Fishin'* 'crew' spread their gear over the verandah and worked on a game plan.

The view had changed and replacing a smooth placid bay was a procession of white horses which arched towards the rocks and threw themselves on the land in a shower of spray.

"Not looking good today, me old moitees," said Paul, "but they're catching a lot of kahawai off the mouth of the Motu and if it's happening today you won't even get your feet wet."

We drove around the sweep of the Motu mouth and down the shingle track to the mouth.

Kahawai are a much valued traditional food source of the Maori and the only non-Maori anglers were myself and a chap named George. George and his friend, Tom, are NZ champion surfcasters and they stood at the mouth of this mighty river and hurled their lures 150 metres off the beach.

Tom's wife, Kath Riri, was my fishing buddy for the morning and a great help she proved to be.

"Just cast and retrieve," she said, "anyway you know what to do." It reminded me of growing up on the shores of Christchurch's estuary and rowing my dinghy out in search of a feed of kahawai.

A silver lure and treble hook, cast, wind, thump and another bullet sped off in search of freedom.

The Motu was just getting a blue look to it after a flood and the kahawai were in the mix of freshwater and salt. A late run of whitebait may have dragged them in and gulls swooped and screeched, pouncing on any morsel that stayed on the surface long enough to be eaten.

The shingle beach gave way to a blue but 'creamy'-looking bay and beyond the sheltering curve the white horses frolicked their way towards Te Kaha.

"What else do you catch here beside the kahawai?' I asked Kath.

"We get shark, rays and snapper, plus the odd kingfish, and whitebait in the season. Usually get a feed of something", she replied.

Cast, wind, whallop and another kahawai was wrestled onto the stones, leaping and fighting until its life was extinguished and it was added to the heap.

After we had a dozen, the team said we had enough and that lunch was in order.

Andy Coleman was the cameraman and Anthony Nevison the soundman and as we filmed lunch they fair drooled in anticipation of their share.

Crayfish, tua tua, whitebait fritters, marinated snapper and Maori bread and then back to Te Kaha.

We snuck out for a quick fish as the wind eased and were on the ocean anticipating great deeds the next day when the sun slid under the breaking cloud and darkness marched out of the eastern sky. You could have hit us with a well- aimed stone thrown from the beach, but even here we caught our snapper and prepared them for a late evening BBQ on the famous verandah.

In the morning the white horses were back and the forecast promised 25 knots of northwesterly.

Rob Cochrane with a very good 12 kilo Te Kaha snapper. Rob's first 20-plus pounder. We set off for an evening fish and decided to target one large snapper. Six metres of water, plenty of foul, burley and tide. A baby squid did the damage.

"Not what we want," said Paul, "but I like a bit of white water to stir things up and carry our burley onto the reef. I have a spot we may be able to tuck into."

On the water it was rough but we found a spot that enabled us to anchor and let the current carry our baits back over the reef. It was starting to look very promising.

Mike Rendle joined us and fished 2, 4 and 6 kilo line. Whizz, bang, see you round, was the Rendle story, although Mike did land some nice kahawai on the ultra light gear.

Paul and I were straylining, feeding out a floating bait and let it drift down the burley trail. The idea is to present the bait as naturally as possible, have the reel in free spool and make sure there is no weight on the bait. When a fish picks it up, let it run with no resistance, give it time to swallow, lock up the drag and hit it hard. In the five metres of water we were in, the result was usually spectacular. Big fish have an inborn understanding or have learnt exactly how to bust you off. They fight to get among the rubbish on the bottom and you must fight to keep them out of it.

We were using baby squid, sanma, pilchards and bonito – all good reliable snapper baits. Our objective was to catch a 20lb snapper. A fish bigger than that is regarded as a real prize.

"How big do the snapper grow here?" I asked Paul.

"Well moitee, my biggest is over 14 kilos or if you prefer, over 30lb and a number of anglers have landed snapper around that size. Te Kaha is home to the big boys."

The Te Kaha Cat pulled restlessly at the anchor, straining to get away. Plumes of white water showered the rocks with spray and the ocean was restless. Gulls swooped in with the breeze, their wings seemingly motionless and yet they raced across the sky with what seemed like perfect control, feathered gliders riding those unseen currents. At our feet the shearwaters lined up, waiting patiently to pounce on our bait or any other morsel that floated in range.

The wind was steady and carried the excitement of the feeding birds and fish and the clean but pungent smell of the ocean. As we anglers say "it felt very fishy".

"Something big here", said Paul, and I glanced across to see line flying off the reel and snaking away in the distance.

"Hit like an express train, think it's a big snapper", he said. "I'm going to hit him, here we go."

Click went the lever to engage the gear and the rod curved and

Darryl Black with another T.K. beauty. We caught eight like this and went home. John 'Stumpy' Black provided the guidance. Stumpy is a man who really knows his snapper.

loaded up on what was obviously a bigger fish than those we had already partied with. Thump, thump, thump went the rod.

"Moitee", said Paul, "it's a beauty but I don't like the next bit. I've got to get him back through all the weed and rock." By then the fish was 100 metres away and didn't look like stopping.

"Damn", this guy doesn't know when to stop. It's a snapper, no doubt, I just hope we get to see it. When the camera rolls you pray for the classic ending with happy anglers and big fish celebrating against the setting sun but I would love a dollar for every catch we have painstakingly set up, gathered all the beautiful shots together and then ping, the line parts and you hope you get another chance. No matter what happens, the thrill of being hooked up is a wonderful thing. The adrenalin flows, the excitement mounts and then you reach a point where you get beyond exhilaration. If a fight with a big fish stretches beyond half an hour you are left with all of your senses wonderfully heightened and the fish, the battle, becomes a total focus.

It is a great feeling and Paul ultimately showed that elation had given way to total concentration. If this fish got away it would not be because he made a mistake.

"Gee this fish has so much line out, I don't believe it", he commented staring intently at the point where line entered the water.

We were at the point where knowledge and skill often make all the difference and impatience usually means over-stressing line. When monofilament gets dragged in and around reefs there is usually some fraying at the very least, more often the fish breaks off and wins the battle.

The longer it went on, the more we all willed that fish to the surface.

"C'mon, c'mon", muttered Paul to no one in particular. Finally a flash of orange and white before a flick of the tail saw another 20 metres of line peel away into the battlefield.

"This is the worst time", said Paul shaking his head. "I've got an idea of how big that fish is now. It's a beauty, a very big snapper but I'm not going to put any more pressure on. If that line's as frayed as I think, this fish could soon be on his bike. C'mon, c'mon", he muttered.

I glanced at Paul, Reg, Mike, plus Andy and Anthony. We were all the same, filled with the excitement, the anticipation that turns non-anglers into converts. This was what it was all about, the thrill that gets into your system and never lets go.

"Close now", said an excited angler, who had experienced many such battles and never lost the thrill.

The beast came up out of the depths, rolled on its side and was swallowed by the landing net.

"Yes, yippee", yelled a face creased into a huge grin. We laughed, yelled, whooped, hollered and looked. What a fish!

"Must be at least 25 pounds, maybe a touch more." The camera rolled and the fish joined the *Gone Fishin'* cast, not on the end credits but as the focus of some great action.

Te Kaha was in my blood and its superb angling drags me back to chase yellow fin tuna, snapper, kingfish and kahawai. This spectacular, beautiful rugged coast is a must if you're an angler or diver.

I'll tell you about the game fishing in the next book, but before the crew left, we wound up throwing my boat in the water and joining a kids' fishing day. Andrew and Darlene were the two juniors who joined me on Saturday the fifth and the bad weather had been replaced by stunning perfection. The kids caught just about everything and because I couldn't help it, I threw half a bonito head out the back of the burley trail and let it sink to the bottom.

Often the big snapper are a little shy and I like to have the back door covered. Half a bonito head may seem like a rather large chunk of bait, but believe me, a big snapper makes short work of it.

What a day; sun, sea, kids happily hauling in all manner of fish and beyond the coastal strip the rugged, bush-covered hills stark and impenetrable, bathed in sunshine but keeping their secrets hidden beneath the luxuriant green canopy. I had a hankering one day to get into those hills and chase a few of the abundant wild pigs.

The ratchet on the bonito head reel started to click, something was picking at the big bait.

I gently lifted it from the holder and flicked the ratchet off. The reel was out of gear and my thumb sat gently on the spool, ready to stop any overrun. Whatever it was, picked that moment to head for faraway places and I was pleased that the thumb hovered above the spool or the line would have disintegrated into a classic bird's nest.

The fish ran, stopped, ran again and on the second run I flicked the reel into gear and let the drag go to work. Thump, thump, thump, the classic snapper signature, the big bonito head had done its thing.

It was a short battle and for taking the kids fishing my own reward was a 20lb snapper. A perfect way to finish the shoot.

Te Kaha is now our family Christmas destination. Everything I love about New Zealand has been parcelled up and delivered to this stunning coast.

Fishing, diving, hunting, scenic splendour and great people. It ain't half bad.

It is great to combine the quest for yellow fin with the hunt for big snapper but as I've said, the yellow fin and marlin have to wait for the next book. A lot of similarities exist between hunting on land and hunting on the ocean and as soon as you realise that you are hunting when you chase big fish, the sooner your luck improves.

Change of light is a classic time to hunt, early morning or late evening and those times are great, big snapper times. The fish I caught with the kids had been a midday snapper but the time I love is late evening.

A good friend of mine, Rob Cochrane, joined us in Te Kaha a couple of Christmases ago and desperately wanted to land a 20lb snapper.

We started 1997 with a new year's day fish that began on Queen

Street. Two other friends, Ross and Robbie Drysdale, had stopped off to partake of festivities and they too were on board. Suzie and Robbie had a competition against Rob and Ross, the result of which was by no means clear, because everyone was so excited about the quantity of good snapper that filled the bin. I was the deckhand for the day.

By lunchtime the team had enough snapper and we delivered the bin to the chiller.

"How about a look for a yellow fin", said Ross, "I've never caught one".

"Neither have I", said Rob.

"Ok, we'll give it a couple of hours and then go in and fillet the snapper."

Filleting snapper can be a real waste because there is so much good eating in the heads for fish stock, or just as another tasty morsel to partake of, the heads are great.

Suzie stayed behind while the rest of us headed off the coast and at the first sign of a work-up, in went the lures. Five minutes later we had a double strike of yellow fin and 40 minutes later both Rob and Ross were yellow fin virgins no longer. What a day, a classic indication of how good this coast can be.

It still left the matter of Rob's 20lb snapper and we left that until the last night.

An hour before dark we headed off. I had burleyed the spot the night before but not thrown a bait.

Quarter of an hour from the beach we were on station.

The sun gathered around it that beautiful orange glow as it descended on the horizon and the small cluster of scattered clouds became fringed in silver. The wind was a barely discernible puff but a chill came from the darkening shore. It was snapper time.

Just Rob and I went on this journey and dropped anchor in four metres of broken reef and weed. If we hooked one, the challenge would be the same as with Paul's fish, the ever-present, broken terrain and chance of a bust-off.

"I'm so excited, my hands are shaking", said Rob.

"Perfect night mate, and this spot is an old favourite, caught two 20lbers here last year."

Over went the burley, plenty of it, with a drift carrying it back over the rocks where the lazy swell broke in a ribbon of white.

"Put two baby squid on", I suggested, "they won't be able to resist them and cast back about 20 metres or halfway to the rock."

We put two baits out and if a fish jumped on either it was Rob's.

The sun dropped over the horizon, the orange glow slunk away and a lazy sort of darkness descended on our spot.

Rob's fish didn't pick at the squid, he just swallowed it and took off. It was another great battle, another close run thing, but 25lb of snapper was scooped into the net and landed in the boat. We had done it, gone out, targeted a single fish and achieved the objective. Rob was in seventh heaven.

"What a beauty − well over 20lb, eh", he said, looking, and all the while shaking his head.

It was two very happy anglers that prepared to head home, but the fish had other ideas. While we cleaned up I flicked another couple of squid into the burley and was instantly fastened to another great head shaker. Thump, thump, thump, whizz, bang, ping, it was all over in 30 seconds − just a reminder that we came for one fish and it was time to head home. Te Kaha had delivered another of its gifts.

The year before, I had met a guy by the name of Rugby Edwards, a sixty year old mountain man who was a New Zealand champion axeman. Rugby is a big boy, fit as a buck rat and looks more like 50 than 60. Rugby was also the sort of pig hunter that legends are made of, so when he invited me for a jaunt up the Motu, there was no way I was going to say no.

"Meet you below the Motu bridge at 5.30 tomorrow morning," he said, "you should be back by lunchtime. I've got a mate, Alex, who'll take us in his chopper. He'll drop us at the top of the hill and we'll hunt down, gentleman's stuff," he laughed.

I was so darned excited I couldn't sleep. All that time sitting out in the boat gazing longingly at the hills and now reward time.

I was there at 5.00, crunching around on the gravel, watching Rugby's headlights wind their way round the hillside. Eventually Rugby pulled up, his dogs safely in a cage on the back of the truck.

"Looks like a great day", said the master, breathing steam into the early dawn.

A faint rhythmic thump and gentle whine grew out of the gathering dawn and Alex plonked the Robinson on the banks of the clear sluggish river. It took two trips but eventually we all wound up on top of the selected hill and Alex shut down the machine.

We were in the middle of nowhere with forested gullies plunging off in all directions and mountains disappearing in a procession of ridges all around us. After the excitement of the ride and noise of the helicopter, we were in almost total silence, just the dogs running back and forth, already shaking in anticipation of the hunt.

"Only breeze is coming out the gully I want to hunt, perfect", Rugby muttered.

"I'll hang around up here for an hour, then take the machine to the bottom of the hill", said Alex, parking his backside on a convenient log.

Rugby and I started our journey down a leading spur, the dogs ranged out and came back to check on their master, or at least they did for the first 20 minutes. Suddenly they were gone.

"We'll wait up here, hopefully if they are onto pigs we should hear the barking pretty soon".

Woof, woof, woof came the combined noise of three dogs intent on catching up with the pigs.

The barking continued and a squeal and agitated grunting added to the racket.

"Didn't take long", smiled Rugby. "I'll get down on that one − you

Paul O'Brian and the most underrated fish New Zealand has ever known. Kahawai, great sport, superb smoked and excellent sashimi.

stay up here. I expect they'll be away again soon. Follow at your own pace when they catch up with number two." And with that he was gone straight down through the trees at a very steady run.

Hmmm, I thought, couldn't be more than half an hour since we left the chopper.

Ten minutes later there was a final grunt and then silence – Rugby had put an end to round one.

Pretty soon the barking and squealing started again, closer this time – the dogs had found pig number two.

This was too much for me and I raced off down the hill towards the racket, swinging around trees and clambering through the supple-jack chock full of adrenalin. A hundred metres down the hill, and a great racket associated with something large and in a hurry, stopped me in my tracks.

The undergrowth shook and a beast cut a swathe to freedom. A huge black boar came hurtling through the undergrowth and skidded to a halt, beady black eyes, fixed on an unarmed G. Sinclair.

The pig ground its tusks and foam dripped from the salivating mouth. More crashing and a second large black pig broke away to my left, passing within 10 metres, but not bothering to stop. Freedom was mouth. More crashing and a second large black pig broke away to my left, passing within 10 metres, but not bothering to stop. Freedom was as far away from people like me as he could get. With a grunt my beady-eyed mate took off after his mate. I was a very relieved boy. That pig looked out for vengeance. With wings on my feet I raced down through the trees, laughing nervously, my head filled with the look of absolute hatred that had been on that pig's face.

Suddenly there was silence, but I had an idea Rugby would come back along the track.

Pigs had been rooting up the ground and had bedded down among the ponga ferns. It was wild pork city.

Eventually the hunter pushed through the undergrowth with a half grown black pig slung casually over his shoulder.

"That was short and sharp, must have been a dozen of them, couple of big pigs somewhere."

"Yeah", I said, "I had a close encounter with both of them. Bloody big pigs and not too happy about this carry on."

"They'll keep, the second one's just over here", he said, pushing through the ferns to reveal a second half grown pig lying in the undergrowth.

"I'll take this one for you, Rugby."

"No, don't worry about it", he laughed, "only little pigs, I'll carry them both." The huge mountain man flung the second pig over his shoulder and we set off down the hill to rejoin our very convenient ride out.

I was back before lunchtime, just in time for a feed, before heading out for a snapper or yellowfin or a dive for crayfish.

What a place, what great people. My adventures on the Te Kaha coast and around the Motu continue and always at the end of the day we sit on the O'Brian verandah swapping stories, sipping on a cold beer and gazing out on that magnificent everchanging view.

12

Preservation Inlet

Graham McGeoch, the late Ray Tinsley and I set off to explore Preservation Inlet in 1984. For Ray and I it was a change from our annual expedition to George Sound chasing wapiti, and for Graham an opportunity to share the magnificent scenery and history that is tucked away at the bottom west corner of the South Island.

We thumbed a lift with one of the Te Anau helicopter pilots, Richard 'Hannibal' Hayes, and wound up dumped on the beach at the head of Long Sound watching Hannibal and Woody disappear in search of deer.

The weather had started out kind but the forecast was not, however, nothing would dampen our spirits, another Fiordland adventure had already begun.

I had purchased a small inflatable to get us around the Inlet and Hannibal had loaned us a 7.5 horse outboard. The thing we hadn't put to the test was whether or not there was enough room in the inflatable for all of our gear and three bodies. We were too excited to care but had a long way to go before we set up camp in Kisbee Bay.

Fiordland during the 70s and 80s was full of characters and one of them was an old fisherman and hunter, George Burnby. George was always 'pulling someone's leg' and although I had never met him he was a bit of a legend.

Another chopper pilot, who must remain nameless, had dropped George and his friend into the inlet a few days before us. The history of Preservation is phenomenal, with the search for gold representing a big chunk of it.

"Dropped old George in the other day", said the pilot, "he's got enough pumping and sluicing gear to start his own gold mine and if National Park Board knew, they'd crucify him. Why don't you pull his leg a bit. It would make a change if someone got one up on George Burnby."

To sweeten the deal, he thrust a bundle of newspapers and flagon of scotch in my hand and we set off for our rendezvous with Hannibal, down near Lake Hauroko.

There wasn't really enough room for everything but we squeezed in George's papers and the flagon of scotch, fired up the little Mercury and puttered off into a westerly chop.

We reasoned that the craft was pretty much unsinkable but an annoying amount of water broke over the bow and spilled in among the gear.

"Only one thing for it", said Ray, "we'd better sample that scotch."

Ray and I had a golden rule. No booze on a hunting trip, but this wasn't a hunting trip and how could we argue if someone had dropped a little liquid refreshment in our lap.

The three of us had a very jolly trip down the sound and were well primed to give George a bit of a fright when we pulled into his campsite.

The old boy was ensconced at the mouth of Dawson Burn, a faint smudge of smoke curled up through the trees, showing us that our target was in residence.

In those days we used to openly flaunt anything to do with officialdom, especially when it related to Fiordland National Park. There were so many examples of mismanagement that it was a bit of a farce. All of us who spent a lot of time on the coast loved the place with a passion and an occasional brush with the park board just added to the adventure. The trick of course, was not to get caught and we were about to catch old George redhanded.

It was illegal to go digging around for gold, especially with the sort

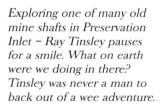

Exploring one of many old mine shafts in Preservation Inlet – Ray Tinsley pauses for a smile. What on earth were we doing in there? Tinsley was never a man to back out of a wee adventure.

of gear George had choppered in.

"I've met the old boy", said Ray, "so you're the Park Board Ranger, give him a bloody fright, I'll hang back with the scotch."

By the time we hit the Dawson Burn beach there was not a breath of wind and the occasional stag was moaning up in the forest.

We were surrounded by forested mountains and cruised a fiord that looked like a millpond. Ray, Graham and I were in seventh heaven. It was a bit of a walk from the boat to the campsite. The tide was low and a rocky beach fanned out into the bay.

Graham and I strode across the stones trying to look purposeful and also trying not to laugh. George's mate appeared out of the scrub when we were still some distance away and then the old chap himself.

"He's got a bloody pistol strapped to his hip", said Graham.

"I hope he's not the nervous type. If we were really from the park board he'd be in a power of trouble."

Eventually our two parties met, out in no-man's-land.

"Are you Mr. George Burnby?", I asked.

"Who's asking?" he spat, his hand fingering the revolver.

"My name's Graeme Sinclair. I've just joined the Fiordland National Park Board and we have reason to believe that you have illegal gold mining equipment in the area."

"Piss off", said George, looking ultra nervous and still fondling the sidearm.

"I am authorised to search the area and confiscate any such equipment", I said, "and what's more, you could be subject to criminal charges."

"Watch it, mate", said Graham out the side of his mouth, "he might shoot us if you lay it on too thick."

By now George and his mate didn't know what to do and Ray decided to enter the fray.

"Here, you silly old bugger", he chortled, "you'd better have a drink – you've just been had!"

"You pack of bastards", said a very alarmed George, lunging for a medicinal slug of scotch.

"What a damn dirty trick. Who put you up to this, bastards", he muttered, ducking back into the scrub.

"That's the sort of trick I usually pull", he said from under the trees. "Scared the living daylights out of me."

It was a long time before we stopped laughing. We just stood on that beach, surrounded by our beloved bush and mountains and could do very little to stop the tears streaming down our cheeks.

George had been well and truly "got" and he and I became good friends after that, but every time our paths crossed he would always start with the same phrase "you bastard".

Late in the day, after a brew and a little tucker at George's camp, we headed round to Kisbee Bay and dragged the inflatable up onto the lawn-like frontage that fringes the old town site.

"Early this century there were two towns and several mines spread around here", said Ray, "but the gold didn't last long and now it's kind

Looking towards Cavern Head from Coal Island in Preservation Inlet – breathtaking. If you want to know what history "feels" like, go to Preservation or Dusky.

of hard to appreciate that anyone lived here at all."

We pitched camp back in under the trees and by the time the work was done it was almost dark. A bellbird sounded its wonderful melodious call and two fantails flitted around the edge of our fire, snatching insects and chatting in their excited, agitated manner.

"It's good to be home", said Ray, slouching back against a long-dead beech tree and cupping a steaming brew in both hands. Darkness crept slowly through the trees until the only illumination was the light from our fire. Graham threw another log at the embers and a shower of sparks leapt in the air.

We were bone tired, it had been a long day and there was little conversation. Three insignificant human beings sat in their little patch of isolation feeling totally at peace. Time in the bush does that, you become independent, selfreliant, very appreciative of the natural environment and very aware that you are not as clever as you sometimes think you are. It is a wonderful, humbling experience.

The bush and mountains, just like the ocean, are never beaten and rarely forgive the arrogant or foolhardy.

Next morning we headed off to Cuttle Cove and explored some old mine shafts that Ray had scouted out on a previous trip. Cuttle Cove was a whaling base long before thoughts turned to gold and tucked back in the trees were a few old barrel hoops that had rusted almost to a point where they were no longer recognisable. They and a bronze plaque are all that remains to remind us of Cuttle Cove's contribution to the whales' plight. It was bitterly cold, a real north westerly storm was brewing and smudges of rain cloud were whipped across the bay.

116

"Once we have a look in these old shafts we'll see if it's calm enough to explore Cavern Head", said Ray. "Boy, can that place tell some stories."

Our little craft rode the swell like a thoroughbred. Quite large seas rolled underneath in the open parts of Preservation but we nimbly snuck into the shelter of Cuttle Cove.

Ray was off like a flash and Graham and I hauled the inflatable above the high tide mark and lashed it to a tree. It would be a long time before anyone found us if we lost our boat. The rain arrived and dripped through the already sodden bush and on the beach the sandflies were voracious.

Graham and I headed off after Ray. We hadn't gone far before a voice summoned us and soon we were peering down a long-abandoned shaft that plunged into the hill. The torch failed to illuminate the end of the tunnel. The old support beams had all but rotted away but that didn't stop Ray. He disappeared down the old shaft. "Never know what you're going to find", came the muffled echo, "must have been tough old buggers that dug these tunnels."

Graham and I stood under the trees as large drops of rain shook themselves loose and went splat on our coats and hats. The old boys and girls that tried to eke out an existence in the forests of Fiordland had a great many hardships to overcome. Sandflies, bad weather, isolation, hard work and little reward were the usual companions for the fortune hunters of Preservation Inlet.

A gust of wind roared through the trees and whistled around the mouth of the old mine. It felt as if we were not alone. We explored a number of shafts before heading to Cavern Head. Our travel guide on the journey was the book '*Port Preservation*' written by AC & NC Begg. It is a wonderful book, long since out of print but it guided us to much of the history we came to explore and Ray knew of quite a bit more.

In spite of the roll, we managed to get in under Cavern Head, an area of indentations, rocks, cliffs and, tucked in behind, a cavern.

Graham and I had dragged along our wetsuits and snorkelling gear so thoughts turned to crayfish. He drew the short straw and fed most of his anatomy to the sandflies before he had donned the protective wetsuit. Over the side he went and within 30 seconds a couple of crays flapped in the bottom of the inflatable. In a couple of minutes we had half a dozen of the tasty morsels and thoughts again turned to the history of Cavern Head. It was the Maori history that had intrigued us the most, in particular the story of Tarewai. Here is the story care of '*Port Preservation*'.

Tarewai was a giant Kaitahu chief of great strength and agility. On one occasion he was surprised on the Otago Peninsula by a band of Katimamoe enemies. The story is told that during the night before he was to have been killed and eaten, he broke his bonds and escaped, leaving behind, however, his famous greenstone club or mere. He was determined to retrieve it and, as his unwary captors were admiring the quality of the weapon, passing it round the campfire, a strong brown hand reached from the shadows to take it. Saying 'This is how it is used', Tarewai lunged to the left and again to the right, killing two of his enemies, then with the others at his heels, leapt from a cliff at a place near Taiaroa Head, still known as Tarewai's Leap. He miraculously survived and lived for his revenge.

The last retreat of the irreconcilable Katimamoe was Rakituma or Preservation Inlet, and it was on the island of Matauira that they made their final stand. One evening, in the middle years of the eighteenth century, a double canoe approached this stronghold. In it was a party of Kaitahu led by Tarewai and his nephew Te Whara-o-te-marama, who declared their visit friendly. Unconvinced, the Katimamoe prepared for battle. One of their warriors swam silently out to the canoe in the dead of night and attached a rope to it, by which means the defenders gently pulled the canoe to the shore. At the last moment Tarewai awakened to the danger, but his men were at a disadvantage and many were killed before they could wade ashore.

However, a few of the invaders, bunched round Tarewai, gained the beach and, weaving and lunging, inched their way to the area of raised flat land below the largest monolith. This was the place where the Maori women prepared their flax for making baskets and robes – removing the long fibres and discarding the green, slimy leaf debris, or toreka, on the ground. Now the Katimamoe warriors, outnumbering the little band and sensing the kill, rushed in from all sides. As he moved back, Tarewai slipped on the flax refuse and was down. They fell on him, striking and stabbing until he lay mortally wounded. With a great effort, however, Tarewai rose and threw himself backwards into the water of the sheltered southern bay, where he was joined by one other who had escaped. In the general melee they concealed themselves behind a rock and then slid silently into the sea.

One exhausted and one dying, the fugitives slowly and painfully floated to Cavern Head, drifting with the tide along the flanks of those forbidding cliffs. There is just one place where they could have landed. Behind a rib of rock which runs down steeply into the water there is, at low tide, a stony beach a chain or two in length. Behind this beach are the dark mouths of three caves. Into the one nearest the landing place the two men struggled, the chief still holding his greenstone mere. Tarewai was near to death but he was dragged or carried into the depths of the cave. His sorrowing companion took him to a deep recess, laid him gently on a shelf of rock and placed his arms and legs tidily in the burial position. After paying his final respects, he gathered what strength remained to him and made good his escape. In the darkness he may not have noticed the steady drip of spring water which bathed Tarewai's face and drained onto the sand below.

In the course of time the Kaitahu heard about the defeat of their war party and Tarewai's death. They immediately mobilised a strong force to travel south in search of vengeance. Maru and Te Aoparaki led the party and were under no illusion as to the actual strength of Pa-a-te-ewhara. They slid into Preservation Inlet during the darkest hours of the night and proceeded past Cavern Head to the harbour beyond. After camouflaging their canoes, they crossed the neck of land to the edge of the bush overlooking Te Whara Beach. In the first grey glimmer of dawn they saw the impregnable cliffs of the fortress and Maru decided to try to lure the defenders into the open. He clad himself in a sealskin and crept down to the sea. In the shallow water near the beach he rolled and wallowed and played like a seal. The unsuspecting Katimamoe, seeing an opportunity of adding to their larder, rushed down to the beach. The bait had been accepted and now the trap was sprung. At the last moment Maru rose up and slew the nearest hunter, which was the signal for his Kaitahu warriors to race down from their concealment in the sandhills to cut off the retreat of the others. Surprised and poorly armed, the Katimamoe were no match for the war party, which exacted a terrible revenge for the death of Tarewai. When the beach was red with blood and the last defender was dead, the victors easily scaled the approaches to the pa, slaughtered those who had been left behind

The old tramway from Cromerty to the Wilson River. If you have a day to spare and exploration on your mind, its amazing what you can dredge up in Preservation.

and burned the houses and fortifications to the ground.

As it happened, it was the pall of smoke from this fire which warned a small party of Katimamoe who were returning from a food-gathering expedition in Long Sound, that something was amiss. They discovered the concealed canoes, seized them and took them to sea. As the flotilla rounded Cavern Head they saw the smoke and ashes of the sacked pa, while the victors, equally abashed, saw their canoes, the only link with their home territory, slowly grow smaller until they disappeared out to sea. Their victory suddenly became hollow as they realised they were marooned, perhaps forever. However, Maru and Te Aoparaki would not admit to defeat and they pursued the Katimamoe fugitives to Dusky Bay, some 20 miles to the north. After a gruelling overland journey, they eventually caught up with them and it seems that most of the men on both sides must have been killed in the encounter. Maori tradition tells us that it was Maru, still in the prime of life, his two wives (presumably the spoils of the victor) and their children who comprised the Maori family described by James Cook when he brought the *Resolution* to Dusky Bay in March 1773. The Kaitahu chief and the Katimamoe women had at last come to terms.

We beached our little craft and found that there was only one place Tarewai could have been laid to rest. It was eerie walking into the cavern and reading the history as we stood in the half light. At the back of the cave the limestone slab no longer supports Tarewai's body. It was long ago removed, as too was his greenstone mere, but there is a real feeling about the place, especially when the wind moans its way around the cliffs and lifts the hair on the back of your neck.

The three of us roared across the waves, heading for Coal Island to pan for gold and supplement the crayfish with a feed of blue cod. By 1890 there were about 70 miners on Coal Island. Initially they worked the creeks on the west side, naming them very conveniently one to four. Then as they pushed further east, Lewis Lonquet picked up a large nugget weighing 600-800 grams (20-30 ounces) on Moonlight Beach.

That really got the gold rush started and we headed straight to Moonlight Beach hoping the miners might have missed something just big enough to lift in the boat. A few tantalizing streaks of dust were all our labours could produce.

In 1892 the town of Cromerty was pegged out to provide access to the distant Golden Site quartz mine in the Wilson River. A tramline was built through the bush and across the plateau. It ferried goods to and from the mine 10 kilometres from Cromerty. By 1895 the battery reached its peak when it yielded 24,762 Grams (875 ounces of gold).

A second township, Te Oneroa, sprang up and a new mine the Morning Star, went into production. At its peak in 1898 the Morning Star battery produced 58,298 grams (2060 ounces) of gold. It was all short lived, the gold petered out, the population drifted away and the

bush swallowed the buildings and debris of civilisation.

Preservation is all the more colourful for its history and exceeded our expectations as one of the most fascinating places we had explored.

There was a deer running along the beach as we entered the bay but our rifles were still in camp, otherwise venison would have supplemented the cod and crayfish.

"Run you little bugger", said Ray, "and don't stop or you'll wind up in the pot."

"It's nice to see them in the wild like this", said Graham defensively.

"Yeah and nicer to see them sizzling in the pan."

Back in camp, the feast got under way, the weather was atrocious, wind, rain, the air was just full of moisture. It crawled under our tent fly and tried desperately to find its way into our sleeping bags. Before leaving camp we had scavenged a huge supply of firewood and stuck it under the fly.

Even in the worst conditions, old dead trees, usually those still standing, provide the best source of dry firewood and we had a good supply.

A tent fly, as opposed to a tent, is just a roof, in our case a large chunk of ripstop nylon that tied down to ground level at the back, was 50 cms off the ground at the sides and open at the front. It was large enough to sleep three of us at the back and leave room to cook under cover at the front. A fire can be a godsend, especially when a storm rages in the forest and every flap of the tent fly sends down a blanket of strained rain. The fire takes the misery out of wet clothing, a camp site churned to mud and food full of sandflies. A fire in the

A Hughes 500C loaded to the gunwales and en route to Preservation Inlet – Fiordland.

bush adds more than its warmth and light – it adds humour and good feeling to three guys who are trying to play cards but can't because all of the moisture makes the cards stick together. Still, our feast of cod and crayfish was fantastic. One thing about Ray, Graham and I was that even when the sleeping bags got a little damp we could still find something to laugh about. Eventually we all drifted off into a soggy, disturbed sleep. Next morning the wind had eased and the rain had turned to showers. Cloud hung low around hills and today was the day we decided to trudge the 10 kilometres over into the Wilson River. We were up at daylight and as Ray kicked some life back into the embers, I stepped out onto the beach. A lone hind stood looking at me, probably mirroring my look of surprise, but not for long. In a couple of steps she was in full flight and crashed off into the scrub.

"Looks like the same animal", said Graham.

"Yeah and here am I wandering around without a rifle. I hope you like blue cod."

This wasn't a hunting trip, it was exploration time, although a feed of venison was on the menu. The history books talk about a tramline that ran from Cromerty up the hill, across the plateau and over to the Wilson River.

We had no trouble finding it and what a perfect track to hike. Someone had surveyed and built it with a very convenient gradient and what a great day we had. The rain came in again, five deer leapt off the track in front of us and we eventually found the old pelton wheel and stampers that help crush the quartz that would be trucked back over the hill. They were hidden in the gorge at the edge of the Wilson River. There is not a great deal left of the Cromerty or Te Oneroa town sites but there is history in the bush here and there. Old equipment, mineshafts, that ingenious tramway and stories such as that of Tarewai and Cavern Head.

Just like Dusky Sound, Preservation adds another dimension to the exploration and adventure to be found in Fiordland.

We explored all manner of locations during the next three days, always with the rain driving in to a greater or lesser degree.

On our last full day we squatted under the tent fly trying to sort out breakfast. Our sleeping bags were sodden, most of our food was past its best, although a procession of cod and crayfish ensured a level of freshness. It rained almost continuously and blew with real ferocity.

"Would have been nice to have seen the sun", said Ray, squelching around our muddy camp, "still that's Fiordland, no point in coming here unless you are prepared to get wet." He poked at the listless fire and stirred the lumpy porridge.

"What's that?" asked Graham staring out through the trees and across the bay.

"Looks like a water spout", I said, staring at a column of water that snaked across the bay and disappeared into the leaden sky.

"Wow, that's impressive", we all agreed, watching the spout work its erratic course. "Wouldn't want to get hit by one of those."

It was a great spectator sport tucked in under the safety of the trees. We all got a funny feeling about the thing at the same time. Suddenly its erratic course became a beeline for our camp.

"It'll stop when it gets off the water", said Ray hopefully.

"I'm not so bloody sure", I said, as the scream of wind lifted several more decibels.

On it came, on and on, until it was almost on top of us.

"Hit the deck", said Ray, as if we needed any encouragement.

We tried to dig our way into the ground as a shrieking, wild, out of control path of destruction enveloped the camp.

For a few seconds everything was noise, wind, debris, a tent fly being ripped to shreds and for the three lads a massive injection of adrenalin.

It was over in seconds, the column shrieking off into the forest.

"Bloody hell", said Graham, "are you guys alive?" We all did a quick systems check and found that no one had a scratch.

"Well, that was entertaining", said Ray, "never been under one of those before."

The camp was a shambles, stuff was up in the trees, spread around the forest and the tent fly was just tattered cloth.

A couple of fantails flitted in out of nowhere, chattering away about the damage and all we could do was laugh.

It was a heck of an experience although it took a while to rein in our belongings. A fishing boat cruised into the bay late in the afternoon to shelter from the storm and Peter Roderiques and crew gave us a home for the night. In the morning we went back to the beach and packed up the gear in case Hannibal was silly enough to fly through the storm and pick us up.

The wind had swung to the south the previous day and it was bitterly cold. Snow blanketed the bush to low levels and we were thankful of a warm fishing boat and happy to have been spared the sodden sleeping bags.

About midday we thought we heard a chopper. The odd break was appearing in the cloud and it suddenly seemed likely.

Sure enough, Hannibal roared into Kisbee Bay and settled the Hughes 500 on the beach.

"You look a bit damp boys", he said, through an amused grin. "I've got the cargo net, might get everyone over to Hauroko in one hit and one of you can stay in the machine for the leg to Te Anau, if you like."

I drew the appropriate straw and in 15 minutes Hannibal was checking the weight of the cargo sling and lifting off for fairer pastures.

What a trip, swaying and lurching through the cloud, wind buffeting the chopper, snow-covered bush disappearing in a seemingly endless canopy.

It was like travelling through a Christmas card, a breathtaking journey in wonderland.

That Preservation trip was the only one that Ray and I did to that part of Fiordland. He passed away and set up camp in another happy hunting ground. Ray was a special mate with a wonderful knowledge and hunger to explore. As we flew out, I longed to find a way to record some of this beauty to share it with people, open their eyes to what a magnificent country we live in. Little did I know that it would be 12 years before I came once more under the spell of Preservation Inlet.

In February 1996 I was in another chopper heading back into Preservation armed with cameras and dive gear. It was a chance to share the dream.

13

Preservation - Return Journey

Trevor Green is another helicopter pilot who made his name chasing deer on venison recovery. Hard, long, exacting flying – often in marginal conditions – certainly separates the men from the boys, especially when the slightest mistake is likely to put you in a box.

Trevor, like Te Anau's Hannibal Hayes, is now best known as a bloke who ferries people into a Fiordland adventure. His base is just outside the little town of Cliften and within sight of the mountain butress that stands guard over the Fiordland coast.

Grant Atkinson, Tarx Morrison and I wound up unloading a mountain of gear in Trevor's backyard, the backyard that doubles as his hangar. Camera gear, dive gear, fishing gear and clothing spilled out of two vehicles and formed quite a heap, but something was distracting Tarx.

"What's that bird?" he asked.

I looked in the direction of the tree he had singled out and saw a very plump wood pigeon swallowing large round berries.

"That's tree top tegel", I said, "or wood pigeon."

As we stood there, another dozen or so swooped out of a neighbouring gum tree and joined their mate for a feast.

Wood pigeons are one of those birds you often hear before you see. Whish, whish, whish, there is no mistaking the sound of the labouring wings that carry the beautiful native around our forests.

"Are they good to eat? Those birds are as plump as chickens."

"Yes", I replied, "they are good to eat, but totally protected. Look but don't touch", I said to 135 kilos of salivating sound man.

There was a time when over on the coast a friend and I had been caught in a storm and run out of food. The thing that probably saved our lives was the beautiful lumbering wood pigeon that came too close to camp. It tasted unbelievable when baked in clay and gave us

Heading into the Fiords – a bird's-eye view of what to expect. Scenery that takes your breath away.

the strength to walk out. That was a long time ago and on this journey to Preservation and Dusky, food was to be very plentiful.

Of the flight in, a couple of things were significant: firstly the weather, which was sheer magic, and secondly the eight deer we saw and filmed on the tussock above the bush line.

"Jimmy Kane shot over 100 deer in that basin in one day", said Trevor, as we screamed into the valley above Lake Monk and gave a hind and yearling the fright of their lives.

"A fluke to see anything there now." We skimmed the next saddle and suddenly Long Sound and Preservation unfolded beneath us. It was breathtaking.

We dropped altitude and swallowed up the procession of mountains, lakes and forest that headed off towards the coast.

The machine flew straight over the Dawson Burn and I thought of old George Burnby and our earlier prank on the beach.

We skimmed low over the Sound and a pod of dolphins accelerated away from the noise.

It was very, very good to be back in Preservation, especially when we had been dumped on a chopper pad and loaded our gear aboard the 85 foot *Cindy Hardy*. Another party quickly scrambled aboard and we left. Very soon the chopper ride was only a memory and ahead of us were four days of diving, fishing and exploring.

The sandflies very quickly found their mark, but once we put to sea they were all but left behind.

"The boys want a feed of crayfish", instructed skipper, Gordon Johnson, once we were in open water and heading towards a likely-looking headland.

126

Even above the sound of the engine, the noise of the birds travelled on the faint breeze. A few puffy blobs of cotton wool cloud sat in the sky and everywhere mountains and valley reached towards the heavens. On a Fiordland day like this you know you are knocking on the door of paradise.

The *Cindy Hardy* is a ship and once I hurled myself off the side the underwater camera had to be lowered down on a rope. As well as Gordon, the skipper, there was a cook on board, Marion, and crewman called "Tracker". A group of eight people represented the charter and my team were add-ons. Fourteen people had plenty of room to spread out and after a dive there was tea, coffee or soup. The meals were huge, the supply of dive tanks endless and the skipper's knowledge of the area seemingly limitless. This is the way to explore Fiordland. My dive buddies on the first splash were Steve and Coral and they gave me something human to refer to as I filmed the cliffs of red coral and the kelp that fanned across the surface.

There had been a tonne of rain before this perfect day and the first six metres were green, the brackish fresh water having spilled into the Fiord via hundreds of rivers and waterfall. The fresh had then vainly tried to mix with the sea, the battle taking place in that six metres of eerie-coloured diving no-mans-land. Beneath that layer was 30 metres of clear ocean that was a little dim after the light had struggled through from the surface. Diving is another adventure in Fiordland, there is nowhere quite like it. Whether hunting a feed of crayfish or scallops, or filming the plant and animal life as I was, the undersea world reflects the magnificent scenery and geography to be found topside. I have heard it described as the "mirror world".

One of the first things you notice is the taste, a leap into the ocean is generally greeted with the salty flavour you would expect, but not necessarily in Fiordland. After that initial *Cindy Hardy* plunge I was marinated in a very crisp fresh water bath.

During descent that changed and I broke out below the eerie green fresh and started filming.

Steve and Coral were hunting crayfish, peering in every nook and cranny, while I filmed that red coral garden. Fiordland is the last place you expect to be exploring coral colonies but they are there, the famous black coral trees plus red and white branch coral. I have said it is like diving nowhere else but the uniqueness of underwater Fiordland has to be seen to be appreciated.

It was a beautiful dive but the cray hunters didn't have any luck. Back on the surface our next pleasant surprise was getting back aboard.

Gordon worked the controls of a Hiab crane and we swam into a specially made cage and were effortlessly hoisted onto the deck. It is a superb system.

As soon as I was out of my gear, Tracker ambled over with the heaviest hand line I have ever seen.

"Chasing sharks, Tracker?" I asked.

"No, just a feed of blue cod, but we don't muck around with that light line nonsense. If you want to get a feed get on with the job", he said, hurling a 2 kilo sache weight sinker over the side. The sinker was followed by 5 mm nylon rope and the two hooks were attached to similar sized rope. There was only one thing of interest to me and that was the long-shanked hooks that Tracker used. Fish like blue cod envelop the bait, suck it right down and are usually hooked in the throat. Long-shanked hooks make it possible to get your gear back without major surgery.

The one thing that struck me about this charter was that it was pure meat hunting and everyone was totally focused on filling the larder. That's the way almost all trips used to be, everyone focusing on plunder and I was as guilty as the next guy. We have learnt in recent years that our resource is not infinite and overfishing has created all sorts of problems.

Sure, we have regulations, but it would be great to see the still bountiful resource of Fiordland looked after a little better.

When it comes to cod and crayfish, I would like to see people take enough to eat while they are on the coast but leave the rest alone.

No chopper-loads of fillets and cray tails. If we adopted that philosophy we would look after the resource and the charter operators would be investing in their future.

Anyway, that's the sermon, and in no time Tracker and Paul Lindsay were hauling in fat, sleek cod. The sun sparkled on a glassy ocean and the fish lined up for the dinner table.

Tracker is in his 50s, has been a commercial fisherman for years, wears a red knitted hat with Tracker written on it (so you don't forget who he is) and on a charter you couldn't find a more helpful guy.

He assists with dive gear, fillets fish, helps Marion when it come to peeling vegetables and is just an all-round good bloke.

When the pile of cod started to look like enough, Gordon climbed out of his wheelhouse perch and shambled across the deck. The bridge looks out across the vast expanse of deck and when you gazed up from the work area, Gordon's round, mischievous face peered back. Someone has given him a statue of a gnome and it also looks down from the Captain's perch. It also has a similar grin and if it wasn't for the fact that Gordon does so much helpful leaping around, you would think that he and the gnome were twins.

Suddenly he was beside me. "Guy from Invercargill found a pretty special colony of sea penns a couple of weeks ago. Do you want to film them?"

"Too bloody right", I said, "I've seen them in George Sound and Doubtful but never filmed them. That would be fantastic."

The lines came in, Gordon climbed back on to the bridge with his gnome and soon we were underway, the bow swinging gently towards a narrow channel that proved to be home to the sea penns.

These animals love tide, it enables them to filter an abundant supply of food and in the current they wave like the beautiful broad feathers that they appear to be.

They can retract beneath the mud but dozens of them fanned

Cindy Hardy *arrives to pick us up in Kisbee Bay. From there we set a course to Dusky Sound.*

Richard Henry's Kiwi Enclosure, Pidgeon Island, Dusky Sound. Richard's contribution to the protection of New Zealand's flightless birds has never been fully acknowledged.

The Elingamite wreck site, West King Island the Three Kings on a very calm day.

Silver coins from the Elingamite. There is nothing quite as thrilling as watching coins pop out of the sediment. We had a ball.

Who said all of the big blue cod are confined to the South? Not Willy Bullock, seen here with a very respectable Three Kings breakfast.

Brian Franks with his biggest ever fish – a little Three Kings Bass "Don't see many fish like this on Banks Peninsula".

Kydd Pollock with a Volkner Rocks kingfish of about 15 kilos. Kydd and Rick Pollock are legends in the battle to find big kingis.

Another White Island kingfish – this time around the 20 kilo mark. The world record caught on a Rick Pollock charter is 52 kilos, also care of White Island.

Mack Seymour and Becky Smith recording a bad tempered White Island. The ruins around them bear testimony to how disturbed this place can get.

Becky Smith with pink and blue mao mao. They school in clouds around White Island and the Volkners. Underneath cruise predators such as the kingfish.

East Cape Road Block!!

All the way around East Cape the scenery is breathtaking. Rhys Duncan and Tarx Morrison catch the tranquillity.

Tarakihi and hapuka filled our day and fishbin on a trip out with Fred Lewis.

Around the Cape it's the pace that gets you. The road isn't reserved exclusively for cars. It is a convenient place to stop and have a chat. "Wait a minute" said the cocky "I'll just shift the cattle off the road".

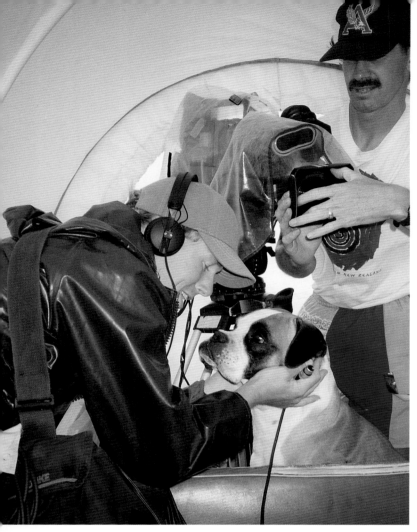

Tony Burrows in action "Tony please don't kiss the talent". Ralph the dog is unconcerned. An entertaining day with Richard Job and Tamure Tours on 90 Mile Beach.

A gathering on 90 Mile Beach compliments of "trail boss" Richard Job. Richard offers a great day out and superb feed.

Grant Atkinson (cameraman extraordinaire) fishing for blue cod with a rope handline. "They ain't going to bust off!"

upward like delicate, apricot-coloured single feathers. Sometimes sea penns are tiny, standing five or six centimetres but these were all at least 20 cms. They are unique to this environment, are beautiful to behold and never before have I seen such a magnificent colony.

Thank God for dive computers, they seem to give you so much time underwater and I dragged out every last second. A couple of the other divers came down for a bit of a look but most of the team were totally focused on crayfish hunting. Among the sea penns were plenty of large fat scallops and I decided to prise one open with my dive knife and see if I could attract a few cod and perch to add a bit of colour to my shots of the sea penns.

Blue cod must have incredible hearing, because as soon as my dive knife scraped against the shell, it was like a stampede, blue cod came charging in from everywhere.

I seemed to be wearing a large neon sign that flashed "Food, food, food". The perch were there too, and as soon as that shell was open, everyone dived in for a scoff. The bigger fish shouldered the others out of the way. In this community, might was right and I could see why cod and sea perch are so easy to catch. If it moves they eat it, if it doesn't move they nudge it until it does and then devour it. I could forgive Tracker for his lack of finesse when targeting a feed because the old cod will never rate as a sport fish, just a very tasty garbage disposal unit.

That dive was a real beauty even if I broke all the rules and spent most of it on my own. Underwater cameramen tend to lead a fairly lonely existence but when I was hoisted on board the cray hunters were in very good humour. Bags bulged with creatures destined for the larder and the final touches were added to a Fiordland banquet.

I had another chat with Gordon and we steamed into Isthmus Sound and a wee historical interlude before anchoring in Cuttle Cove for a much needed rest.

The sun started to sink with real purpose and a faint breeze flowed out of the forest and rippled the surface of the sound. The mountains stood up stark and clear, contrasting dramatically with the late afternoon sky. Jackets went on and an involuntary shudder shot up my spine. Fiordland was reminding me to stay humble, to make the most of the weather and the opportunity.

One of the things that Graham, Ray and I had explored was an old chimney in Isthmus Sound. It is made of bricks and is built against the side of the hill. The structure was designed to help extract gold from quartz ore, but as smelters went, it doesn't seem to have been too successful. The quartz itself contains gold all right, but not enough to have been viable, just like many similar gold mining activities in Preservation during the 1890s – a brief, hopeful, but ultimately forlorn interlude, that has been all but swallowed up by a patient forest.

Next morning our explorations continued, the Cuttle Cove whaling station, Moonlight Beach on Coal Island and then the towns of Kisbee Bay.

In recent years someone has built a lodge at Cromerty occupying a couple of building sites on what used to be Gala Street. It is a superb building, a unique thing to find in Fiordland National Park. We called in to have a brew with the caretaker, a friendly little chap called Peanut.

"Must be a bit lonely living here?" I enquired, gazing across the expanse of the bay and onto the forested slopes of Coal Island.

"Fishermen and chopper pilots stop off to say gidday", he said. "One of the chopper crews dropped in a little fawn the other day. Shot the mother and gave me the little one to look after."

Sure enough, he disappeared inside and returned with a very uncertain- looking stag fawn.

As we left, Peanut didn't seem like a happy hermit, in fact he didn't really seem happy at all. He lives opposite the grave of the almost forgotten prospector, explorer William Docherty, who stayed on as the gold petered out and was buried on a little island in the bay. We paid our respects to William, who had died on 20th March 1896. Maybe I imagined the feeling of sadness, perhaps the changing weather was altering my normally buoyant mood but as we steamed towards the open sea and a passage to Dusky, Preservation seemed to be brooding. I got the feeling that Preservation Inlet was ready to be left alone.

Cindy Hardy ran out towards the ocean and picked up the first of the swells that rolled out of the southwest.

"Sea's up our bum", yelled the skipper, "be a good trip." As if in agreement the bow rode high and plunged into the back of the next swell. Tonnes of blue ocean split, shot skyward and cascaded over the deck. Occasional showers rolled off the mountains of Preservation and the Fiords looked dark and forbidding but out on the ocean the sun shone and *Cindy Hardy* soon settled into a rhythm that ate up the miles. Captain Cook sighted and named Dusky Bay in the *Endeavour* in 1770 but could not make landfall. He returned in the *Resolution* and spent a month in Dusky in 1773 exploring, charting, replenishing supplies and staring in awe at the magnificent country. As we steamed into the mouth of Dusky Bay, I too was in awe. It was not my first trip out of the open sea but it was one that afforded the clearest view. It reminded me of the words of William Wales, one of Cook's officers.

"For every island, of which there are almost an infinite number, is a mountain, and the country a heap of mountains piled one upon another, until you lose their tops in the clouds."

The appearance of Dusky is unchanged, the adventures endless and the scenery breathtaking.

Our cray hunters were itching to get back in the water so our first dive was tucked in behind Dusky's southern headland.

The rolling swells with the white breaking tops were left behind and the blue ocean was devoid of any fresh water layer. After the heady lunge off the side of *Cindy Hardy* a look into the depths revealed crystal clear visibility and enough boulders and crevices to put a smile on any crayfish hunter's face.

I had trolled a lure from Preservation in the hope of hooking an albacore or two, but by the time the vast bulk of the ship had been brought under control, I would have been spooled. It was a token gesture and no albacore was silly enough to have a go.

There were crayfish everywhere and a couple supplemented the roast chicken and vegetables that Marion prepared for dinner.

We had been travelling, exploring and diving for some time before we choppered in to Preservation and there was no way I was going to waste a minute of the time in Fiordland.

After changing out of dive gear and having a hot shower, I found that we had anchored in historic Pickersgill Harbour where Captain Cook had been.

I climbed up on to the aft deck, looked up at the mountains, shook my head in wonder and started filling in my diary.

Apparently I promptly fell asleep and the devious buggers I call friends covered me in incriminating signs and filmed me until they got bored. I like to check the footage at the end of the day, make sure we haven't picked up any camera faults and there it was – a whole heap of G.B. Sinclair out to lunch with half the crew taking turns to make me look like an idiot. I've got a long memory, guys.

I was too shattered to know the difference.

Marion's feast was fantastic and I wasn't the only tired camper, so after dinner everyone drifted off to their bunks.

Tarx and I were sharing a cabin, which was a big mistake, because he snores like a bastard. And that is exactly what it is − a real bastard − because in a confined cabin there is no getting away from it. Every time he "wound up" I battered him with a pillow until he woke up. The battle raged for hours until we were both so exhausted we fell into a restless sleep. In the morning we were not exactly rested but it was another brilliant day and although fishing was on the agenda, Tucker, Tarx, Attie and I headed off to film Richard Henry's house site and kiwi enclosure on Pigeon Island.

Richard was another hermit on a special mission. He was employed to catch flightless birds such as the kakapo and kiwi and release them on Resolution Island. Rats and the mustelids (stoats, weasels and ferrets) were decimating the mainland bird population and Richard saw himself as the saviour given responsibility to protect these magnificent creatures. Richard Henry devoted over 14 years to his work, living on Pigeon Island from 1894 to early 1909. He shifted

The Cindy Hardy *deck is always cluttered. A bin full of crays in a holding pattern just prior to entering the galley.*

over 700 birds to the supposed safety of Resolution Island but one day in 1900 he came face to face with a weasel and it broke his heart. The mustelids had arrived on Resolution Island and it seemed as though his years of work had been in vain. He stayed for another eight years but the battle was lost. So many attempts to intervene in Fiordland's destiny or harvest her resources have ended in tragedy. Sometimes because of greed and slaughter, as is the case with whales and seals, sometimes because the reality doesn't measure up to the dream, as is the case with the miners and prospectors.

In Richard Henry's case, someone was devoting a fair portion of their life to a wonderful cause, but right from the start, it too, was doomed to failure. Those aggressive little animals don't know the difference between the rabbits they were introduced to help control and the birds we are desperately trying to protect. To them it's all tucker. If you want to know more about Richard Henry, read "Richard Henry of Resolution Island" by Susanne and John Hill. It is a fascinating story.

The little peninsula where Henry lived, housed his birds and stored his boat, was an absolute picture. Most of the trees are youthful second growth slowly claiming back the signs of habitation but there is still enough left of his home to provoke thought and respect for Richard Henry's work. Back in the dinghy we headed round the corner into Facile Harbour and the scene of New Zealand's first recorded shipwreck. The *Endeavour* was scuttled here in 1795 and today is just a few old copper-clad timbers and piles of ballast stones. Parts of the ship were used to help complete a new vessel and other parts to convert a ship's long boat. For a time 244 people lived in Facile Harbour and their story is also fascinating. Tales such as that of Richard Henry and the *Endeavour* have far greater significance when you learn about them during a visit to Dusky than they ever would by simply reading their stories.

On that sparkling clear morning I set out to film something of the *Endeavour*'s grave but my camera battery died and the boys returned to the *Cindy Hardy* for a replacement. I spent the time exploring the ship's old bones in three metres of water. I cleared some of the sand, and shiny copper sheathing gleamed in its beautiful polished way.

By the time the lads returned I had something to film, but for a time I lay on the smooth surface of Facile Harbour, listening to the birds and imagining what life would have been like for those stranded here over 200 years ago.

The thing I find special about Fiordland is that you can literally immerse yourself in it. Hunting, diving, fishing, exploring and relaxing combine so well with individual challenges or the pleasure of being in good company. During the afternoon I broke a few rules and took Grant Atkinson, the cameraman, for his first dive. Attie does such a good job and he had for a long time expressed a desire to try diving, so he and I went on a dive just for the hell of it. (No cameras.) He caught a crayfish and released it, saw black coral trees, scallops and a wide variety of fish. He was only in 10 metres of water but as soon as he broke the surface, the ear to ear grin told the story. "Wow, that was fantastic, unbelievable", and so on. Diving has a habit of doing that to people, especially when conditions add the sort of magic that exists in Dusky.

We steamed off for a blue cod fish and along the way a Robinson Helicopter peeled off the tops with two dead deer slung underneath.

The 'Robbie' landed precariously on the back of a boat with a modified stern platform and the crew went to work refuelling. Within 10 minutes the 'Robbie' was up and away, swooping up one of the valleys adjacent to our drift and searching for more unfortunate deer.

The cod were huge and we wound in a good feed. I used my rod, Tracker and the crew the huge hand lines of committed meat hunters. A cruise ship appeared out of the Acheron Passage and set a course for the open sea. A massive cruise ship in the wilderness of Dusky Sound didn't seem to have a place really. They were passing through, having entered the shelter of Breaksea Sound to the north, but all those people would see is the geography, snap a few pictures and disappear.

The essence of Fiordland is in the experience, that immersion thing again, when you eat, sleep and breathe the place, not slip through on a cruise ship.

Marco Polo, she was called, and a pod of dolphins broke away from her bulk, probably unable to keep up, and came to investigate the anglers.

I was back in my wetsuit in a flash and, armed with the underwater unit, had a 40 minute frolic with flipper.

By the time I got back on board, the blue cod quota had been filled and Gordon slid over for another chat. "I know", I said, "the crayfish hunters are getting a bit twitchy."

"Yep", he replied, "but I'll put you in a really pretty spot with plenty of black coral."

He climbed up to his spot beside the gnome and we headed towards a sunny cliff on the north eastern side near the Acheron.

Paul Lindsay was my buddy, and Gordon was right, the location was superb. Not only were there dozens of black coral trees standing snowy white off the cliff, but a school of respectable trumpeter cruised by for a look. The late afternoon sun broke through in shafts of dancing light and a million pilchards streamed by in a seemingly endless school, the sun reflecting off their silver sides.

Hmm, I thought, some very large predator would have a field day with this lot. In every crevice there were crayfish, but Paul and I took only pictures. The cray bags would be bulging on the decks and the hunters would be happy without us adding to the heap.

I was happy just to be here filming all this stuff. How Ray Tinsley would have loved to have been on this trip. It seemed like years since we had shared adventures in Dusky, Preservation and the fiords further north, it was a long time ago, but at the same time it was just yesterday.

Cindy Hardy anchored in Duck Cove. Darkness crept through the trees and just when it seemed that the day was over, the Robinson came hurtling around the corner - a stag slung under its belly on a long strop. The machine roared and clattered over our anchorage and disappeared off in the gloom.

The cabin windows were frosted and the smell of Marion's cooking floated around on the faint breeze. A blanket of stars crawled from their hiding place and the forest became part of the night, it was time for a feed of cod and crayfish, banter and a couple of beers. I joined the animated discussion in the warmth of the galley. It was the last night of the trip.

The morrow dawned slowly through a leaden sky.

"Turning to shit", said Gordon, "35 knots of north west."

Trevor was due to pluck us out of Cascade Cove at midday.

Not far from the mouth of Cascade, but a little seaward, is an island and on the island were a whole bunch of seals.

"They weren't there two years ago", I said to Gordon.

"No shortage these days," he said, "you want to see them on Five Fingers Peninsula or Breaksea Island."

I filmed the seals in a place I had dived two years before and the fish had gone, presumably scoffed.

Seal numbers around the coast are increasing dramatically and today, when nature's food chain is interrupted by the harvest of man, I couldn't help but wonder what sort of seal population represents a balance.

Will total protection kill the seals with kindness? Will the population get to a point where the animals start starving to death? I don't know, but I hate to think that we would start killing seals with good intentions described as kindness.

The seal issue will become a scrap of major proportions - just wait and see.

I alluded to some of these points in the Dusky Sound show and boy, did I get the hate mail.

Protection is a very emotional argument, I just hope we have the sense to identify what's best for everyone. It all seems so simple when you are swimming with the seals in Dusky.

At midday a faint whine grew louder and the Squirrel roared in under the cloud. We loaded up, said our good-byes and were whisked away from Fiordland.

"Until next time", I muttered to myself, as we swallowed up the forest and mountains and headed east towards better weather and a fishing tournament in Bluff. Fiordland had shined on us and the adventures are on tape, a couple of shows that rank up with the best. Have I convinced you to visit this place yet? I certainly hope so.

On our return to Preservation we slipped into Dusky Sound and came face to face with the cruise liner Marco Polo. *The last thing you expect to see in Fiordland.*

14

The Three Kings

I always get excited at the thought of heading away on a 'shoot' but some places and some adventures are so darned exciting to plan that they mean the added inconvenience of sleepless nights.

The Three Kings always has that effect on me, whether filming or not, because I have shared so many fantastic adventures to this 'anglers' eldorado'.

The next book will describe the fantastic big game fishing found around these wonderful remote islands, but this story is about another eldorado, the search for *Elingamite* treasure.

The steamer *Elingamite* was wrecked on West King on 9th November 1902, and in the days that followed the sinking, 45 people lost their lives. The 2587 ton *Elingamite* steamed a regular route between Sydney and Auckland, usually taking an uneventful five days. On this occasion Captain Atwood's ship ran into heavy fog. A passenger from Sydney, Steven Nell, found himself gazing through a thick bank of fog "at one of the most beautiful sights my eyes have ever witnessed . . . It reminded me of a transformation scene in a theatre. A thick, heavy bank of cloud had come down the side of a hill. It did not touch the water and was clear enough 20 or 30 yards high. The scene very much resembled a snow clad mountain.

"Charmed, I stood looking at it for some seconds. Then it struck me we were headed straight for it. As I gazed in awe, the cry "Breakers ahead" from the forecastle was followed by the alarm signal to the engine room. "Full speed astern"."

The ship's engines stopped, but for some reason did not go into reverse. Gently, in a moderate swell with a light wind from the north-west, the *Elingamite* grounded on a rocky shelf 50 km north-west off the New Zealand mainland. She sank within 20 minutes and all was confusion, some passengers and crew struggling to reach lifeboats or rafts, and a few already dead.

Yes, there are massive schools of fish at the "Kings" and yes a few thousand birds hovering overhead help to give the show away.

Everyone in the water who was alive was eventually picked up, but only one lifeboat was fully provisioned. In the fog, lifeboats and rafts became separated. One boat with 52 passengers reached the mainland near Houhora. Three others sought the land on the other side of West King, where there was no landing, but the occupants succeeded in scrambling onto Great King, 10 kilometres to the east. Seventy survivors huddled together on a rock ledge. Help came in the form of the *Zealandia*, which had been alerted by a whaleboat that put out of Houhora where the first boat had raised the alarm. A missing raft was found at sea five days later, eight of the original occupants having died of thirst or the effects of drinking sea water. They were blistered and burnt, ravaged by wind, sun, salt and sea.

One lifeboat was never found, its occupants disappearing in the vast expanse of unforgiving ocean.

In this area the Tasman Sea and Pacific Ocean meet. Vast lumps of ocean are pushed around by huge tides and rise up over underwater ledges and mountains. The ill-provisioned lifeboat and its desperate occupants just disappeared.

At the subsequent enquiry, Captain Atwood was blamed for the disaster, although he was later exonerated when it was established that the Three Kings were charted out of position.

The *Elingamite* eventually rolled down the cliff to about 40 metres and was smashed to pieces in a procession of Three Kings storms, but she was never forgotten.

Her attraction lay in the hold, £17,320 of gold and silver coins. It was the treasure that attracted salvagers, the first expedition only 10 days after the wreck. Most of the early salvage attempts were driven away by huge seas, treacherous currents or near disaster.

The seventh expedition, in 1907, was the first to experience success. In January of that year, diver E. Harper went down from the auxiliary schooner *Huia*. Soon after, the ship reported "Good Luck, have recovered £1500. Hope to recover the lot. Heavy conditions at present prevailing making it impossible to work."

When Harper resumed diving he continued to find coins but he also started to get 'deep water pains', and was warned to keep future dives short. They didn't know a great deal about the potentially lethal effects of the bends in those days.

On 23rd January 1907, making a third dive for the day and staying down for over half an hour, he complained of chest pains. When he came up he collapsed and died.

Harper had that morning brought up £800 in coins – half in silver, half in gold, bringing the total so far recovered by the *Huia* to £2500.

Now that coins had started to be found, a steady stream of them came up – £700 and £300 more to the *Huia* – and then £700 and £200 to the *Claymore* on two separate expeditions. Tragedy struck again when another diver surfaced with cramp in the arms and pains in the feet. He died the same night. People were growing wary of the *Elingamite* and no further expeditions took place until 1957, when Les Subritzky dived from the *Greyhound*. He didn't even reach the wreck before being swept out to sea. Les surfaced in a heavy swell a long way from salvation and was very lucky to survive the ordeal. By the time the exhausted diver was reunited with the *Greyhound* there was no way Les was going back down on that wreck.

I hadn't even heard of the Three Kings or the *Elingamite* until, at

The Harold Hardy – *preparing for a slow chug to the Three Kings at the start of our search for gold on the wreck of the* Elingamite.

the age of 14, I picked up a book called "The *Elingamite* and its Treasure", written by Wade Doak.

From that day on, the Kings and a dive on the *Elingamite* became one of my dreams. In later years, while chasing marlin, I steamed past the wreck site several times but rarely did it look diveable. Those huge swells that caused problems for salvage expeditions rolled in out of the Tasman and slammed into the cliff. They were not hospitable. Kelly Tarlton, Wade Doak, John Pettit and a number of other guys had been working the *Elingamite* site since they had rediscovered it on a spear fishing expedition in 1967. They had pulled up a lot of silver and a little gold but had never found the "mother lode". Kelly had calculated that the remaining treasure was the size of a car and although good quantities of silver were found, that mother lode remained elusive.

Wade Doak wrote in his book "The *Elingamite* and its Treasure" of the first dive at the beginning of their successful salvage.

"We dropped down from the madly tossing surface (off West King) to the relative quiet of the wreck site; the gold seemed to be already in our grasp. At the bottom at 150 feet we swam around looking for our bearings. Each diver in his silent blue world registered a private feeling of dismay. The powerful current billowing in our faces was changing visibility rapidly from 40 to 80 feet in gusts. When we had fixed the position of the initial silver find, visibility had been 150 feet. Now we had no way of determining that position. With rising fears we searched among the similar rocks, probed hopefully in the wreckage, and fossicked in crevices. Kelly found two threepenny pieces in a crack. I seized a golden looking cat's eye jubilantly. We surfaced in the rip ride. It was hard to break the news to John Pettit and John Gallagher, waiting to descend with a golden glitter in their eyes; we'd failed to relocate the coin deposit.

"Divers become accustomed to quick reverses of fortune, but when 10 minutes later those two divers broke the surface and came aboard, and John Pettit reached into his sack to flash a golden half-sovereign under our noses, we were bursting with excitement. Over 100 silver coins spilled out on the deck. He had refound the cleft. In prospecting nearby he had picked up the golden coin somewhere but, not recognising it immediately, could not say exactly where it had been. However, a small buoy was now bobbing six feet above the coin deposit, and that single coin made our hopes more buoyant than ever. It was the morale booster that galvanised us into five days of hard diving."

Looking back John Pettit says; "Those were great days. We were frightened lest they might end."

But end they did, even before the tragic death of Kelly Tarlton in 1985.

As a diver, Kelly inspired me, he seemed like one of those rare adventurers that saw obstacles as challenges and always looked for the way ahead.

His "Underwater World" on Auckland's Tamaki Drive is a

wonderful legacy to this unassuming achiever but the place that always gets my attention is Kelly's museum of shipwrecks in the Bay of Islands.

It was the thought of filming something that would record the adventures of Kelly and his mates that finally spurred me to action. That, and the fact that two of Kelly's colleagues, Ken Dury and Malcolm Blair, were planning an *Elingamite* expedition. When the offer was made I roped in another of Kelly's mates, Willy Bullock, and suddenly we were in Houhora loading gear aboard the old *Harold Hardy*.

"She's an old concrete barge", a mate of mine had said.

"A big slab of uncomfortable bloody concrete. They make toilets out of concrete and that's what she feels like."

"So you didn't have much of a charter then?" I enquired.

"Weather turned to shit and she rolls like a pig."

I have a profound respect for Ken, the skipper, and although I knew the *Harold Hardy* was not the most attractive beast on the ocean, and perhaps a bit slow, she certainly knows her way to the Kings and back.

The weather forecast said 10 knots variable and a great big high pressure system had decided to park over northern New Zealand. Forecasts don't get much better than that − it was like a dream come true.

We left Houhora at 8.00pm and steamed all night, a slow but steady chug in our concrete home.

Ken Dury is in his late 40s, he has a vast experience on the ocean as a salvager, fisherman and charter operator. He is a squat, solid, quietly spoken chap with a ruddy round face. Ken doesn't miss a trick and is the sort of solid reliable chap you want to have around in a crisis. Ken also has a tremendous knowledge of the *Elingamite* site. Older, taller, equally as experienced and just as quietly spoken, is Malcolm Blair. Malcolm is a dedicated wreck diver with enthusiasm that is similar to what Kelly's must have been. The thing I have learnt about Malcolm over the years, is that he is totally focused, very analytical and always happy to share his accumulated know-how. He was relief skipper on this trip, freeing Ken up to dive. Malcolm worked several wrecks with Kelly Tarlton, including joining him on the Auckland Island expedition that searched unsuccessfully for the gold lost on the *General Grant*. The third experienced chap was retired commercial diver, Willy Bullock. Rosemary Tarlton once told me that Willy was a diver who Kelly held in very high regard, another level- headed man for a crisis.

Willy is the sort of guy who just fits in, no bullshit, no agendas, just a damn nice companion whose stories of commercial work are astounding. Joe, Ron and Brian were the other divers, Rhys Duncan was the cameraman and Aaron Hughes the sound operator.

We were prepared, we were excited, we had planned endlessly and now a final sleepless night as we ate up the gentle swells and narrowed the gap between Houhora and West King.

Getting ready to dive the Elingamite, three 40 metre dives a day, chasing silver coins and the possibility of gold. It was a fantastic trip to film.

In the early morning the *Harold Hardy* was on site, a gentle swell rode up the sheer black cliffs of West King and spewed back off the rock in a ribbon of white foam. Gulls wheeled and dived, riding invisible currents, or sat with their mates on a rich ink-blue ocean. Schools of trevally and mao mao seethed here and there as the anchor clattered down into the grave of the *Elingamite*. We had arrived at one of my dream adventures.

Two 40 metre dives were planned on day one, the first a swim over the wreck and the second a dedicated dig for gold and silver.

Rosemary Tarlton owns the wreck and it was her permission that had put the final stamp of approval on the trip.

I had butterflies as I geared up, had to slow myself down, concentrate on being methodical, this was no place for a diving accident.

"I'm excited", I said to Willy.

"So am I", he replied. Great, I thought, even the pro's still get that little burst of adrenalin. It's part of the passion that dedicated divers and anglers carry in to their sport.

The first thing that struck me when I leapt in, was the cold. Way off the northern coast of New Zealand we were talking subtropics, but huge currents and upwellings drag in cooler water. The deeper we went, the more profound the cold, but the thing that amazed me was the visibility. During the days of our expedition it was always 30 metres – at times over 40 – and that is very clear water.

Kelly was nicknamed "Gelly Kelly" because of his liking for gelignite. If something was in the way or a bit stubborn, stick a charge under it and, hey presto, problem solved. The *Elingamite* had been

142

well and truly blasted by the time we turned up, but no amount of explosives could compare with the ocean's handy work.

Over 90 years of being pounded by a procession of storms had smashed the ship to pieces. Some large slabs of steel remain but, boy oh boy, the site is a veritable junkyard.

I don't know whether it's my superstitious nature or not, but during that early dark dive under the shadow of the cliffs, I felt that this old ship was yet to claim her last victim. Maybe it's the isolation or knowledge of the tragedy, perhaps it was the cold, but that first impression never went away. This is not a place to take risks. Our second 40 metre dive focused on coins, gold or silver – we didn't care – and the thrill of waving your hand across the sediment and having coins pop up is hard to describe.

The boys had rigged and buoyed a safety line from the *Harold Hardy* stern down to the area we were working. A spare dive tank was tethered at six metres complete with regulator. If someone ran out of air or suffered a malfunction, the tank was backup. At the end of dive number two the current raced across the wreck site. As I decompressed at three metres the safety line vibrated like a violin string. We fought to hang on and I thought of divers like Les Subritzky who had been plucked away in the current and almost lost.

The *Élingamite* was certainly not for the fainthearted. Eventually we joined the excited throng on *Harold Hardy*.

Bags were emptied and coins rolled out on the deck. A couple of dozen assorted half-crowns, florins, shillings, sixpences and threepences, but no gold.

We didn't care – it was treasure.

Inside the Harold Hardy – *the smell of mouldy wetsuits hanging in the air. You don't want to be with anyone who is too house-proud.*

"I think we'll forget about any more dives in that current", said Malcolm "asking for trouble."

"What about heading off for a fish?" I suggested.

Surprisingly, everyone thought that was a great alternative and the anchor was winched aboard and we zipped away downcurrent. A large green buoy remained on the spot, with a river of current breaking clean over it.

"Glad I'm not hanging on that line now", I said to Willie.

"I see what you mean", he replied, with a grimace. The cliff reached up stark and beautiful under a late afternoon sun. Tide lines stood out like roadways, carrying the ocean this way and that, but no wind tore at the surface and the swells had eased to a gentle metre roll.

"Weather looks as though it'll hold for the next day or two", said Ken.

It was perfect.

We only fished for half an hour – it was plenty of time to catch a feed.

Ken positioned us for a drift in 130 metres of depth and slackening tide.

The tackle was simple, a classic ledger rig with a heavy sinker on the bottom and two 8/0 hooks with big baits.

As soon as the sinker hit the bottom, we hooked up, instantly.

It was great fun and fresh blue cod, giant tarakihii and golden snapper soon landed in the bin.

When it was clear that there was enough for a feed, the lines came in and we "set sail" for our anchorage in Cascade.

After an all night steam, a couple of serious dives and a good feed, everyone hit the sack.

Before I knew it, the sun was threatening to sneak in to a perfect Three Kings day and no one was going to waste a minute of our search for *Elingamite* treasure. The crew was up at "sparrow fart".

For the next three days the weather remained perfect and we burrowed under rocks and sediment, lifting dozens of silver coins but Willie and I could find no gold.

At one point we left the wreck site and dived on a pinnacle with clouds of tarakihi, mao mao, kingfish, soft corals and other marine multi-coloured garnishings. We were caught under the Three Kings spell, this was everything I dreamt it would be.

On our fourth evening we fished again with the same result. The current highways crossed this way and that, schools of fish boiled and the island chain cut a jagged line across a late afternoon sky. It was perfection. A whale spouted beside us a couple of times before continuing on its journey.

Day five dawned a little sluggishly, a change was on the way. In the morning, Ken always fired up the BBQ and we started with a hearty breakfast. Bacon, eggs, sausages and fish, good diving tucker.

I have a vivid recollection of the eggs slopping around on a hot plate, sliding this way and that in the swell, yokes breaking one after another and mixing with the clear slime that slid across the white base that had already cooked. It tasted much better than it looked and the smell of all that food drowned out the stale odour of damp wetsuits and close confinement.

I stood beside the barbie chatting to Ken on that last morning.

"Been a great trip."

"Yeah, best weather I've seen on the wreck site in 14 years", he answered.

"Do you ever get sick of the place."

"No, there's something special about diving and fishing here, everything is bigger, brighter, cleaner. It hasn't been raped yet and besides, every charter is different. There is no other place like this anywhere in the world."

The sausages sizzled, the islands brooded and the ocean shifted restlessly. Things had gone very smoothly so far.

"Spent some time in the islands", Ken continued. "The natives had some great names for things – in fact the sausages reminded me. They couldn't get their head around sausages, so they called them tube steaks, and binoculars were a problem, too hard to say. The answer – far lookers. Great people, everything's simple."

As we ate breakfast, the wind tugged at the canvas awning on *Harold Hardy*'s stern.

"C'mon", it seemed to say, "you'd better get a move on."

Back on the wreck site, the ocean was starting to change gear and the occasional large swell rode up against the cliff.

We dived and plucked coins out of the crevices, no gold for Willie and I.

The sea and wind built steadily throughout the day and we started bouncing around like a cork. This was more like some of the old film I had seen of Kelly's crew at work. It was not the swells rolling underneath us that caused the problem, but the backwash as tonnes of water rolled back off the cliff. I was taking a break before our last dive when there was a hell of a crash and water cascaded off the stern.

"I think we're sinking", said a normally unflappable Rhys, as he carried his big round eyes into the aft cabin.

We weren't sinking, but a huge wave had rolled back and tried to envelop the *Harold Hardy*.

Suddenly the anchor dragged, we had divers in the water, the safety line took the weight and was as taut as a bow string but threatening to break. Everything was very quickly coming unstuck.

"Shit", said Malcolm, "we'll have to get the weight off that rope. If it breaks ,the boys lose the safety line and we lose the spare tank." Malcolm had responsibility for *Harold Hardy* because Ken was diving.

In the end, we started to swing onto the rocks. Our divers were due to return, but we reasoned that they would like a floating home, rather than another wreck.

To save the ship, the safety line had to be cut, our drift had taken it under the propeller.

Signs of success. Silver coins start to fill a bucket, but where was the gold?

Malcolm fired up the engine, we cut the line and slipped into gear, easing out of immediate danger.

"Quick, chuck a float out the back on a long rope", said the new skipper, "if those guys surface in this tide they'll be round the point before we know it."

Close to 100 metres of rope was paid out and supported by a distant buoy. The divers surfaced in the foam and slop and lunged for the rope.

In a few minutes they were safely aboard.

"I ran out of air", said Ron. "Thank God Ken's a miserly breather. What happened to the spare tank and rope?" he said.

Ken had a backup second stage on his regulator. A spare second stage means that someone else can breathe off your tank.

It was a close run thing, the safe outcome attributable to a couple of level heads on old campaigners, who knew how to navigate through a crisis.

We had a very tense 10 minutes and it seemed as though the Kings wanted to be rid of us, but Willie and I decided to go ahead with our last dive. No cumbersome underwater cameras. Two underwater scooters, a fast trip to the bottom, a quick scratch around and out of there.

With the safety rope gone but with a solid knowledge of landmarks, we took off into the rolling, pitching depth.

At 40 metres the surge still tried to suck us out of our crevice and roll us down the slope. The surge and suck threatened to rip off my mask and tear out the regulator. This was definitely a finale.

Willie and I used the underwater scooter blast to clear debris and

146

anything likely we just threw in a bag. Now the wreck site was cold, gloomy and very angry. It was time to get the hell out. We hit the surface and many hands dragged us back on deck.

"What a surge", I said to Willie.

"Yeah! Even at 40 metres, really impressive", he laughed.

"Well if you think it's big, it must be bloody big", I laughed back.

"Let's see what we got", he urged.

The bag was opened and out dropped the coins and right in the middle was a little gold half-sovereign.

I looked at Willie, he looked at me.

"Did you put that there?" I asked.

"I don't know, I just kept firing stuff in the bag like you."

It was unbelievable, our last frantic dive and out rolled a gold half sovereign. We'll never know which one of us threw the sovereign in the bag.

The wreck was telling us to go but tried to entice us back at the same time. People who have seen the *Elingamite* story on television and have seen the way the little gold coin pops up, always ask me if that was a jack up. The answer is no, that's how Willie and I came to be in possession of our small chunk of *Elingamite* gold.

That trip was everything I hoped it would be. As we steamed back towards the shelter of North Cape, the cork came out of a couple of bottles of wine and we toasted people like Kelly Tarlton and special places like the Three Kings.

We had all had one hell of an adventure in a very special part of New Zealand.

*The "new" Pursuit – purpose-
built for the White Island,
Bay of Plenty trade.*

15
White Island

It adds to the thrill when you fish under the shadow of one of the world's most continuously active volcanoes.

Parked kilometres out in the Bay of Plenty, White Island acts like a weather vane, the angle of the smoke and ash cloud providing an indication of wind strength and direction.

White Island is a moody place, its various eruptions having claimed the lives of workers in the sulphur plant and scaring the living daylights out of countless other explorers and fishermen.

To the Maori, White Island, or Whakaari, was a rich source of food, the island seabird colonies supplying plump and tender nestlings and the ocean a vast-array of fish species.

Every year, thousands of seabirds came to breed, both above and below ground and by November recently-hatched chicks were prime table fare.

Birds were preserved in their own fat and transported to the mainland. Steam vents meant that the food gatherers had readymade ovens to assist in catch preparation.

White Island became attractive at the turn of the century because of the abundant supply of sulphur.

The Maori were first to appreciate the mineral qualities of sulphur, collecting it from the crater to spread on mainland vegetable gardens.

Sulphur and superphospate go hand in hand and for a largely agricultural nation, the fertilizer was a way of life.

The mining of sulphur on White Island had a checkered history, 10 men, buried under a large slip and then a slowly deteriorating financial position causing ultimate collapse.

Today the ruins of the old sulphur works add to the mystique of the island, the bird colonies to its beauty, and the attendant ocean remains one of the most productive fisheries in New Zealand.

We first filmed White during December 1993, although I had enjoyed a number of previous trips on Rick Pollock's *Pursuit*.

Morris Savelle took us out on the charter vessel *Vincere* and by the time we 'threw' the pick, a dying sun had lit the crater cloud a brilliant orange. Without too much imagination it seemed that the island itself was set to explode and slip back under the ocean.

There were a couple of commercial boats at anchor in Crater Bay and Steve Haddock's *Ocean Invader* slipped in through the darkness.

In terms of hours spent fishing, a White Island trip is hard to beat because after the evening meal, deck lights are illuminated and bait flies flicked in to schools of koheru, mackerel and flying fish.

Full live bait tanks mean the best possible chance of kingfish action and sometimes that activity can be mind blowing.

Our crew transferred to *Ocean Invader* at daylight and we set off in search of great camera action. First stop was a deep water drop on a couple of pinnacles known to produce good bass, blue nose and gemfish action. When I say deep, I'm talking about dropping a heavy sinker into 200 metres of water.

Above the sinker there are usually two circle tuna hooks which are designed to help the big beasties hook themselves and even hauling

A nervous crew prepares to up stakes as White Island's ash cloud ambles over to get better acquainted.

a couple of empty hooks out of 200 metres can be a reasonable workout. This sort of fishing is pure meat hunting as on mono filament line, which is very elastic, you don't feel any bites. The procedure is to drop the gear to the bottom, count to about 30 seconds or a minute and crank back 30 turns on the reel. If you come up tight after those 30 turns, you are either onto a fish or hooked on the bottom. If it's a fish you are going to get a serious winching workout.

The day was perfect, a five knot NW did nothing more than whip the sheen off the surface, the sky was cloudless and the team from Tokoroa, who represented the charter, were fizzing in anticipation. It was a day out of the box.

"Listen up", said Steve Haddock, "we're drifting the spot, I'll tell you when to drop your gear, stay on the starboard side of the boat and spread yourselves along the rail. Good luck", and he dived into the wheelhouse, spun the wheel and studied the sounder intently. Steve and other skippers like him are superb when it comes to giving instructions, providing recommendations and generally maximising the value of your charter. Steve now runs *Zambucca*, a big fast beast based in Whakatane.

When the call came to drop the gear, six lines snaked off into the ink-blue void and six anglers were filled with anticipation. The biggest bass I have caught on one of these excursions was 42 kilos, but some are caught a lot bigger than that. It may be meat hunting, but 42 kilos of bass was a lot of eating. During the next hour we wrestled 3 bass, 2 blue nose and 3 gemfish, or hake, from the spot. Certainly enough for a feed. Quite a lot of anglers who fish the deeper trenches and pinnacles are changing from monofilament to nonstretch "super" lines like dyna-braid, spectre, and spider wire. The lack of stretch and small diameter provide some real benefits – you can even feel the bites – but watch the stuff on your hands, it's so thin and strong, it can cut you to ribbons. Another tip that Steve passed on during the morning, was to thread your hooks from the point side or front of the hook, not the back. Having hooks prepared in that way helps them set. In the case of a circle tuna hook it improves the hook-ups significantly, in fact it is something I do religiously. After the meat hunt their target became kingfish or, as we affectionately call them, kingis. Pound for pound they are one of the best battlers around, they possess a wonderful desire to survive and unless you get right into them, they tear off onto the reef structure they live around and bust you off. The joint all tackle world record kingi comes from White Island, 52 kilos, and many other line class world records have been hauled in.

When we steamed over the kingi spot the picture on the sounder was that of solid fish, a great red mass that moved from just below the surface virtually to the bottom at 30 metres.

"Looks good", mumbled Steve, "solid fish and you have a choice of live baits or dead flying fish. Use a four ounce ball sinker to help get your bait down. Spool it out in free spool and use your thumb to control the descent. You'll know when your luck's in because something, hopefully a kingi, will pick it up and you'll feel it take off. Don't wait too long, smack the drag up and lift the rod in a solid strike, then wind like shit. Don't give the fish any slack line. Work hard, boys," and off he went to attend to the business of positioning *Ocean Invader* for the best drift.

That tip about not giving fish slack line is a beauty. A great many people strike a fish by vigorously wrenching the rod tip skyward, which is fine, but what they do next is not. For some strange reason a lot of anglers strike and then throw the rod tip back down, which has the effect of transmitting slack line to the business end.

When you strike, as in live-baiting kingis, hit them hard and start winding with the rod still up in the air. Don't throw the tip down and then start winding, it is a great way of releasing your catch. Keep the pressure firmly on the fish.

Another way of ensuring that you maximise the pressure, is to have the drag correctly set. You need to know how much pressure is needed to haul line off the reel but avoiding a bust-off. With heavier breaking strain line, in particular, a great many anglers have too light a drag setting, a few too heavy and not that many at the desirable level. In game fishing the rule of thumb is to set the drag at one third of breaking strain, but when live baiting kingis, I go heavier, as you only get one chance to turn them away from the foul ground and to the gaff.

Even if you are intending to release a kingi, gaffing it in the mouth, preferably behind the bottom jaw, makes life easier for the crew and the fish. A hole in the membrane behind the bottom jaw soon heals.

So there we were, armed to the teeth, technique discussed and sorted out, the five knot NW now puffing up to 10 and the sea and sky battling for the darkest blue. It was idyllic. We were near the Volkner Rocks and not far away. White Island threw its cloud of ash hundreds of metres above the crater rim. Grey cloud tinged with orange streaks spewed from the earth and the desolate crater wore its cloak of brown/grey earth and wind.

A bit of scrub clings to some sort of existence near the gannet colonies − the birds adding a splash of colour to the desolate scene.

There was no doubt about where we were. One angler had most of the kingi luck, Bruce Hemingway landed three and was smashed off by a real brute. G. Sinclair landed one and was smashed off by two. It is very exciting fishing with the odds about even when you are among fish over 20 kilos.

That was our trip, short and sweet and yet what we learned and filmed was exceptional.

People always ask how long it takes to film a show and the answer varies according to a couple of very important criteria, the weather and the fishing action. Everything on that brief 24 hour sojourn was perfect but it seemed a little like unfinished business, so when Steve phoned up to say he'd purchased a new ship a couple of years later, the temptation was too great and we were back on our way to

"White".

Zambucca is a ship, 20-odd metres of fishing machine that is fast and spacious.

On this excursion we took saltwater fly gear and decided to combine fishing with diving. The stay was also extended to two days. We hit the bass with limited success and the kingis with good results, but one of the highlights for me was a dive just around the corner from Crater Bay. At some point the volcano had hurled a massive house-sized boulder out into the bay and now it is a garden of infinite variety. I love diving when you get to a lip or drop-off and slide down in the depths. The top of the boulder sat in 10 metres, covered in kelp with butterfish, red moki and parrotfish snaking their way through the undergrowth. Jason, my buddy, and I finned through the kelp forest and dropped down the boulder cliff hitting bottom at 22 metres. The whole of one side of the boulder was a 20 metre long cave, pretty as a picture and home to spanish lobsters, spiny crayfish and packhorse crayfish, the three lobster related species that live in New Zealand waters.

It was the only dive I've ever experienced at White where I didn't see kingis, usually a school appears from somewhere, buzzes the divers and heads off to investigate something else of interest.

Kingis are very inquisitive but not so inquisitive as to go cave dwelling.

The guts, caves, ravines and drop-offs of White Island offer some superb dives, and when combined with the fishing, can literally "blow your mind". Several of us were keen on saltwater fly fishing – an extension to the sport – which is only just taking off in New Zealand.

Kydd Pollock prepares to release a healthy kingi. I would love to see some of the fish that broke off that day. Live baits proved lethal.

153

It was February and the yellowfin tuna were charging around the Bay of Plenty scoffing feeds of anchovies. They were joined by skip jack and albacore – just what we wanted to target with saltwater fly, and at Steve's suggestion we left White Island early on the second day and headed back towards Whale Island, the scene of all the tuna action. I don't want to get too heavily into the tuna as the next book is devoted totally to game fishing, but we sure as heck gave those old fly rods a workout.

The great thing about *Zambucca* is the deck space, plenty of room to flail away with a saltwater fly and dance around in pursuit of your fish.

We caught skip jack and found a meat ball of anchovies with yellowfin smashing through every now and then.

"Bugger the fly", I said, "I'm into 15 kilo stand up game fishing gear." A feed of yellow fin would be an ideal way to finish the trip. The wind was getting up but the anchovies were seeking shelter under the hull. I hooked four or five anchovies up and delivered them to the frenzy of feeding tuna.

Whallop. I was hooked up and 15 kilo line snaked off into the depths. "Yahoo", came the standard sort of Sinclair celebration, there is nothing like hanging onto 30 kilos of yellowfin unless it's 40 or 50 or 60.

After 20 minutes I had the fish near the boat, describing typical yellowfin circles, as it lay on its side and swam round and round.

Unfortunately, it swam around *Zambucca*'s huge rudder stock and the line got caught up. Not so tight as to cause it to bust-off, but jammed enough to mean that unless something was done soon, the fish would certainly break free.

"Don't worry", said Jason, the deckie, "I'll go and free it", and with that he took off his shirt, grabbed a mask, snorkel and fins, and leapt into an ocean full of large predatory beasts, including sharks, that all happened to be nearby and all very hungry. In a second the line was free and Jason, his limbs still attached, was dragged back over the side. The film crew loved *Zambucca*, as even in a reasonable sea, she was stable and they had plenty of room to move.

Within five minutes the yellowfin was gaffed aboard and we headed for Whakatane. Yet another very productive White Island trip was at an end.

Our most recent sojourn took place on Rick Pollock's new *Pursuit*, another new beautifully appointed, purpose-built charter vessel commanded, in this case, by Rick's son, Kydd Pollock. It was back to the kingfish and a few wee surprises.

We caught kingis up to 20 kilos under the shadow of a very upset White Island. Vast plumes of ash shot out of the crater and at times we found ourselves dodging the ash cloud. There is something unsettling about White Island in a bad mood, but that rich blue water and awesome kingfish action has a way of soothing the frayed nerves. The other White Island tradition is a deep water drop for bass and blue nose and although they didn't play ball, we caught a fish called a raised bream. I've never seen one before and they are amazing. Our other first on that trip was a spotted gurnard caught while hauling in a feed of tarakihi. We have filmed in the Bay of Plenty often and obviously will again because the area is rich in variety and full-on when it comes to action. Add in charter vessels of *Pursuit*'s standard and the unique backdrop of an active volcano, and suddenly the package is rich in television opportunity.

One of the boys from *Exide*, Andrew, joined us on *Pursuit* and although he is an Aussie, which is almost unforgivable, he did the only sensible thing and succumbed to a disease called fishing fever. If you ever want to turn a 'some time', take it or leave it angler, into a passionate grinning machine, then park their backsides on *Pursuit* for a couple of days.

The White Island excursion puts you into excellent angling for large fish and there is nothing like hands-on experience to teach you a great deal in a short time. This area and in fact, the whole Bay of Plenty, serves up an inexhaustible supply of angling options. It is a prolific fishery where most of the charter skippers impose extra restrictions on the amount that can be taken home. You always leave with a good feed, but usually the greater percentage of fish are released.

There always seems to be something new to film around White Island and there are still half a dozen shows I would love to complete on some pretty amazing species.

I cannot recommend charter vessels like *Zambucca* and *Pursuit* highly enough. They combine that rare and beautifully matched combination of great crew and wonderful boat.

If you can get a booking you will not regret the experience.

White Island produces a few surprises. Andrew Duncan with a Rays Bream.

16
Out and About

Sometimes it's not just a place or character that sticks in your memory, it is a journey, a procession of people and places, all enchanting and absolutely unique.

While filming series six, one of our major excursions took place in Hawkes Bay and around Mahia to Gisborne and East Cape.

By the time we drove out of Napier, the crew had been on the road for a week and in every stop people wanted us to party all night and fish all day. It's a slice of heaven for a couple of days, particularly if you happen to be on holiday.

"C'mon, just another little drink."

"No thanks, might just slide off to bed", you ultimately wind up saying.

"What's wrong with ya, call yourself a fisherman."

"Yeah, I do actually, and I'm sure as hell going to enjoy tomorrow sober, catch you then", and without waiting for a reply, we're out the door leaving some local chap looking for someone else to get pissed with.

We're all pretty social animals but if it became a nightly session there would be very little effective work done. At risk of upsetting a few of the more staunch local drinkers we usually call it a day but every now and then you can't help yourself. I guess it's called being human.

Mahia was one such place. We bunked down with Ray and Leslie Thompson in a farm cottage with views all over the place. Rolling pasture, plunging valleys, fingers of bush, fishable creeks and panorama that reach beyond the peninsula and right out to sea. The Thompson's farm stay takes it all in and fills you with excellent meals and lungfulls of air that is so fresh it is like an adventure entree.

We peeled off the main highway to Gisborne, followed a sign that said Mahia, snaked our way up a shingle road and splashed through

Rhys Duncan being attacked by wild animals on the Mahia Peninsula.

the legacy of a downpour into the drive.

I got out and promptly stood in my first piece of cattle shit. It was not the last.

A lean, middle-aged bloke ambled towards the wagon, wide-brimmed hat dragged down with a list to starboard.

"See you're making yourself at home", said Ray, as I scraped my shoe with a stick. "You pay extra if you take it away", he added with a chuckle. All you have to do is look at Ray Thompson to know that if you have a sense of humour you're going to have a lot of fun because he'll just drag it out of you.

"Bloody feast being prepared for tonight, Leslie's up to her armpits in it. Few of the locals coming over for a chat and to point you in the right direction. May as well have a brew eh."

We needed no encouragement as this rough-as-guts character took us in to meet "the other half". The Thompson homestead is a stunner, but guests stay in a separate farm cottage, a renovated old place under pines near the cattle yards. It is downright luxury.

"Got a few cattle to sort out", said the cockie, "so I'll saddle up and show you the way to the cottage and then take you down to the creek for a trout. Plenty of good fish down there but this rain may have buggered it up. We'll go and see, eh?"

Sounded pretty damn good, we all agreed, so with the aforementioned brew and a few of Leslie's cakes pushing seriously on the belt buckle, we went off to round up cattle and settle in.

We were here to fish, but saddling the horse and stepping in cattle shit somehow seemed like an appropriate start. Heavy grey lumps of cloud did their best to hug neighbouring hills, but blue cracks came and went. The scrub and farmland was drenched, washed clean by recent rain, colours vibrant, the air fresh, every breath a lungful of rural intoxication.

We drove while Ray rode across to the yards. He knew the camera was on him, knew he needed to watch his language, clean up his act a little bit. "You buggers", he said, leaning heavily on the reins, his horse spinning in the mud, loose clods of earth flying off the hooves. "How can I muster cattle without swearing at the dogs?"

"Have a go", I said.

"I love my dogs", he added, "but they won't do a bloody thing unless I yell and scream a bit."

"Have a go", I encouraged, "they must know what to do after all this time."

With that he galloped off through the mud, dogs just let loose marking their territory, doing all of the things that dogs recently released from captivity do.

"C'mon", shouted Ray and the team obediently fell in behind. Horse, man and dogs looking like a well-oiled machine.

We stood there filming the cattle action, just to add a little something to the show. Ray was hooked up to a thing called a radio microphone which is totally portable and has a little transmitter attached to it that will record good sound up to 80 metres away without cables. It meant that Ray could gallop around, herd cattle, say nice things to the dogs and the whole chit chat was recorded.

All went well initially, Ray let a whole bunch of beasts out of the yards but the dogs didn't quite do what was requested. Ray tried hard; "C'mon . . . . . you bast . . . . ., good fellah get away. GET AWAY NOW, jeez", he would mutter through clenched teeth! We all thought it was a huge joke and when Ray, the rampant beast and dogs disappeared behind the sheds, we kept filming the beautiful view. Ray decided that because he was out of sight there was no need to suck up to his dogs any more and besides he knew nothing about radio mic's. If he was out of sight the camera wouldn't hear what he said . . . right? WRONG, when Ray climbed into his dogs, the voice ran right over the beautiful scenic shots we were filming.

"You bloody mongrels", he bellowed, "you useless bloody bastards, get away, back, Jesus, I'll have a piece of you . . ."

Well, by then we were rolling around, no more Mr nice guy, the cocky was taking charge. The dogs came into line, the job was done, Ray was pleased and we thought it was just great.

"Right", said the returning rider, "let's see if we can find a fish." Everyone was very pleased.

The journey to the creek was a 4 wheel drive excursion on a slick track and the large sluggish river was bloated and mud-brown. There would be no fish rising there tonight, but we sucked in more beautiful air at the head of a scrub-covered gulley and admired a river that promised good fishing when the weather was better behaved. A feast awaited our return, a fresh, home-cooked meal, a roast that would give the cholesterol gauge a bit of a tickle up, but with all that fresh air, was just what we needed.

A few locals were having a merry old time when we turned up. The sound of laughter floated around the valley, steamed windows hinted of warmth and shelter from the stiff breeze that whistled along homestead ridge. I opened the door and was hit by laughter, warmth and the delicious smell of country cooking. A number of the vocal chords were already well lubricated and the crew and I just kind of fitted in.

Stu and Bruce were there, complete with stories about a place called the Loughlin Bank, a serious chunk of fishing real estate parked out off the Mahia Peninsula.

"If the weather gives us a break", said Stu, "you won't know what hit you. We get a lot of big bass and blue nose on the bank, it's amazing."

He dragged out the customary photographs that proved that the fishing would be great so long as the weather was in a reasonable mood.

We talked about fishing, farming, local history and all manner of things that tore a bit of a hole in the alcohol supply. It was one of those nights that just happened to be really good fun.

Naturally Ray was in good form, and so was Leslie, as she and a friend put the finishing touches on the feast.

"Bit of a delicacy for you tonight", said Ray, thrusting a plate of steaming curried blobs on the table.

"Beautiful", he added, firing one of the fleshy-looking offerings into his mouth.

"What are they?" asked Becky.

"Just a few oysters", came the reply.

"Don't look like oysters."

"Try one", urged Ray, but Becky wasn't too sure and fortunately wasn't so keen on the curry.

I dived in. "Beautiful", I agreed, reaching for a second curry-covered blob.

Ray had a grin from ear to ear. "Know what you're eating?"

"Yeah I do", I was pleased to inform him. Prairie oysters, mountain oysters – call them what you like – but they start out as lambs' gonads, or lambs' balls to the uninitiated. Very tasty, and of course the locals decided that the old lambs' bollocks trick had to get a few of us conned.

It was great to have done your time on a farm and know a few of the cocky's tricks.

We had a great night, but next morning the wind stiffened a touch and binoculars showed white caps whipping across the bay.

We joined Stu and Bruce, pounded our way towards the bank, got a line wet and the cameraman as sick as a dog. It was as rough as guts and the trip had to be aborted, just one of those things when you try and film a fishing show.

The team was due in Gisborne later that night, so we spent the afternoon charging around the farm on 4WD bikes, looking for a stag that was holed up in a patch of scrub.

The sort of fishing you can get out of Gisborne – bass and blue nose.

It was just one of those extra little things you can do when a farm stay is your angling backstop and the Thompson hospitality and tucker is downright amazing.

Once we hit Gisborne the last thing on our mind was tucker, we were full of it.

The thing we were very keen to do was of course, catch a few fish and the man that was going to do the job was local entrepreneur, Fred Lewis.

Fred's a pretty wealthy sort of bloke, but it didn't stop him cooking breakfast next morning and loading us on his 9 metre *Blackwatch* rocket ship.

As private fishing boats go, the *Blackwatch*, a superb Aussie design, is hard to beat and when you stick a few hundred turbo-charged horsepower under the hatches, it ain't going to take long to go fishing.

I kind of like Gisborne, as a city it still retains the feel of a town, has great beaches and fishing on its doorstep, a fantastic, very active fishing club and it's not far to the isolation of places like Mahia.

As we raced out to sea, the wind was trying to muster a bit of strength, but fortunately failing. The sun shrugged and headed over the horizon to add a silver sheen to our passage. Sea birds scattered out of the way or wheeled across the sky, carving up vast tracts of ocean in search of breakfast. The swell was just a lazy roll like driving across small undulating hills that heaved their way towards the distant shore.

It was good to be alive as it always is on a morning when you are on the ocean and that ocean has decided that you deserve a decent day.

"Spot we're going to is called Westpac", said Fred.

"Westpac?"

"Yeah", he said, "just like money in the bank, specially on a day like this. You watch, you'll catch a feed of tarakihi first, then a few hapuka."

As the throttles eased, I spotted a boiling mass of bait fish, seething in a foaming frenzy over what was obviously the spot.

Westpac is a reef system, or rocks that rise above the sea bed and, like all such rocks in the middle of nowhere, attracts the life necessary to set up a food chain and become residence for a variety of tasty fish. This one proved to be a beauty. We threw over a weight with a buoy attached to the other end of a length of rope. With no wind to speak of, we just sat with the boat out of gear and engines rolling and before long our drift became obvious by looking at how we moved in relation to the weighted buoy. It's a simple trick that helps you to drop anchor and position the boat exactly where you want it.

Today, modern electronics work wonders, you can drive straight to the spot using marks on your GPS (Global Positioning System), your colour sounder shows where the fish are in relation to the rock or bottom and a bit of rope, a weight and a buoy take the guesswork out of how your boat will lie at anchor.

Westpac, or money in the bank, produced tarakihi within five minutes. One of my favourite tarakihi rigs is a bait fly system, that can be purchased from all good tackle stores, and is manufactured by Black Magic Tackle.

It is called a Tarakihi Terror and it's just dynamite.

One of Fred's mates was a dab hand at sorting out the catch and this craft had a series of underfloor fish bins already filled with ice and just waiting for the tarakihi. A bucket of saltwater completed the slurry and fresh fish, after being spiked in the brain, were laid to rest in this improvised marine chiller.

"You know", said Fred, "for every hour a fish lies on the deck in the sun, it ages equivalent to a day in the ice. Sometimes you wonder why people bother eating their catch. If it sits in the heat for two or three hours, it deteriorates so much that it's hardly worth eating."

After catching and filming enough smaller fish, we changed to heavier stand-up game fishing rigs and went to work on the hapuka.

I used a pre-rigged Black Magic hapuka rig just because I had one and they are so convenient to use.

Down snaked a couple of big solid baits and whallop, over went the rod in a heavy, satisfying arc.

"This is great", I found myself saying.

Sooty shearwaters ducked over the side and a couple of huge albatross sat back and waited for a feed. What beautiful birds, these ocean wanderers, large captivating creatures that give you a thrill by virtue of their presence, their stern business-like look in keeping with the sheer unflustered majesty of their being.

In less time than it takes to describe the scene, my first hapuka was gaffed aboard and placed on ice. The crew would not be going hungry. We didn't have to pull up the anchor, merely changed our gear, went up a few hook sizes and increased the amount of bait. That was all that was required to change the menu at the Westpac smorgasbord. The rest was just a procession of angling entertainment. When it was decided that we had had enough, up came the anchor and we headed for home. En route I dragged out the saltwater fly rod and had a go at a massive school of trevally. It was superb, with the engines at idle and the boat out of gear, we drifted into an acre of trevs. I flicked the fly, retrieved a tiny amount of line and was hooked up. It was that simple, and after a very solid scrap, an equally solid trevally landed on the deck.

"That's a beauty", I said, leaping into the cabin to check out the record book. "Might be a New Zealand record on fly", I said to Fred.

"Might not either", he added, nodding in the direction of the aft deck.

There on the filleting board was my potential record trevally – one side already whipped off and filleted. Unfortunately they don't acknowledge records that are weighed in pieces and when someone has very efficiently filleted record trevally.

The team were "back on the hard" by mid-afternoon and sitting in the magnificent Tatapouri Fishing Club by the time the sun began its final slide. Late afternoon sun reflected off a cold glass of amber liquid and we all reflected on a particularly good day. Westpac was most definitely money in the bank.

Next morning we completed our final stop before rounding East Cape and heading for Te Kaha. Our destination was breathtaking Tolaga Bay – one of the real gems to be found nestled against the coast. Another beautiful beach, forested hills, a delightful town, headlands, cliffs and islands. Tolaga Bay possesses the sort of thrown-together geography that makes your heart beat a little faster. Instinctively you know the fishing and diving will produce results a notch or two above pedestrian. Add to the equation a bloke named Bert Lee, a guide with a hunter's passion and vast local knowledge, and somehow it seems reasonable to expect you're going to have a ball.

The trouble was, there was only an afternoon available for us to take advantage of the Tolaga Bay offerings, but that didn't faze Bert one little bit.

"Love to catch a few kingfish, Bert, caught heaps of hapuka and tarakihi in Gisborne yesterday and a few kingis would finish things off

Tarx Morrison fondling Ray Thompson. He's actually rigging a radio microphone. It does get a bit personal.

nicely."

"Shouldn't be a problem", offered the guide, with a knowing sort of grin, "there's a spot out here where we'll have a jig this afternoon and I doubt you'll even get a lure to the bottom before you hook up."

"It's that good?" I asked.

"Yep, it's that good."

I needed no further encouragement, and in record time Bert Lee had us racing across a lumpy ocean towards our kingi rendezvous.

On the spot there was a reasonable swell building and the other boat that accompanied us was already, after a matter of seconds, hooked up to what a still-smiling Bert informed us must be a kingfish.

"Have a look at the sounder", said the skipper, pointing to the electronic screen mounted on *Ospreys* dash.

Almost the entire picture, from 10 metres deep to over 50, was bright red. When the screen shows red it means you are getting a very solid reading – so solid that the bottom produces a red picture – but for 40 metres we were looking at solid fish, wall to wall kingfish. It looked as though the last part of our journey was about to deliver exactly what we wanted. What took place was a couple of hours of frenetic fishing, red hot kingfish action and a serious sort of competition between Bert and I. Somehow he had the knack of hooking bigger fish, not much bigger, but just enough to even up his lop-sided smile and make him particularly cheeky. It was great fun and if you ever get a chance to fish with Bert Lee out of Tolaga Bay, chances are, you'll have a ball. The guys on the other boat had trouble with a mako shark tearing off large chunks of their kingfish,

164

but they too, ultimately shared this amazing kingfish action.

In conditions like this, kingfish just cannot resist jigs, drop them towards the bottom and if you don't hook up on the way down, put your reel in gear and wind as fast as you can. Sooner or later some big old kingi will devour your jig.

After a couple of hours the wind had pushed up an offshore swell big enough to make filming a real handful.

Large blue mounds of ocean rolled out into the open ocean white crests shaking loose and filling the air with spray.

It was time to punch our way back towards that breathtaking bay and another feed of fresh seafood.

From the Thompson's farm stay on a windswept Mahia to the kingfish of Tolaga Bay, our journey had taken in a great chunk of beautiful coast, outstanding fishing and unique characters. Weatherwise we, just like anyone else, had to take the good with the bad but, even when the weather drives you off the ocean, you can always find good company, someone who will share a laugh, a feed and maybe even a quiet drink. It's the sort of stuff that adds character to outdoor New Zealand.

17

The Far North

The far north is like another world, with vast tracts of unspoilt beach, rolling hills and unique geography that enables visitors to bounce from east coast to west with incredible ease. The far north is also very laid back, the people kind of cruise along at a quiet pace and the hassle of the city is left for outsiders to worry about. We've filmed a few shows in this wonderful part of New Zealand, a couple of which really stick in my mind.

An ex-Mongrel Mob member who traded in his patch for a horse and cart was the first Northland character to really get my attention. Richard Job, tattoos everywhere, the real "tough sticker" models., a big smile and a desire to run his horse and cart along 90 Mile Beach.

"Just out to give tourists a bit of fun", he told me, "maybe catch a fish, gather a feed of tua tuas and have a cook up on the BBQ attached to the cart." This was real covered wagon stuff. A trot along this endless beach, rolling sandhills to the right, surf to the left and nothing but sand and heat haze in front. It was great fun just slowing down, feeling the wind in your face, soaking up the roar of the sea and hearing the jingle of the harness and clomp, clomp of hooves on hard-packed soil.

"What do you think?" enquired Richard.

"You've got something really special here mate. This is fantastic."

"Well, wait till we dig up a feed of tua tua, man. Just steam them open in the shells. Beautiful", said Richard, smacking his lips, and flicking deftly at Mo's reins.

We clomped along for a while, the horse operating on a kind of auto pilot that suggested she was comfortable with the routine and really enjoyed the experience. Ralph, the dog, just kept pace. The fishing was kind of challenging. We donned wetsuits and waded out into the surf, before heaving our baited hooks as far through the breakers as we could. It felt good being pushed around in the waves, feeling the power of the sea, occasional waves breaking higher than the rest and showering us with spray. There was no one else on the beach as far as I looked – surf, sand, haze, the breeze carrying its sea smells and the taste of salt – every sense soaking up all that was on offer.

"Be bloody lucky to catch anything in this sea, man, but wiggle your toes into the sand and when you feel a lump, reach down and you'll either pull up tua tua or toheroa. Eat 'em straight out of the shell, real choice. If it bites, you're into a swimming crab. Give you a hell of a fright".

Sure enough, I twisted my feet, encountered some resistance, and up popped the tua tua.

"Just slide the shells in opposite directions", suggested my mate, "and they pop open. Try them, delicious."

So we stood there, up to our knees in water, waves crashing everywhere, surfcasters bending and straining against the drag of the ocean, scoffing a feed of tua tua. Life, as is usually the case in this situation, did not seem so bad.

We got kind of carried away, digging up a feed, firing a few shellfish in the bucket, sharing a few laughs and throwing tua tua at Rhys, the cameraman, and Tony, who was trying to give us good quality sound above the roar of the waves.

As Richard suggested, it was bloody good fun.

Every now and then we looked up the beach to make sure Mo, the Clydesdale, and Ralph, the dog, were still waiting patiently on the beach.

They had obviously decided that we were having too much fun or maybe they were just bored.

"Hey!" said Richard pointing up the beach, "bloody horse is heading off." He leapt out of the surf and took off after an ambling horse and dog that were disappearing into the shimmering and very distant sand.

We were still all alone on the beach, and without the old nag, home was a very long way off.

Paul, Tony and I stood there laughing as Richard muttered off in pursuit of the beasts. It looked bloody funny, but eventually we all found ourselves together at the back of the wagon, the BBQ hotplate fired up and an assortment of tucker sizzling away quite happily. The aroma of fresh seafood drifted away on the breeze, a BBQ in the middle of an endless sandy beach seemed like heaven. Fresh bread, hot tua tuas, butter dripping between fingers and the taste? – just the best. Those are the things I remember about a half day on 90 Mile Beach with Richard Job. Little did I know, but all of this was just a warm-up. Another character waited for us on a farm above Herekino Harbour, but we stopped at a roadside tavern for a quiet beer and to cleanse away the taste of salt. It was early days in the filming of *Gone Fishin'* but a few of the locals, all Maori blokes, ambled over for a quiet beer and a chat which became a game of pool, a few more beers and a lot of laughs.

That's one of the great things about filming a fishing show, you meet so many neat people, and with fishing, you've always got

Richard and GS dressed to kill. The fish obviously heard we were coming and bailed out.

something in common, no matter where you are. The beers had a soothing effect, so by the time we turned up at Tui Inn Farm Stay, we were in "the groove". Grant and Tangi Devan farm above Herekino Harbour, have a separate cottage for hire, serve up huge meals, great company, plenty of laughs, wicked home brew and more fishing on horseback. It's an excellent combination in a rugged, beautiful part of the country. The views around the farm are stunning, rolling scrub-covered hills to the east, and farmland and distant sandhills with a fringe of mangroves around the harbour. Late on that March afternoon when a chill rose out of the valleys with fingers of shadow, the sky painted red and gold, we found ourselves tucked inside the farm house with Grant and Tangi feasting on Maori bread, fresh meat and vegetables off the farm and paua cooked with cream.

"Better wash it down with a brew", recommended the host, hoisting the cap from a very volatile, but quite tasty, home brew. It was a fitting end to a day that had started on the 90 Mile with Richard, Mo and Ralph, the dog.

Next morning dawned fine and clear, but a brisk westerly pumped its way across the harbour and danced in the tussock on the hills.

"Could be a bit rough on the coast, especially if you want a feed of paua and crays", said Grant, hauling on his trusty steed's girth strap. With a heave, the horse let out a bit of air and the belt slid up a notch. We looked at a distant ribbon of white, a procession of breakers hammering the coast. Grant remounted, flicked the reins, and we headed down the hills towards the harbour. We rode, bait, lunch and spare gear tied in sacks over the front of the saddles. Grant carried his surfcaster like a lance, Northland's equivalent to a medieval knight. Once we hit the flat, our course followed the retreating tide across the mudflats and through the mangroves. The hills and seaward sandhills that had provided such a wonderful view now crowded in around the harbour. It felt isolated, as though it was there only for our pleasure, because there was hardly a house as far as you could see. What there was, however, was another rider, waiting patiently at a point where the track narrowed to sneak beneath a bit of a bluff.

"That's my mate, Don", said Grant, pointing at the rider with his 'lance'. "Don'll give us a bit of a hand with the gear and help get your cameraman over the hill. He's also a bloody good fisherman."

Don didn't have much to say at first, I think the camera put him off, but he warmed up a bit later in the day.

The closer we got to the swells, the more they humped up and threw themselves onto the rocks. Shit, I thought, another day trying to make a fishing show out of nothing. We were becoming experts because our budget didn't allow us to hang around until the sea flattened down. It was today or nothing.

"Reckon we'll do all right in that surf?"

"Not bloody likely, should have been here yesterday, could have water-skied out there."

Grant rigged a sinker that slid up and down the 15 kilo main line. A swivel was tied at the end and then a metre of trace finished off with a hook. The sinker could only slide as far as the swivel and the trace with hook attached was left to waft around in the surge.

Before he cast, Grant spat on the bait.

"For luck", he said, "you need a bit of luck when you go fishing". He leaned in to a cast, the old bamboo rod creaking and groaning as if it would snap.

"Got this rod out of my father's shed, had it stuck up in the rafters, ideal for this fishing thing, cost me an arm and a leg", he added with a laugh.

Don, the big burley mate who lived under a broad-brimmed black hat, was warming up and adding his bit of advice.

"Too bloody rough", he quipped helpfully, "might be better over the hill – one of those guts might be a bit sheltered."

"Yeah, we'd better shift, because Sinclair pointed at the fish."

Don just sat and shook his head as though I was just some dumb townie.

"So what?" I asked, "the damn fish don't know."

"It's rude to point at people with your finger and it's rude to point at fish with a straight finger."

"You won't have any luck now."

"You're pulling my leg", I said incredulously, but I was the only one laughing.

"If you want to point at the water, which is where the fish live, then you have to do it with your finger bent like this", added Grant thrusting his hand and semi-extended, bent index finger in the direction of the unrelenting, pounding fishless-looking surf.

Another half hour saw a couple of marble fish and a banded parrot fish snaffle our tua tua bait before the surf pounded it to pulp. Armed with the new secret weapons, spitting on the bait and pointing with a bent finger, we headed over the hill to a spot that I hadn't contaminated with my ignorance.

The horses were loaded up with extra gear, tripods, spare battery cases and all manner of junk.

Rhys, the cameraman, and Tony, the soundman, climbed up the hill to film our procession with the harbour and massive sandhills around the old Ahipara gumfields as our desolate backdrop. With the westerly whipping in off the sea and the spray hanging above the ribbon of foam, the view was breathtaking.

The higher we climbed, the better it looked.

Don decided that I was walking the horse a bit too slowly. I wasn't aware of him sneaking up. I was too preoccupied with the view.

"Give you a hand", he yelled, as the plastic pipe he held whistled through the air and smacked my trusty steed, Phantom, right on the ass.

I heard the call, the sound of plastic on rump, then suddenly the world did a somersault and I landed in the scrub.

No one waited to see if any damage had been done, they just fell all over the place laughing.

Don had certainly come out of his shell and was marked as a man to watch and, if the opportunity presented, a man to get even with.

With nothing more than wounded pride, I caught up with a very circumspect *Phantom*, who obviously didn't trust me anymore and became a little flighty.

The sound of sniggering drifted in on the breeze and turned to laughter again when I stopped to give Tony a ride.

"You stupid townie buggers", laughed Don. "That's no way to get on a horse. Climb on from the uphill side. I don't know", he half mumbled, half laughed, as he continued down towards a surf-filled bay that held very little promise.

Tony had been trying to climb on the back of the horse from the very steep, very low down, hill side of the track. I hadn't even thought about it, deciding that if anyone else was going to cartwheel into the scrub, it wouldn't be me.

Just a little tip, team, if you're out doing your John Wayne impersonation, mount the horse from the high uphill position, it gives the locals less to laugh about.

If it was possible, the next spot was rougher, more exposed, less fishy-looking and all that came to the hook were a few more very hardy and according to Grant, very tasty, marble fish.

"Don't stand where the rocks are wet", chided the guide, "that means there's been a wave there bro, and only a matter of time before you get another."

"When's the best time to fish off the rocks then, an outgoing tide?" I asked.

"When it's calm bro, when it's calm."

I decided to shut up and watch the huge rolling breakers drag my

GS and Tony Burrows heading across to where the fishing is good. Herekino Harbour − Northland.

line into the bay. Eventually we packed up, decided the fishing was not going to improve for a couple of days, and headed back over the hill to Herekino Harbour. It was becoming hot, thirsty, hungry work.

"Feel like a bit of tucker, plenty of fresh mussels and tua tua down in the harbour", advised Grant, nodding in the direction we were heading.

Rhys is one of the fittest, hardest-working cameramen you'll find anywhere, but even he was starting to wilt in the heat and the thought of a brew and bit of a feed perked us up no end. Down beside the water, Don dragged some rocks into a rough circle, Grant retrieved a rusty old BBQ hot plate from the scrub and the rest of us dragged in a supply of firewood.

The scene was set for a BBQ, Herekino Harbour-style.

"I'll just get the mussels, plenty out there, big, fat and juicy", offered Grant, climbing out of his clothes and into the water.

"Like Crocodile Dundee", added Don, watching his mate dive for our lunch, "already got a whole heap of tua tua." He threw another chunk of wood on the roaring, crackling fire that shimmered heat and sparks high into a late afternoon sky.

"The hot plate looks as though it'll kill you with all that rust", I said, sceptically.

"No, no, only use it to heat the shells open", he indicated, pouring a bag of mussels onto the plate.

Clouds of steam joined the sparks and shimmer, and then an aroma drifted around on the breeze and landed in the taste buds.

It was the delicious smell of half-cooked shellfish being prepared on the beach where they had been gathered. It was garnished with our stunning surroundings and supplemented with our hunger and

Herekino Harbour – a beautiful unspoilt part of the country well supported by the Devans and Tui Inn Farm Stays.

fatigue. It was the smell of heaven.

"Feel like a lemonade", said Don, thrusting a full bottle of Sprite in my direction. I had briefly forgotten how thirsty I was.

"Fantastic", I said, instantly forgiving him for getting me bucked off the horse and reaching for the bottle.

I wrenched the top off, tipped the bottom towards the sky, took a couple of huge greedy gulps and thought that someone had blown the top of my head off.

"Jeez, what the hell's that?" I croaked.

"Local moonshine", laughed Don, through tears of laughter, "honey mead, you're not supposed to drink it that quick, you won't be able to get up."

The stuff was pure rocket fuel and for the second time that day, I had been well and truly had.

"Better watch it", added Grant, "bit different – that honey mead. If you have enough of it, your legs just go on you."

I had to close out the show, feeling just a little inebriated.

What a day, the locals had certainly had their fun, but we too had had a ball. As soon as those mussel and tua tua shells opened, we whipped them off the hot plate and climbed into a feast.

It was the second day of fresh tua tua but it seemed like an eternity since yesterday's excursion along the 90 Mile with Richard Job.

The far north is a wonderful place, lightly populated, with some of the most amazing secluded valleys, harbours and beaches.

It is an area that I love to visit and recommend highly, but just watch some of the locals, they don't take any prisoners and are always in the mood for a party.

18
Whitebait

I grew up on the shore of Christchurch's estuary and my father was a commercial fisherman. His father was a boat builder or shipwright, and in the late 1800s his father (my great grandfather) was building and racing yachts all over the country and winning a great many accolades. His father in turn (my great great grandfather) was also a shipwright in Lyttelton and, according to the stories, a pretty loose unit.

So here I am, a fisherman and loving it, treating every day as though it is a privilege, drinking in salt air and with every lungfull wondering what little adventure the day will throw at us.

Filming *Gone Fishin'* happened by design, it was a planned event, not just something that I stumbled over. It was also a major team event early on, but there were a lot of defectors after the first series made a sizeable loss.

I guess if you have a passion for something, you tend to hang in a little longer than those who want a quick result.

It is a philosophy that is the common ingredient in all successful anglers, real tenacity, a belief that if you hang around for another minute or so it may be an investment that produces the sort of catch you dream about.

As a kid grovelling around the estuary, I used to spear flounders and eels, catch kahawai, mullet, spotties and even elephant fish in season but there was one time I used to live for – the whitebait season.

For some reason I could wander around for hours, scooping up whitebait in groups of half a dozen, and think it was just Christmas.

I used to stalk a small shoal of bait and my heart would pitter patter with excitement. The estuary also produced ample flounder – Dad and I once caught over 100 in a single drag. I remember dragging them home in a wheelbarrow and feeding the neighbours.

We didn't have a fridge in those days, in fact our hot water had to be boiled in an old copper. There wasn't much money, but there was plenty of fish, and because my mother was a Coaster, whitebait were put forward as a culinary masterpiece.

What a bugger, a childhood dripping with sweet pan-fried flounder and whitebait patties. Most of the spots I used to catch "bait" in are still there and I stopped along the causeway between Mt Pleasant and Redcliffs four or five years ago. Three viaducts, as we called them (they are really culverts under the road), flow under the causeway and as a much older G. Sinclair peered into one of his childhood haunts, half a dozen whitebait came scooting in and pressed themselves against the rocks. I felt the old thrill — over what — half a dozen fish that require sharp eyesight to even see them. It almost seems ridiculous, but they still do that to me, maybe it's that West Coast blood that Mum threw into my veins.

As time went by, my focus shifted from fishing with rod and reel and developed to an obsession with hunting and diving. We dived for fishing sinkers along the causeways, wound up spearfishing around Taylors Mistake for butterfish and moki, and eventually scuba dived out of Akaroa and off the Kaikoura Coast. Thinking back, we were a bunch of ratbags, growing up with our parents' attitude to a resource that seemed without end. We waded in and harvested all sorts of stuff, taking pretty much as much as we could. The whole idea was to get the biggest, the most, and to hell with any regard for the future, the stuff would always be there for the taking.

Same with hunting, I was a terrible poaching bugger right from the start, but overriding that I found that I had a great love for the places

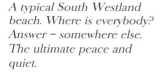

A typical South Westland beach. Where is everybody? Answer — somewhere else. The ultimate peace and quiet.

I walked, swam and explored. After you've won the same race 100 times, you wind up asking yourself why you bother racing.

I guess that's why I've finally settled on a philosophy that says "take enough for a feed and put the rest back" but it took me a long time before the significance of limiting my catch really hit home.

During my late teens I was a diving instructor, commercial hunter, and eventually a sales rep for a pharmaceutical company. The company's name was Pfizer (the Viagra company, but they didn't have the drug in those days).

Why they employed a ratbag like me, I will never know. Someone must have seen a glimmer of promise, but all I wanted was a job with a car. I had flipped my Land Cruiser onto its roof with five deer in the back. Too much accelerator coming out of a creek bed and too much weight in the back. She flipped front over back, landed in the creek, engine seized before I could turn the key off, and I was lucky to get out with my life. Bugger.

So suddenly I was a drug rep for a pharmaceutical company, peddling my drugs to doctors in Canterbury, Nelson and the West Coast. I wore a tie but I had the company car and still travelled to many of the places I loved.

The first time I went to the West Coast was during the whitebait season.

I had a nice new car with a boot full of glossy literature and drug samples and the back seat was adorned with clever city clothes. It looked slick and clean, right up until the time I went out the back of a West Coast town call Ahaura. A labyrinth of forestry roads made for some great spotlighting. I drove around in my new car, waving a spotlight. The car wound up a little dented, the paint work a tiny bit scratched and two deer bled all over the boot. It was a bit of a mess but it made wearing the tie a bit more bearable, and besides, I was still doing what I loved and it was my first trip away.

The other great thing was that it was Monday and I still had four more days, including a stopover with the rellies in Westport.

Sure, I had a quota of doctors to chat to and sales targets to meet, but it didn't take long to find out that some of them were hunters and fishermen. We'd chat for ages about sport and for a couple of minutes about drugs. It was very enjoyable. By the time I got to Westport I was getting the hang of things, but the company car had aged about ten years.

One of my cousins, Donah Low, was very excited about the whitebaiting.

"Been a good week", she said, "getting about 10 pound a day".

"Ten pound?" I couldn't believe it, my heart had always done somersaults over shoals of half a dozen.

It was too much for me – I had to get some of this action.

The tide was early next morning, daylight in fact, which gave me two and a half hours to fish before I called on Dr. Predergast at 9.00am. Donah, Charlie and their son, David, took me down to the Oruwaiti to fish the family stands.

You wait for the tide to push upriver in a section that is sufficiently high to catch the last couple of hours of the incoming. White spotting boards are placed on the river bottom and we used the long-handled drag net that I had grown up with. I was filled with anticipation. My thigh gumboots carried me across the stream to my own little spot on the river. The Oruwaiti was stained in the way that so many West Coast rivers are, the water clear but the colour of underdone black tea.

A wonderful forest hugs the grassy riverbank where flax bushes poke up here and there. It is a beautiful place with endless bird song and forested flat land sneaking back towards rolling hills and coastal mountains. Farmland borders the roads and dairy herds make a twice daily excursion to the milking shed.

The Oruwaiti is a real gem and I was fired up about the idea of catching whitebait in quantity. Imagine ten pound of whitebait, I kept thinking. Could I really be that lucky?

The lazy passage of the river finally slowed, then stopped, and then the tide started to muscle its way upstream but I had seen no 'bait', none. It was, however, a perfect morning, a great way to delay the inevitable tie and good pants that waited in the car. I was grateful for the thigh gumboots and my Swanndri, that great chunk of woollen clothing which is a bit like a sleeping bag with a hood. In those days every bushman worth his salt wore a swanni. Suddenly I saw Donah stiffen, shift her weight and glide the net downriver, across the spotting boards.

Hmm, might be in for some action after all, I thought, registering the fact that it was already 7.30am and I had work to do at 9.00am.

I was gazing at the white spotting boards and all of a sudden they went black. Must be something wrong, I remember thinking, but already my net was gliding down towards the all-but-obliterated spotting boards.

Couldn't be whitebait, not that many, no way. The net grew heavy and I struggled to lift it. Whitebait streamed down the mesh sides, cascading into the bottom of the net.

In one scoop I had about six pound, not six whitebait, and my heart was doing somersaults.

I whooped and yelled, pouring the catch into a bucket that very quickly was starting to look too small and still the whitebait flowed over the boards.

Everyone was into it. A lot of excited chatter rippled along the bank as the whitebait wave descended on more and more fisherfolk. It was a day of dreams, sure the old timers would probably consider it an average day but everyone was incredibly excited, especially the lad from "over the hill".

At 8.45am good shoals were still coming and I had filled the best part of two plastic buckets that each held two gallons.

At 8.55am guilt got to me and I threw the net on the bank and waddled off towards the car.

I pulled up outside the surgery in my gumboots and Swanndri,

Part of the feast. Leap into the surf, wiggle your toes and the tua tua pop up – Magic.

If the fishing is slow, the chops and sausages hit the hot plate. Richard Job in action.

The Oruwaiti, near Westport, a great little spot.

Simon Baumfield (camera) Anthony Nevison (sound) beyond the call of duty and valiantly fording a Westland river.

Grace Trolle, a cook up in South Westland. Up the river, into the pan and down the hatch. Too bad you can't hear the sizzle and taste the proceeds.

All right – just to really upset you, here's a close up. Just enough egg to bind the whitebait together.

The Poor Knights or, more correctly, North Reef, produces some outstanding fish.
The Poor Knights (now a reserve) is a brilliant place to dive. Snapper time.

Off the mouth of Nancy Sound trolling for southern blue fin tuna. It never seems to amaze me just
how close to the coast the fish are. The Continental Shelf butts right up against the mountains.

Tim and Butch with Peter Shaw's southern blue fin. 60 kilos gutted and gilled. We had to drag it off the rock. I have never caught fish like this so close to land.

Sandee and I making the most of chilled southern blue fin tuna and a wee hydraulic sandwich.

Solander Island rises up out of the Southern Ocean.

Ian 'Grizz' Miller trying to decide between paua, oysters and crayfish. Tough one Grizz.

Big and I mean big (5 kilo) blue cod from Solander Island. Grizz Miller again.

Solander Island again − this time in close proximity. An awe-inspiring place.

Gurnard – The Kaipara always serves up a feed and very nice they are sizzling in the pan.

Filming at Kaipara Harbour land based episode. The four wheel drive trip along the beach is breathtaking.

Mack Seymour filming one of the South Westland locals in his office.

feeling a little brassed off that it was still happening on the riverbank and I was leaping into a doctor's surgery.

Pfizer had a pretty strict dress code that didn't include gumboots and a Swanndri. To make matters worse, another immaculately dressed rep was already ensconced in one of the waiting room chairs.

We all used the same kind of doctor's bag to carry literature and samples, and as this particular lady looked me up and down, like something that crawled out from under a rock, her eyes came to rest on the bag.

You could see the old brainbox working overtime – "No, he couldn't be a rep, how incredibly uncouth".

"Gidday", I said, "Graeme Sinclair, the Pfizer rep, how's your day?" I enquired.

The smile was fleeting and the look cold.

About then the surgery door flew open and the doctor waved me in.

My going first did nothing to improve my relationship with the other rep.

"Gidday doctor", I said, "Graeme Sinclair, the Pfizer rep."

"Sorry about the dress code, but the whitebait are running on the Oruwaiti and when we finish I'm heading straight back. Do you want a couple of pound?"

Well, he and I understood each other immediately, and within five minutes he had taken note of the drugs I was peddling and I was out the door.

I made my five calls at odd times during the day and by mid-afternoon wound up on the Buller with my cousin David.

Whitebait anyone?

We had a ball, our combined tally for the day amounted to 137lb, a far cry from scavenging a feed out of the estuary.

Sales of my products on the coast increased dramatically, in fact during that first year I sold enough in my combined territory to win a trip for two to Hawaii, all expenses paid. Not bad.

Once *Gone Fishin'* took off I was keen to get back to the coast and film some of the characters I had met on sales trips. One of them is my Uncle Ian, who no matter what the season, always drags a feed of whitebait out of the freezer and sorts out his nephews' hunger pangs.

The catalyst to a couple of whitebaiting shows occurred when a friend of mine, Daryl Crimp, the Nelson cartoonist, phoned up to say he had a new idea for a show.

Crimpy has a radio show on Friday mornings dedicated to fishing, and someone had phoned, wondering what his favourite method of catching whitebait was.

Crimpy thought they had to be joking, after all whitebait are caught in set nets or drag nets. So he said longlining.

Longlining for white bait, hilarious, but the other party believed him, and so did a few other people. Suddenly, with the support of local sports shop owner, Tony Entwhistle, a real longline was born that people could view in the window of Tony's store. The hook was set and the believing public taken for a real ride.

All of this took place before Crimpy's phone call.

"You've got to film a show on longlining for whitebait, a heap of people believe it. Imagine how many we can fool if we put a story on television."

How could I resist? Plans were made to meet Crimpy in Westport and film the show.

We were also invited to the opening of a new store in Greymouth so decided to film in Greymouth and travel up to Westport a day later. The fishing was not too good when we arrived for the store opening so we concocted another little ruse. I managed to persuade the local radio station, who had a mobile studio parked at the new store, that we wanted to run a whitebait patty cooking competition.

I told them that we needed to film this event but in reality the crew and I were hedging our bets. All we were after was a free feed, but when the word went out on radio, we had a huge line of people form up behind the BBQ, each clutching a bowl of whitebait and various ingredients.

Some of the recipes were great, some were not, but we gorged ourselves on whitebait and kept our end of the bargain by filming most of the offerings.

Late in the afternoon I purchased a net, and on advice from one of the locals, we headed down to the breakwater on the south side of the Grey River. Lumps of cloud hung over the hills and the wind whipped up a fair sort of sea at the river mouth.

"Drive until you find a couple of white rocks", the bloke had said, "usually there's a gap about there, clamber over the rocks and drag your net repeatedly downstream. You should get a feed."

We drove down and there were whitebaiters everywhere. Any decent rock had someone standing on it, either gazing longingly into the murk or dragging their net.

Having had prior experience, I was all fired up and confident we could haul in the next day's breakfast. The only thing that was a little unusual was why the locals had conveniently left this gap. Perhaps they look after visitors particulary well?

We fished away quite happily, Anthony Nevison, Simon Baumfield and I. Simon was our second cameraman, a real character himself and was in Greymouth because Grant Atkinson had been rushed to hospital the previous night with a kidney problem. Every time we dragged the net in we caught a few whitebait in among a jellied-looking mess. After a couple of hours our breakfast was in the bucket, with all sorts of other floating debris, and we climbed back up onto the breakwater and into the tooth of the gale.

Another chap was parked there but he was outside, leaning against the car. Dressed in an old yellow plastic raincoat and trying desperately to roll a cigarette, we picked him for a local.

"Afternoon", he said, "you from over the hill." Over the hill means anyone not from the coast. It could be Christchurch or Chicago, regardless, you're from over the hill.

"Yeah, how'd you know?"

Bits of tobacco flew off in the breeze and old yellow coat looked at me with a crooked sort of grin.

"Oh! You can usually tell that someone's from over the hill when they start fishing near that sewerage outlet", he replied, waving his arm at the bank on the other side of the road.

Simon, Anto and I exchanged disgusted looks, said thanks, and nonchalantly started loading gear in the wagon. We drove off into the blustering squalls muttering and mumbling about the bugger who had put us crook.

My last sight of the local was of a yellow-coated individual still trying to roll a smoke on the sheltered side of his car while we beat a hasty retreat.

We didn't eat the whitebait.

Next morning the team headed north to our rendezvous with Crimpy all the more determined to film the longlining for whitebait show because of our encounter with the sewerage outlet.

That evening we set up at the mouth of the Nile River which plunges into the sea just below the old gold mining town of Charleston.

I have fished the mouth of the Nile with the first push of an incoming tide on numerous occasions. It is a beautiful, wild, windswept chunk of real estate and ideal for our purposes.

Crimpy had made a longline using tiny wasabi hooks and a wine cork as a float.

I scooped out a small shoal and hooked a couple of the hapless bait onto hooks so it looked as though the longline had done its worst. The other hooks were loaded with cheese, which Crimpy claimed (on camera) were the best bait. Helped by a wee nip of scotch, the rest is history, and the longlining for whitebait show rates up with the best, primarily because so many people thought it was true.

Most people regard it as a huge joke but a few people complained bitterly and felt that we had cheated them by filming something that wasn't accurate.

Of course we had taken them for a ride, that was the whole idea. No sense of humour, some people.

19

The Poor Knights

The first time I dived the Poor Knights was in July 1981 and I remember being astounded by two things – the visibility, which seemed endless, and the abundance of marine life. I grew up, diving on Banks Peninsula, where three metre visibility was a cause for celebration, so to wind up in 30 metres at the Knights was a real shock.

Dave Miller and Graham McGeoch were my companions, and all of us had trained in dirty water.

Over the years I have watched the Knights improve as both a fishery and dive location. I was one of the blokes who staunchly supported the idea of limited fishing around parts of the Poor Knights, and still do.

It was logical for us to film a couple of shows that combined excellent fishing with stunning diving and of course, the Knights was a sitter.

Charter skipper Pete Saul has an old chugger called *Lady Jess*. She is one of the old seven or eight knot sedate cruising vessels that plied the coast when everyone was in much less of a rush. *Lady Jess* is also a lucky old boat that catches more than her share of fish, so it was a pleasure to chug our way out to the Knights and rendezvous with the sort of filming we frequently dream about.

We left Tutukaka Harbour and plied a course over a lazy roll and ten knots of puff that was easing to nothing.

"Well, you picked the weather", said Peter, "and North Reef has been fishing well for kingfish. Someone nailed a nine kilo snapper out there over the weekend."

"I'd settle for a few kingis and a decent dive."

When the weather is a big slice of perfection and someone tells you the fishing is a bit of all right, it is hard to contain your enthusiasm. Every time I head out on an ocean like glass, I find it

The northern end of the Poor Knights. Now a reserve but offering outstanding dives in countless locations. Perhaps some of the best diving in the world.

hard to stay calm. Dragging in big lungfulls of fresh salt air, the throb of the diesel, the lazy roll of the ship yielding to swells that march relentlessly over a distant horizon. Add to the whole thing a thrill which reminds you that what is about to happen will be full of surprises. Our first dive was at Northern Arch, a beautiful natural slice through an otherwise uninterrupted cliff, and on that day it was full of stingray.

Suzie and Pete buddied up, Warwick Wrigley, the cameraman, who is a keen diver, was tearing his hair out. He was desperate to leap into 40 metre visibility and cruise the arch but sometimes a cameraman's lot is filled with frustration.

"Please mate, I'll only dive for a while, leap out and film you guys coming back. It won't take long, I won't miss the shot. Dock my pay, anything, just let me jump in."

"Listen", I said, "if you stop putting on that pitiful act you can join us on the next splash. Let's make sure we nail this one and then everything else is a bonus."

As soon as I leapt over the side I felt guilty. It was perfect, clouds of mao mao, golden snapper, demoiselles, kingfish, and of course, huge cruising stingray. Spectacular, and added to the fish life were the multi coloured walls of the arch, dripping with sponges, anemones and soft coral. If ever you enjoy the beauty of a dive on the Knights make sure you are armed with a torch. Colour underwater is very quickly dissipated so that staring at rock walls through a mask yields a world of blue and grey. Red, orange and yellow very quickly disappear under 10-20 metres of water, but throw in a beam of torch light, and all of those rich colours leap back at you. Diving with a decent torch offers huge rewards and for someone like me, filming with the aid of 200 watts of pure fizz, the marinescape looks absolutely stunning.

Filming underwater that day under Northern Arch was unforgettable. I remember suspending myself at about 20 metres and the biggest ray of all, with a wing span of about three metres, cruised straight for me.

It was great filming this massive beast gliding straight at me. On and on, until I thought shit, he's not going to stop. He came straight at the camera until at the last millisecond he veered clean over the top of the camera and banked away the way he had come. It wouldn't have missed by any more than 10 centimetres. It's a great shot and was a real thrill, although for the rest of the dive I was preoccupied with the thought of getting topside and replaying that segment just to make sure that it measured up. It did. With that sort of footage "in the can" it was time to chug over to North Reef and have a go at the kingfish.

It's a short hop and by the time I had stowed dive gear, Pete was saying that he could see schools of trevally and kingfish packed over the reef. The wind had dropped right out and the swell was easing by the hour. Every disturbance of the ocean stood out starkly and could be read like a book.

"Trevally over there, Graeme, and looks like a big school of kingis further out", instructed Pete.

"How big are they on average?"

"On average pretty small, say 10 kilos, but I know there are fish there 30 or 40 kilos, it's just a matter of getting lucky. You'll get smashed off several times this afternoon so make sure you flatten the barbs on those poppers or we'll have kingfish swimming around towing all sorts of junk."

If I am popper fishing I invariably flatten the barbs. Most poppers are floating plugs with a scalloped head. They are designed to move erratically when retrieved across the ocean, looking for all the world like a disabled bait fish. Kingfish cannot resist them. Poppers are usually armed with two treble hooks, so that anything you are anticipating catching and releasing, winds up stuffed full of barbs.

I like to remove one of the trebles and flatten the barbs. If you are a good angler and keep the pressure on, chances are you will get the fish to the boat, but throw any slack line, make any sort of mistake, and your quarry will punish you with its freedom.

Popper fishing for kingfish, or any other species for that matter, is incredibly visual. You see kingfish shouldering each other out of the way just to be first to devour the artificial bait. If an angler wants to crank the adrenalin meter up a few notches, all that is required are poppers and kingfish. I defy anyone to keep a lid on their enthusiasm when greeted with that combination.

Lady Jess cruised into the edge of the seething boiling schools of fish and I flicked out a popper. I prefer a Penn 8500 or 9500 reel loaded with a minimum 10 kilo line for this job – usually 15 or 24.

Kingfish have that wonderful ability to drag you straight into foul ground and bust off. It is a trick that they have mastered and one way to give yourself a chance is to put sufficient pressure on to drag them back into mid-water. It is something you cannot achieve with light line. The other part of the tackle combination is the rod, and my preference is a good stiff stick like the Penn Spinfisher range. For the 8500 and 9500 I use the heavy 10-15 kilo Spinfish or coupled with a 9500 and backed with 15 kilo line. I have tagged and released 120 kilo striped marlin with this rig so I trust its durability completely.

After four or five winds, kingfish started to line up and jostle for position behind the popper. Advancing bow waves showed that others were zipping in for a go at what they thought was tucker.

God help the predated when it comes to surviving in the ocean because as soon as anything starts behaving like fodder, its life expectancy can be measured in heart beats.

Another couple of winds, hook-up and down went the popper, attached to a kingfish that was lunging straight for the rocks. Fortunately this was one of the 10 kilo models and it didn't take too much effort to wrestle him back to mid-water.

"Put on all the drag pressure you can and haul him out of there because he'll go again, especially when the boat comes into view."

"Sizz" sang the 8500 and a delightful arch was suspended on the Sportfisher.

"I think we're in for an amazing afternoon, mate", I suggested to the skipper, and the great thing about having a camera in those situations is that you get the shots to view over again.

The sight of kingfish lining up behind the popper is something I will never forget, but half a dozen poppers were not enough that day and after we had tagged and released six fish, including a couple on jig, the poppers had gone.

It took about an hour, but it was 60 minutes of constantly hooked-up excitement. When the poppers had gone I dragged out a couple of my smaller, but very expensive, marlin lures. They are designed to pop and fizz at about seven to eight knots and I was certain that I could wind that fast.

Rigged up and cast, it took seconds to prove that they worked and a few seconds more to get smashed off and lose $40. One more go, the same result, and there was no way I was going to sacrifice more hard-earned cash. I have since done the reverse and trolled poppers. That approach has also proved to be very successful and I have caught yellowfin tuna, mahi mahi and giant trevally in the tropics all on trolled poppers. It is well worth a go.

Although our poppers were history, our afternoon on the Knights was not and as the sun slid towards the western horizon, shafts of orange-gold streaked the sky.

"It's snapper time", claimed the skipper, "after releasing those kingis it won't hurt to nail a couple of pan-sized snapper. Better than sausages."

Our planned anchorage was Rico Rico cave back on the Knights and thoughts of the sound of sizzling snapper fillets echoing around that massive cave made my mouth water.

Once we had dropped the anchor and started carving up bait, a flock of shearwater positioned themselves on the stern to swoop on any titbits.

A big slab of skip jack tuna threaded on a couple of 6/0 Black Magic hooks snaked away into 40 metres of rugged snapper terrain. There was just enough tide to make things interesting. Late evening settled on the ocean, its breath a faint whisper, occasional patches of gliding ripples danced briefly on the swells and died away.

We were filled with anticipation and sure enough, within 10 minutes, Pete's rod curved gracefully towards the sea and loaded up.

Nod, nod, nod went the rod tip, and suddenly Pete Saul was grinning from ear to ear. "Snapper!" he said.

"You beauty", I encouraged, all the while muttering "c'mon, c'mon" to the unseen fish. The thrill of fishing for school fish like snapper and kingfish is greatly enhanced when your mate hooks-up, because hopefully it is only a matter of time before the same blessing is bestowed on you.

Pete hauled in a nice pan-sized snapper, re-baited the hook and was soon back at work. The skip jack tuna was doing its thing.

Just before dark I had a visitor. Something was mouthing the bait. Obviously at that point I had no idea what, but the reel was in free spool with my thumb putting just enough pressure on to prevent an overrun if a fish took the bait. And it was about to. Without further ado, something with real grunt picked up the bait and roared off, typical big snapper behaviour. The trick is to let the fish run, usually it stops, swallows the bait and takes off again so that the second run is the one that waves a flag saying set the hook. This is what my trusty denizen did, all on camera and just as the last band of orange-gold was being chased over the horizon by darkness. Just enough light left to film one last flurry. When I set the hook, the rod described a lovely graceful arc and recorded several big thumps – exactly what you would expect from a serious snapper.

"What do you think?" asked Pete.

"Seems like a big snapper but that would be too good to be true." Surely not, I thought, that would be the perfect end to a hell of a day.

Nod, nod, nod went the rod. Smile, smile, smile went G. Sinclair. It was a great battle, to and fro, gain some line, then lose it but in the end a huge snapper materialised out of the gloom and Pete whipped the net under it.

If you watch *Gone Fishin'* you will understand what sort of noise I make – all whooping and hollering – well this was the command performance. I couldn't believe it, 10 kilos of snapper just on dark and firmly parked on camera. Sometimes you have to be lucky. An elated crew on a happy little ship steamed back to the island and the shelter of Rico Rico cave. When you first visit the Poor Knights, one of the favourite charter boat tricks is to steam inside the cavern, turn around and sneak out again. It is always a buzz, but to drop the pick and spend the night there, lifts the thrill of the cave to another dimension.

We had enough fresh fish for a feed and six of us, plus a tonne of gear, crammed into a not over-large cabin. Not only did the sound of fresh fish echo around our home but the smell hung in the air. There was not a breath of wind to disturb the tranquility of Rico Rico cave.

Shadows cast by our cabin and deck lights danced over the walls and voices came back with faint echoes. This was a fitting end to the kingfish and snapper action out on North Reef, but there was one further activity planned. After a bit of a scoff, Warwick, the patient cameraman and I, were leaping in for a night dive.

It doesn't take long for a boat to develop a bit of an odour when it is loaded with humanity, fish, bait, wet dive gear and is low on hot showers. The team of musty men and one woman sat down to fresh fish, bread, vegetables and – for the non divers – a wee glass of Chardonnay or a Lion Red.

"Looking forward to this dive, bloody hard watching you buggers dive and catch fish", suggested a much happier cameraman.

"Well, that's what you get the big bucks for, but let's check out the night life, compliments of Rico Rico cave."

We kitted up and leapt into the big blue. I love diving at night, especially to film, as it most certainly is another world. Fish that cruise during daylight hours are literally asleep, the classic example being pink and blue mao mao that curl up on a convenient rock somehow or suspend themselves with hardly a movement. Crevice dwellers, such as crayfish, are out wandering around scavenging up a good feed and in a place like the Knights, where they are protected, they show no fear of clanking, bubble-blowing balls of noisy light that descend on them to film their otherwise private business. When I dive at night I always feel very relaxed, although the predators are hard at work, the pace seems a little less frenetic and the threat less obvious.

It is great to hit the bottom, film for a while, become orientated and then switch off all the lights. Sometimes the noise of a boat generator hums through the black or cabin lights dance on the surface but often the darkness is so complete as to be total. Sometimes you see your buddy moving around in his or her personal cocoon of light, but at other times there is that pressing darkness and a sea of noise. The ocean at night is filled with crackles and pops, the sounds of surge and things that go bump in the night.

It is just a wonderful entirely different environment in which to literally become totally immersed. I love it, and after watching Warwick moving around in his cocoon of light for a while, obviously wondering where I had disappeared to, I flicked the camera lights back on and focused my attention on an octopus that went through a massive series of colour changes, if not a heart attack.

That trip to the Poor Knights was a great reminder to me of how complementary diving and fishing can be. Have a dive in crystal clear water, blessed with abundant marine life, and then head off and catch just enough for feed. A night dive adds the finishing touch and the whole experience is unforgettable.

The unique situation that enabled divers and anglers to co-exist around the Poor Knights has ended.

I think it is a real pity because I have seen the islands continue to improve as a dive location. Areas that totally exclude fishing were great because there were other areas open to limited angling but the chapter is closed and no longer will people be able to enjoy the Knights in the way that we did with Pete Saul and *Lady Jess*. The divers will love it, the charter operators who fish out of Tutukaka will not. I love the idea of reserves, especially when their implementation takes into account what is best for all users. In other words, it's nice when the largest recreational activity in the world (fishing) gets a fair hearing.

Enough of the politics, let's go fishing.

*Rico Rico Cave − an
outstanding Poor Knights
anchorage.*

20
Fiordland

In 1998 I didn't visit Fiordland, my second home. It was the first time in over 25 years that I did not spend some part of the year in this magic piece of real estate and there were two reasons.

The first was that I had major commitments to TV3 weather as their regular presenter and the second reason was that my health had deteriorated to a point where I was spending a great deal of time in a wheelchair.

It was not that I didn't want to go, especially when one of the local fishermen, Dale Coker, was updating me constantly on what sounded like outstanding blue fin action. The reason was that I felt that my health and the wheelchair would somehow hold people back and indeed, during that year, a number of people that I would have regarded as good friends, backed right off. It was a bit lonely for a while, my father died, my partner left me and took my son, multiple sclerosis was giving me a wind up, and TV3 didn't renew my weather contract. As each little challenge presented itself I thought bugger it, life is what you make it, and as long as I am around to draw breath I will make the most of life's opportunities and get through the challenges.

Some friends have shown themselves to be wonderful, and of course life's passage isn't always plain sailing, but late in 1998 I resolved that I would be involved in another filming adventure in Fiordland, even if my bum was still parked in a wheelchair.

I had been keeping in touch with commercial fisherman, Blake Scott, who works a large chunk of crayfish quota in the southern Fiords.

Blake owns a Western Australian-built Marko which occupies 60 ft of ocean, and he didn't care what sort of disease I was battling, if I thought I could hack it, the call was to come on down.

The trip was planned for April 1999, and as that time drew close,

Sandee and Peter Shaw
sharing crayfish – Of course
they have smiles on their
faces.

we had finalised our team and started preparations in earnest.

Once you get yourself on to the coast and out to sea it is important that planning has been meticulous, not so much in terms of food, because all manner of luxuries can be wrestled from the ocean. It is everything else that needs to be triple checked and backed up, filming equipment, tapes, batteries, back-up handy cam, dive gear, fishing gear etc etc.

Blake phoned several times in the weeks prior to departure. "Not looking good", he would say, "water's too warm and the blue fin haven't shown up, sure you want to come down?"

There was no way in the world I was cancelling that trip, broken limbs wouldn't have kept me away.

Several of my team had never set foot in the place, my partner Sandee, my niece Becky who was sound recordist, and her partner, Mack Seymour, the cameraman. It was also first time for Peter Shaw, Sandee's dad, and the trip was our 60th birthday present for Pete. It was a birthday he won't forget in a hurry.

The final member of our team was Ian Miller, long time friend and dive buddy who also owns a dive equipment supply company called Pro Dive.

I hadn't seen *Jewel*, our home for the week, and when Blake phoned again a couple of days before departure to say that MAF Fisheries had cleared him to have a couple of paua divers on board as well as tanks, our number hit nine and I wondered where everyone would fit. I shouldn't have worried!

It is the anticipation of a trip like that which really stirs me. Fiordland winds me up, it enthralls me, fills me with awe, it gets my ticker pumping. For weeks I had been warning the crew about the weather "on the last trip it blew every day – often over 50 knots, occasionally over 70, and rain? Classic cats and dogs stuff. Be prepared, you haven't seen rain until you've spent a week in Fiordland."

From the time we landed in Invercargill in calm clear conditions, to the time we left a week later in clear, calm conditions, the weather was perfect, so good in fact, that the new wet weather gear didn't get out of the plastic wrapper.

On the way around the south coast towards Manapouri, we stopped just short of Tuatapere and filmed the trees that are bent to the shape of the wind. They all hunch over in a protective grove looking as though they are permanently shielding themselves from a major meteorological onslaught. It looks as though the seaward side has been sandblasted, the branches, twisted, bare gnarled, it's a great look, but when those trees stared back at us, there wasn't a breath of wind, just a stunning view west to the Fiords and south to Stewart Island.

I was intent on the trees when I heard a strand of number eight fence wire strain and ping, the noise repeated itself, and I was just in time to see Ian (Grizz) leap the fence and follow Sandee into the neighbouring paddock.

"What are you doing? The cockie will have your guts for garters."

"Won't be long", said Grizz, "paddock's full of mushrooms."

Well, the temptation was too great to resist, and within 20 minutes the team returned to the van with half a chilly bin of fresh, wild mushrooms.

We arrived in Manapouri just in time to ferry across the lake and film the magnificent sunset that was creeping across the western sky.

The temperature slid a few degrees, the polar fleece jackets went on, and our breath formed a slight mist in the crisp clear air. Our first sandfly zoomed in for a feed but even they were few in number and lacking in appetite. For the rest of the week they presented no problem, even on the notorious Fiordland coast.

It was the perfect start and the forecast stretched out ahead of us with a benevolent fine weather and wind, 10 knots variable.

As we started to unload the van, Mack got in position to film the scenery.

"Shit", he said, sounding like someone who had just discovered sandflies, "bloody cameras playing up."

"What's the fault."

"I don't know, but it's eating tapes like cereal."

"Bugger", I concurred and nothing we could do would fix it. From the top of the hill above Manapouri Marina, Mack phoned TV3 in Auckland and a replacement was organised to fly to Queenstown the next day. He had a friend arrange to drive it through to Te Anau and if all went well, Becky and Mack would chopper in with the new camera and join us in Charles Sound the following night.

As if to add insult to injury, that sunset begged to be filmed, it draped the still autumn scene in a canopy of red and gold, a very warm welcome to Fiordland.

We farewelled Mack and Beck and belatedly set off on our journey across Lake Manapouri. A van met us in West Arm and transferred what was left of us over the Wilmott Pass and down to Deep Cove.

My first challenge was to get from the van down a narrow little track across one vessel and onto *Jewel*. *Jewel* was rafted on the other side of the charter vessel *Genesis*.

"No bloody worries", Brian, the skipper of *Genesis* said, when told of the challenge. "I'll carry you!" He's a big burly lad, which is just as well, because I'm over 90 kgs, and he hoisted me over his shoulder like a sack of spuds and strode off down the twisty, steep little track towards the boat. I just bounced along, laughing like a lad expecting at any moment to wind up on my bum. Nothing untoward happened and I was eventually dumped on *Jewel's* deck. It was 10.00pm and the adventure began. Mushrooms helped garnish the steak, and before our gear was stowed, Sandee and Pete were cooking up a feast. The smell of cooking filled the cabin, a rich warm smell, complete with a mouth-watering sizzle. Outside, Doubtful Sound was totally at rest, glaciated peaks reared above our anchorage, their outline stark against a star-studded sky.

A thousand horsepower leapt into life at 5.00am and I stumbled up into the wheelhouse and plonked myself down beside the skipper.

It was pitch black, but chart plotter/GPS, colour sounder and radar combined to carve a safe passage through the darkness.

I couldn't sleep anyway, half the team snored and I was choked full of excitement. It is great to feel so passionate about things, so keen that just to be in a place like Fiordland is adventure enough. On this trip things were even more exciting because so many of the team were experiencing the place for the first time.

Our paua divers, Tim and Butch, had a great sense of humour and fitted in immediately, we were a happy crew.

"Worried about the lack of blue fin", mumbled the skipper, "Dale Coker got one 90 kilos up near Milford a couple of days ago but the water's four degrees warmer than at the same time last year. It's about 16 degrees Celsius – needs to be 12."

"Don't worry, laddie", I encouraged, "even if we don't get any fin something will pop up that we can film. The main thing is that we're here and the weather hasn't shit itself."

Our course took us down Malaspina Reach and Pendulo Reach. Although it was Cook who named Doubtful Harbour, the first Europeans to enter the sound were Spaniards under the command of an Italian. Alessandro Malaspina was in command of two Spanish vessels, *Descubierta* and *Altrevida*, which spent five years sailing around the world. The explorations of Malaspina are highlighted by the Spanish place names in and around Doubtful.

Jewel cruised the inside of Secretary Island and into Thompson Sound. Captain John Grono named Thompson during a sealing

Filming on the vast aft deck of Blake Scott's 60ft Marko – Jewel.

expedition in 1810 at which time he slaughtered 10,000 fur seals. Cook had returned after his 1773 visit with reports of vast seal colonies and it wasn't long before the slaughter began in earnest and the seal harvesters virtually wiped them out. Today seals are in healthy numbers in many parts of Fiordland.

Daylight rolled over the eastern mountains and greeted us as the first swells lifted our bow near the mouth of Thompson. Bush-covered mountains laced with valleys and topped with snow grass plunged into the Fiord or rolled on down to the open coast. The swell was large and lazy, a procession of breakers slammed into the coast and mist hung in a ribbon over the shore.

"Better get some gear in the water", said Blake, "just because other buggers aren't having much luck doesn't mean that we won't."

We trolled four lures, three of which were Yo-zuri squid about 10 inches long with chin weights to keep them just below the surface. The hot colour the year before (and the year before that) was amber, so they were rigged with one hook right up in the body and a second trailing at the back of the lure skirt.

Blake had a tonne or so of his paua quota to fill, but the lift on the open ocean meant that any paua would come from inside the Fiords. Our first stop was at the mouth of Nancy Sound.

There is a lucky rock thereabouts, lucky for blue fin and lucky for an array of bottom fish.

"Got some huge cod here the other day", said Tim, "you might want to ask Blake if he'll stop."

I was uncertain what to do because we still had no main camera but I did have my trusty little VX1000, the Sony digital. It's a fantastic little camera so I decided to let the rest of the team fish and record the action. On a crisp blue day it is hard to tell the difference between VX1000 footage and the Betacam that we use for television.

The team tied a sinker on the bottom and used a couple of circle tuna hooks or 8½/0 wasabis on dropper rigs above. Trace was 200lb, the bait, anything you could find, usually barracouda and in 50 metres of water the baits lasted about half a second before something large and voracious latched onto them. Spool the line down, bite, bite, bite, whack, lift the rod up hard and hook-up.

"I want to try some of this blue cod you've been raving about", said Pete.

"Doesn't look as though you've got long to wait", said Butch, "judging by the bend in your rod."

Sure enough, two huge cod about three kilos each were hauled from the depths and plonked on the deck. We fished for half an hour, catching blue cod and trumpeter as the swells slid on under the hull, rolled over and smashed themselves onto the coast 60 metres away.

Trumpeter are not something you catch everyday and neither are three-kilo cod, but the thing that lifted the occasion towards superlative was the backdrop. Those mountains and Fiords have a habit of stealing the show. Tucked into a nearby Fiord the paua divers grabbed a couple of sacks each while Pete operated as dinghy boy, following the snorkellers around the coast, helping them empty their bags of succulent shellfish.

"I feel a feed coming on", I said to Grizz, "wait till you try my paua chips."

"Paua chips", laughed Blake, "wait till you try my paua patties."

Pete dropped a couple of sacks on the deck, reported that there wasn't much of legal size in the shelter of the sound, and zoomed off to follow the paua divers on their continued quest.

"How long does it take a paua to grow to legal size, Blake?"

"A five inch paua takes five years to reach that size", he replied, "they're pretty slow growing but we are restricted to a quota. Once we catch our allowance that's it until next year, just like the crayfish."

Late in the afternoon we scurried off to another Fiord to rendezvous with Hannibal's helicopter and plucked Becky, Mack and camera from their comfortable hotel room in Te Anau.

We ultimately anchored in Charles Sound and cooked up a feed of cod. Sandee and I left the snorers to it and stuck an airbed on the deck.

Day one ended with us gazing up at the heavens. We were anchored in a little cove, water lapping lightly on the hull, trees reaching to the heavens, and the last thing I remember was a shooting star, a thing of magic that raced across the heavens.

"Make a wish", mumbled my partner, as we drifted off to prepare our bodies for the next day.

The day dawned slowly, we were wide awake watching trees and mountains grow out of the darkness and stars fade away. Fine and clear, ten knots variable. Out on the coast the swell had eased. We trolled around Nancy and Charles, the water temperature frustratingly warm, but Tim and Butch kitted up ready to give the paua diving a serious go.

Grizz grabbed a feed of crays and then set about doing the dinghy boy job.

Lunch consisted of a dream feed, fresh crayfish and paua chips.

For interest my paua technique is to beat them with a hammer or piece of wood (just the large muscular foot), cut them into chunks, say 5mm thick, roll them in flour and cook them for a few seconds a side in a hot pan. They usually come out so tender you could cut them with your lips.

After a serious nose bag and because the swells had eased further, the paua divers opted to work the open coast.

I lay down in the wheelhouse and nodded off. The paua divers headed off with Grizz acting as dinghy boy. Grizz was mad keen to catch a blue fin but because it looked so unlikely he agreed to support the divers.

The very next thing I knew was that the angler's alarm clock was ringing. There is nothing like a howling ratchet on a Penn International to drag you out of a deep sleep.

I was instantly awake, on my feet and shambling into the wheelchair, which in turn raced off towards the stern.

It was a double strike. Pete was hanging onto one rod and the other was bent over, sitting in the holder.

"Where's Grizz?" I asked.

"Off paua diving", said Blake. "you'd better grab the rod."

I got a hold of the rod all right and sat there in a very comfortable mobile fighting chair scrapping with another albacore. We had hauled in a few large albacore, but this was Pete's first game fish and he was not unhappy about the opportunity.

"Pulled a fair bit of line", I mumbled to no one in particular, "maybe they're blue fin", I yelled at Blake.

"Could be", he hailed from way up forard in the wheelhouse, "but more likely albacore in this water."

My fish was close within ten minutes, it tugged and jerked on the 24 kilo line, dragged off less line and was tiring.

"I'm not sure about this albacore", I mumbled to Mack and Beck who were recording all the action, "wouldn't be surprised to see a blue fin. Swivels up Blake."

We were short of crew. Poor Sandee had never been game fishing before and we had thought she had plenty of time to learn the ropes. Mack and Beck were filming. Pete was on one fish, me on another, so that left Blake to drive, lead the fish and gaff. Everyone else was off getting paua.

The skipper raced out of the wheelhouse, grabbed the leader and the gaff, hauled for all he was worth and suddenly 20 kilos of blue fin was flapping on the deck.

We kind of looked at each other with real surprise.

"It's a blue fin", we both exclaimed.

"Only a little one", I added, "but it's still a blue fin." I remember being very excited. We had expected to catch none, and even though the fish was certainly on the small side, it was still a southern blue fin tuna. I was rapt.

"Your turn, Pete", I urged, as another silver missile slid towards the gaff.

Over the side came 20 kilos of albacore. Our double strike became one of each of the Fiordland tuna species.

"Fantastic", said Pete, "biggest fish I've ever caught."

The smile said it all, it wasn't the albacore that was hooked, it was a bloke turning 60 that had just discovered the joy associated with the sport of game fishing.

"Well done, Pete, well done", laughed the crew as a small inflatable roared over the swells and the paua team returned.

"What's going on?" asked Grizz.

"While you were gone we nailed a double strike."

"Albacore", he suggested, staring at Pete's fish still lying on the deck.

"One albacore and one blue fin, the blue fin's already in the slurry. If you'd been here it would have been yours."

"Bugger", mumbled Grizz, "don't they know the water's too warm."

Both fish had taken the amber Yo-zuri squid on 200lb fluoro-carbon leader.

Grizz, the dinghy boy, retired from the job of measuring and bagging paua and decided to concentrate on a southern blue fin.

"I really want to catch one of those things", he added, and the purposeful look only served to highlight his determination.

Snorkelling paua is a physically demanding job. You survive by holding your breath and fight a constant battle with a heaving, untamed ocean.

Paua is worth in excess of $30,000 a tonne and a good diver in the right place can wrest a tonne a day. Blake has six tonnes of paua quota which, if conditions allow, can be nabbed in short order. Our problem was the swell that late in the afternoon lifted again. Huge rolling mountains of water glided serenely out of the Southern Ocean. They were born in the roaring forties and furious fifties well to the south and here they were throwing themselves on to Fiordland's coast. Some of them were massive and I'm sure a few paua clamped themselves a little more solidly to their rocky home. If they didn't they too would be bashed upon the shore. We anchored for the night in Blanket Bay, having sneaked in to collect some groceries from a fisherman who had visited Deep Cove.

Daylight hunted us down heading out the mouth of Thompson en route to Nancy Sound and "lucky rock" where we hoped to fluke another blue fin. As soon as the gear went out, large albacore tried to run away with our lures. We released the lot, no point in taking more than a feed.

Grizz had the honour of taking the first strike because he was the angler most enthusiastic about catching his first blue fin and with every strike we expected blue fin.

At 8.00am we had a double strike of serious intent.

"If this is a bloody albacore", said Grizz, reaching for the nearest rod, "it's a damn big one."

Pete found himself on rod number two, both were hooked on amber squid and both quickened the pulse.

One of the most amazing things to me was that we were trolling about 100 metres off the shore, right on the coast.

Most of my game fishing takes place miles offshore but not in Fiordland. Those mountains are like a magnet, even the fish are drawn to them.

"Lucky rock", affectionately called Nancy's Nipples, was right beside us, and at times we had to tow the fish out of the surf where they were threatening to join the paua and crayfish. I have never been hooked-up on large game fish with a more spectacular backdrop.

"I'm going to get right up this fish", claimed Grizz, "let's find out if it's a big albacore" and on went the pressure and away went 100 metres of line.

"That's a bluey", said Grizz, "it sure ain't no albacore, not to be pulling line as easily as that, but I'm still going to get it in quick."

Old Grizz went to work hard. He pumped away, lifting and winding, heaving and wheezing, inching line back little by little.

We had a full crew on the job, Butch was going to gaff and Tim had the job of grabbing the leader. Pete just kept good pressure on his fish while we went hard out to capture Grizz's prize.

Twenty minutes into the scrap and only 40 metres of line lay in the water. Suddenly a very large blue fin in the 70-80 kilo bracket rose up out of the deep and thrashed on the surface. Grizz leant back, it thrashed foaming white water all over the place and suddenly it was gone.

We were all stunned. "Hook's pulled", said Grizz, winding slowly and filled with disbelief.

He was gutted. "That's fishing", and with that he took his rod, jumped in the inflatable and set off to troll his single lure out the back of a very tiny boat.

The rest of us had no time to reflect, Pete was still on his fish and although we hadn't seen it, the expectation was that this fish was also a beauty. Once again we found ourselves challenged by the rocks as the fish tried to find the gap between Nancy's Nipples and the shore. At 45 minutes the leader was up and you could have heard a pin drop.

"It's a very big fish", I said to Blake, after watching another massive shape rise out of the gloom.

We all willed that fish towards the waiting gaff, surely we wouldn't lose two great fish in the space of half an hour.

At 50 minutes a massive beast was being hauled on the leader, in went the gaff, then a second and 70 kilos of blue fin thumped onto the deck.

"Yahoo", I yelled, "unbelievable, it's a beauty Pete", and everyone else chimed in with congratulations. Pete just grinned "50 minutes", he stated, "50 minutes".

Immediately the crew went to work. The fish had been landed onto a mat and now it was bled and a spike placed in the brain. The gills were removed and the guts drawn out through the gill cavity. "Belly flaps are sought after in Japan", explained the skipper, "beautiful fat cuts ideal for sashimi so you can't gut the fish by slitting the belly flaps in the traditional way. A good fish could be worth $100 per kilo so this one may fetch $6000-7000. You have to be careful though, I've heard of guys sending fish to Japan and having them rejected. In that case you wind up with a bill. Who knows, but we've got five days to get this fish to Japan."

We tried everything to get Grizzler his elusive blue fin, even cubing with pilchards, but all to no avail. Our anchorage that night was in Dees Cove next to another charter boat. When we pulled alongside they were tailing crayfish and filleting dozens of fish. It was like a little fish processing plant.

One of the guys said that they could take six crayfish each per day so that's what they would bloody well do. The law allows it so that's what would happen. I think it's a shame. To me no one should leave Fiordland with more than a feed say, for example, one day's take of things like cod, crayfish and paua. Eat what you like while you are there, but don't rape the place.

Breathe in the special air that heightens your senses and caresses your lungs, drink your fill of mind-blowing scenery, but don't take more than a feed of the Fiordland resident population, otherwise one day you will wonder where they have gone.

As we were enjoying a beer and a little blue fin sashimi cut from my fish of the day before, one of the female members of the neighbouring charter came over for a chat. She was very friendly.

"How's the trip going?" I asked.

"Not enough crayfish, it's really hard going", she said.

That spoke volumes to me. Too much is made of going to a place like Fiordland to take large quantities of seafood. It's a senseless waste.

Anyway, enough of that. We awoke to another beautiful day in paradise and organised to drop the blue fin back at Deep Cove so that it could continue its journey to Japan. From there we were setting off on the second half of our journey, one that would take me to places I have never visited. It would turn out to be a whole procession of beautiful days in paradise.

Just out of interest, our blue fin wound up weighing 60 kilos gutted and gilled. It was a beautiful fish and arrived in Japan, but due to some sort of skullduggery, was rejected. After the hassle of getting it out, Blake called the fish Saga 1. Saga 1 ended up costing Blake's fishing co-operative $700.

He sent the fish to Japan and the Japanese sent him a bill for $700. You have to be joking, but that is one of the hassles of trying to send high value fish to a fickle market. I would love to see more of this magnificent eating fish for sale in the local market.

You have to taste it to believe it.

The source of a couple of serious meals.

21
Chalky & Solander – New Ground

Saga one, the hapless blue fin was deposited in Deep Cove and our bow turned down Malaspina Reach towards the open sea. All we knew was that *Jewel* needed to be moored in the Southland port of Riverton three days hence. As for where we were going, who knows?

With the weather the way it was, the only certainty was south, and along the way places like Breaksea, Dusky, Chalky and Preservation all displayed a vacancy sign. The only thing that differentiated the Sound from the open sea was the swell, that large lazy roll, but there was no breeze to ripple the glass-like sheen. It was perfection.

We had seen one pod of dolphins further north, the odd mollymawk and albatross plus a few shearwaters. A killer whale, a solitary male distinguishable by its massive dorsal fin, had frolicked briefly at the entrance to Nancy Sound then disappeared. The further south we headed the more prolific the marine life. It got to a point where off Breaksea Island we were surrounded by shearwaters, albatross, mollymawks and dolphins, a regular summit conference. I have never seen so many big, beautiful birds in all my life, everything wheeling, diving, toing and froing in a wonderful display.

The albatross is a real stunner, a majestic soaring creature with a stern countenance, they leave me in awe.

According to "New Zealand Birds" MF Soper . . . Few birds so capture the imagination as do the albatrosses, particularly the wandering and royal albatrosses of the Antarctic and Subantarctic seas, for these huge birds – the royal weighs some 20 to 25 pounds and has a wing span of about ten feet – have made as their home what are to us some of the most inhospitable seas in the world. Truly oceanic, able to stay continuously at sea for years, albatrosses return to land only to breed. Some of the wonder that albatrosses have always had for man is reflected in their scientific name *Diomedea* (from Diomedes, a Greek hero of the Trojan War, who, after the fall of Troy, was accompanied on his travels by large and gentle – in the sense of noble or well borne – sea birds said to be his fallen comarades reincarnated in bird form), a name obviously chosen to serve as more than just a scientific label.

In New Zealand waters the term 'mollyhawk' is conveniently applied to the smaller forms, all of which have black backs, and the term albatross to the two 'great' albatrosses, the wandering and the royal, the adults of which have white backs.

"Shall we duck into Breaksea?" asked Blake, "We'll cruise the Acheron Passage and anchor for the night somewhere in Dusky."

"What are the options, skipper?"

"Well, we could push on to Chalky, plenty to explore and I know you've spent time in Dusky."

Chalky Inlet was the only Fiord I had not been in, so the idea of seeking out that particular haven was very appealing.

The decision was made a few minutes later when, way in the distance, a whale spouted classic "thar she blows" stuff. It was easy to see how someone in the crow's nest of a sailing ship could spot them miles away when we were able to do so from the deck of *Jewel*, virtually at sea level.

The spout hung in the still air like a billboard pinpointing the leviathan resting quietly underneath. Blake swung the wheel and the bow carved a gradual arc across a glassy sea that eventually had us bearing down on the spot. We had moved away from the concentration of dolphins and birds, although a few of the more playful mammals slipped through the water off the bow. Within a few minutes they too had peeled away to rejoin their families closer to the coast.

The whale spouted again, now much closer, and that glorious cloud of whale breath hung in a beaded white mist above the sea. A gigantic black log lay almost motionless on the surface. "Sperm whale", I volunteered, looking at the characteristic profile.

We glided even closer, the whale totally unconcerned until we could see every wrinkle, hear every sound, hear the whoosh of escaping air and stare in wonder at the beast and its misty signature. The skipper flicked the Morse into reverse as this whale was in no mood to vacate the premises.

We lay briefly, almost motionless, alongside a whale of similar length to *Jewel*'s 60 feet and watched another misty breath blast its way into the afternoon tranquility.

"Easy to see how they were harpooned in the old days", said Grizz, "especially if they behaved like this."

As if sharing the sentiment, many tonnes of black beast heaved and slid gracefully into the depths.

"Wow", was about all we could say, "that was really something."

The ocean, in its wonderful and mysterious way, throws up some incredible surprises and a sperm whale blowing its clouded breath and lolling among the southern swells was certainly an amazing experience for us.

Butch and his buddies – Two more Solander Island blue cod bite the dust both about 5 kilos.

"I see a lot of whales out here", informed Blake, "but no one spends any time way off this coast."

Our path had moved us a little closer to Chalky so that was it, our anchorage of the night selected, we pushed on.

Late in the afternoon, when the sun was dragging the curtain of evening into a dying day and a bleeding sky held promise for the morrow, another pod of dolphins and many hundred birds came to say goodnight. When the sun slid and the curtain fell we were full of the day's performances and felt that real joy for life that comes with exquisite days in outstanding places.

"Bloody good to be alive", mumbled Grizz. Nothing more needed to be said. The game fishing gear had been wound in and the throttles went down. Eight knots became 14 and the miles slid rapidly under the hull. The sea became restless and the ship's motion like that of a twitchy colt, she pranced rather than planed, and every now and then a wave caught the bow and unseen spray showered the wheelhouse screen.

"Bit of a breeze, can be bloody filthy out here. That's Cape Providence", said Blake, pointing at a spot on the chart plotter a few miles ahead and to the east of us. Earlier in the day Tim and Butch

The rusting hulk of the Stella *in Chalky Inlet.*

had dragged a few mutton birds out of the freezer, crammed them in a roasting dish and flicked them in the oven. Now here we all were crammed in the wheelhouse with the distinctive odour of muttom birds filling our nostrils as the hull pitched this way and that.

Fortunately I'm not prone to sea sickness and don't find the mutton bird smell offensive but Beck and Sandee were turning green.

"That smell is disgusting", said Beck. "Don't know how you can eat something that stinks like that", added Sandee, as we slipped off another wave.

The smell drove them from the cabin, it was that or puke and two miserable looking seafarers deposited themselves on a bench aft of the cabin.

The breeze added to the restless ocean by dragging spray across the deck and every now and then we fell off the top of a wave but nothing would entice the girls back into the cabin with the mutton bird smell. No bloody way. All around us was black, the ocean remained restless but our thoroughbred craft sought out the mouth of Chalky Inlet and guided us into an anchorage that reflected a rising full moon.

There was no breeze in Chalky and the evening breath was but a cool whisper as Sandee and I sought the comfort of our air bed and lay back to stare in awe at stars jostling for space in a galaxy called the milky way.

"There are so many stars they seem to touch each other", said my partner, "it's beautiful and thank God I don't have to smell those damn mutton birds. I'll never eat one as long as I live."

The non-mutton birders had dined on blue fin sashimi and blue fin steaks washed down with a quiet beer or Chardonnay so no one was complaining.

"Grizz ate a couple", I said. "Glad I'm not sleeping in the forard cabin because when they start working on his gut everyone's going to need fresh air." We laughed and slipped off to our dreams.

At daylight, Pete and Mack leapt into the inflatable and set off towards a likely-looking valley to hunt. In typical Fiordland fashion huge forested mountains reared up towards the main divide, a river snaked its way through the wilderness and deposited itself at our feet. Towards the coast the mountains retained their canopy of bush but became rolling hills and tucked in our anchorage at the head of Cunaris Sound (an arm of Chalky), mist was pushed in streaky clouds across the bay. It was indeed a day of promise, and that is very much the way it proved to be. Grizz started the ball rolling by catching a couple of school hapuka (groper) while we waited for the hunters to return. I entertained my fantasies by grabbing the Betacam and filmed the anglers who supplemented the breakfast menu. I guess I'm a latent cameraman and actually film the underwater segments but the chance to grab the big Betacam unit is something I am always keen to do. It is also good to be aware, first hand, of some of the challenges that a cameraman is faced with when filming something like *Gone Fishin'*.

The hunters returned empty handed, but before *Jewel* left Chalky and headed further south, we had some business to attend to.

Grizz plucked a feed of very respectable crayfish from the crevices of the Sound, then in a secret spot, hauled in some oysters that were every bit as succulent as the famous Bluff variety.

"Whatever you do don't tell anyone exactly where these oysters are or the other fishermen will kill me. The commercial fishermen know about the spot and all of us just take a feed. If everyone knows where it is they'll wipe it out."

Blake, the spot will remain nameless, but the memory of that delicious feed of fat juicy shellfish will stay with me for a long, long time.

On the way to the open sea, we cruised by the rusting hulk of the *Stella*, a once proud little ship that serviced the coast, but rolled over and died with part of an also doomed fish freezing plant. Fiordland has always been reluctant to tolerate attempts to establish a human foothold on her unblemished shores.

On the way out of North Port, with the *Stella*'s grave astern, Blake decided we needed a little bit of fun.

"Want to go surfing?" he enquired, "there's some foul at the mouth they call the Boulder Bank. I set pots there but it's an exciting surf break and *Jewel* surfs pretty well."

His smile was a challenge, and when you handle a vessel as well as Blake, we all knew there was going to be a lot more fun than danger. As we nosed towards the more open mouth of Chalky, two things became noticeable, one, the chalk-like cliffs that are responsible for the name and two, the large surf rolling over what was obviously the

Boulder Bank.

The surf rears up in the middle of otherwise uniform swells, perhaps a pile of glacial moraine creating a structure that irritates the ocean. Whatever, in short order we found ourselves careering down the face of a sizeable wave in our 60 foot surfboard. It was just great, everyone whooping and hollering, laughing and cackling. To date on the trip I had been feeling really clever, zipping all over the deck in my wheelchair, timing my runs to take advantage of the swells, but when *Jewel* slid across the face of a superb looking wave and slipped sideways down the face, G. Sinclair and wheelchair rolled over and parted company.

There were a few other crashes, a scream, a lot of laughter and we crested the wave and moved back out of the surf.

Everyone just cracked up and laughed their heads off. They had finally got me out of the chair, but let me tell you, it was worth it just for the ride.

I dragged myself to my feet and kind of grinned at everyone. By then we were all just good mates and thoroughly enjoying every experience that was adding to our little adventure.

"This is my home turf", said Blake, when we cleared Chalky and once again entered the world of large lazy swells.

"I work 300 pots in this area. You wouldn't think it, but on a good day it's usually blowing 30 knots and we work in over 70. My crew wears ski goggles when it gets around 70. There's usually so much spray that he wouldn't see anything without them."

"How rough does it have to be before you give up and dive for cover?" I asked. Blake looked at me with a half smile.

"We don't give up, only ever had to shelter once on the way round the coast, but we spent a few hours tucked away, then it eased a bit and we pushed on."

We were talking about one of the roughest chunks of water in the world, an area that encompasses the western extremities of Foveaux Strait, Puseygeur Point, West Point and a host of shallows and shoals. What Blake and his crew accomplish in a typical rock lobster season is most certainly not for the faint hearted.

The crew headed further south, the beauty of Fiordland slipping astern and finally the South Island dissolving into a smudge. The water was still warm – 15° – and our expectations being that the further south we went the colder the water, and more likely we would be to catch southern blue fin.

Directly ahead another smudge rose out of the ocean. Solander Island was directly in our path and I was dead keen to fish these slabs of rock before a late anchorage at Stewart Island.

Dolphins and birds were once again everywhere. They thrilled us, entertained us, had my companions and I marvelling at their use of the elements. The albatross is at one with the currents of air and may spend up to five years at sea before the mating urge guides it back to the rookery of birth. Dolphins look effortless in their handling of ocean currents and seemed to reflect our light hearted mood. One more day to revel in and explore this strangely benevolent ocean. Most of the trip was behind us but a couple of adventures were still in store.

Late in the afternoon we drew close to Solander Island which is really two main islands named in 1770 by Captain Cook.

I doubt that too many anglers had dropped a line around this storm-ravaged chunk of rock and all of us were keen to see what was concealed in the depths around the rim of stone.

When you are under Solander Island the cliffs rear up out of the sea, stark, battered monuments to nature's relentless power. On the seaward side there is no growth until you get about 30-40 metres above the ocean. Salt spray and huge waves have wiped the rock clean. All sorts of birds nest here: gulls, shearwaters, albatross and, strangely enough, gannets. I had not realised that they nested this far south.

Scant, stunted vegetation adds a little greenery to the view, but by and large Solander is rock. Around the western island, on any sort of ledge, seals had taken residence and the sea constantly rose up the cliffs and was sucked away in white lacy tendrils into the face of the next swell that rode up and was sucked away. Half a dozen lines snaked into the depths. Mack tried to film and Beck made the most of the challenge of recording good sound when 1000 horsepower roared under her feet. As soon as our lines hit the bottom we were attacked and almost instantly a couple of the team hooked up.

"This feels all right", said Butch, his rod bent like a staple, "but I wouldn't like to say what it is." Other rods loaded up in similar fashion and an expectant crew waited anxiously to see what we would

"Thar she blows" – a sperm whale exhales off the Fiordland coast. If wildlife and marine mammals are your thing, the Fiordland will captivate you.

pull in around one of the last chunks of dirt before Antarctica.

"Will you look at the size of those", I urged, as two massive blue cod were dragged onto the deck. They were huge, I have never seen cod like them and in very short order others were thrashing around on the deck.

"Weigh one", I suggested, keen to see how big these unbelievable cod were.

"Five kilos", came the call. Five kilos is one hell of a blue cod, they were as big as Grizz's school groper from the morning fish.

We had been visited by the odd barracouda so that was what we used for bait, a couple of slabs of couda, onto a hook in the classic ledger rig with a sinker on the bottom and two hooks above.

An orange/red/golden sunset chased the sun over the horizon and with the end of the day came the end of the fishing. We had a feed.

It suddenly felt like the end of the trip and I, for one, did not want to go home. What we were filming was magic, it was one of those trips of a lifetime, but Stewart Island beckoned, so we were on our way.

Unlike the night before, this passage was calm and the team wound up having wheelchair races up and down the aft deck. It was hilarious and as a few people found out to their peril, my sporty little wheelchair is pretty tippy.

I have described the beauty of Stewart Island before and next morning we were there harvesting a feed of oysters to take home. Nine of us on board, 50 oysters each, that's 450 which we dredged up in about an hour.

Jewel was anchored in Riverton by lunchtime and we were heading to the airport and home. So ended one of the really special filming excursions. It had proved to me a couple of very important things, not least of which was that Fiordland and the southern coast have to be one of the most beautiful parts of the world.

The other important reminder was that a disease like multiple sclerosis and time in a wheelchair should never be an excuse to stop living. Good friends help overcome the challenges and the right attitude will always pull you through. I was not, as I had once feared, holding people back. Far from it. I felt very much part of the team and have my hand up for next year's adventure, yet another opportunity to share the beauty that resides on our doorstep.

22

Just a Stone's Throw From Auckland

In January 1995 we started filming the third series of *Gone Fishin'*. I was keen to include a selection of material that was handy to Auckland and highlighted what a great variety of fishing there was just a stone's throw from the "City Of Sails". People from "out of town" view Auckland in terms of motorways, congestion, pace, sprawl and a world that stops when it hits the Bombay Hills. While my heart is still in the south where I was born, there is no denying that for the angler/boatie, Auckland is a bit of a paradise, a real springboard to all sorts of mischief.

One of the early episodes we filmed had been out on the Kaipara Harbour, well not actually on the harbour, but surfcasting just inside the heads. Mark Kitteridge and I had done the stint before and for series three I got a hold of John Farr to try out some new gear in this very productive spot.

Surfcasting the Kaipara Harbour is a great little adventure. It starts by roaring along Auckland's North Western Motorway, heading down Rimmers Road, a left turn just short of Helensville, navigating a few bush roads that culminate in a 4 wheel drive charge over the sandhills and onto the west coast. From there a great expanse of beach stretches many kilometres up to the Kaipara Harbour. Access along the beach is best two hours either side of low tide, and if you cock it up, the bodies of dead cars stick up out of the sand here and there to remind you that it's a long embarrassing walk home. Once you hit the Kaipara, follow the packed sand around the lagoon, choose a spot and go surfcasting.

John Farr and I, plus two local lads from Kumeu, had decided to film a couple of surfcasting techniques and a recent tackle innovation. The two techniques related to casting and we are talking extending your cast from 100 metres to 150 plus (the best guys are up around 200 metres). Surfcasting off the beach is often about

Not "Grizz" Miller's kingfish but one the same size as that which he shot at Channel Island to win us the "Ultimate Seafood Challenge".

distance so learning the pendulum cast or the South African can be of great assistance.

John Farr knows how to pendulum cast, I don't. The only time I tried it I bloody near killed myself, fortunately the South African is much easier. Our tackle innovation was a sinker called the breakaway and it has special dropper rigs attached above to stop tangles and eliminate the problem of softer baits separating from the trace.

All of this stuff represented the "guts' of one *Gone Fishin'* episode and my advice if you want to know more, is to trot along to your local tackle store or surfcasting club. That's how you'll begin to learn these techniques.

The other note of caution regarding the Kaipara is that parts of the area immediately behind the sandhills are used by the army and air force for bomb practice.

They raise a flag if any life-threatening activity is in progress but we hadn't seen a flag and got a bit of a surprise when, midway through our set up, the army arrived.

A couple of sign written 4 wheel drives gave the show away so we couldn't tell them we were from the Holmes show and anyway a number of the assembled battle fatigue-clad bods watched *Gone*

Fishin'. We didn't ask whether we were supposed to be there, just greeted them like long lost friends and shoved a camera under their collective noses.

"Welcome to *Gone Fishin'*", one of them said like a real T.V. pro, "fishing out here can be a real blast."

We all thought that was pretty amusing, baited our lines and with half the New Zealand army watching, I stepped up to cast my breakaway rig miles out towards the fishy inhabitants of the harbour.

The breakaway rigs were like gold, we only had two, although we weren't short of sinkers.

Casting into the Kaipara as the tide races out you need a sinker that anchors itself to the bottom. Large flat ones are pretty good and so too are the breakaways. They have spikes protruding from the base that break away or fold back when you retrieve your line, it makes retrieval virtually drag-free.

Well I stepped up, Mr *Gone Fishin'*, the clever angler, and got in position for the South African cast of the century, which involves a great extended arc and plenty of effort.

Sinews tightened in forearms, biceps flexed, a colgate smile was flung in the direction of the camera and New Zealand army.

Thirteen feet of surfcasting rod curled, the sinker started to drag the sand, and then accelerated out and over the Kaipara.

"Crack" the sinker and trace shot at least 150 metres out into the tide, but at that point they were no longer attached to the line. The clever angler had forgotten to check that the line was clear, part of it had been wrapped around the tip and surprise, surprise, it had snapped.

Spectators collapsed in heaps and laughed their heads off as a sheepish G. Sinclair ambled back to the truck to rig another set of gear, minus the valuable breakaway rig.

The army forgot about evicting us, we had brightened their day considerably. Eventually baited hooks arrived where they should have and the guardians of our fair shores set off to blow things up.

Typical of the Kaipara, we caught snapper, kahawai and gurnard on pilchards, sanma and squid.

Such spots abound and at times you can net mullet straight off the beach among the surf. Mullet, when fresh, are superb bait and great smoked.

Surfcasting offers great angling options to people who hanker for a land-based adventure and now with the popularity of kite fishing, lines can be taken great distances offshore and huge fish landed straight onto the beach. The other thing about surfcasting that appeals (as well as being the ideal treatment for sea sickness) is getting there. The journey along such stretches of beach as that between Woodhill Forest and the Kaipara Harbour is brathtakingly beautiful, a wild ride into good fishing with the roar of the surf ever present and fresh air an intoxicating accmpaniment.

Casting for distance is not required when you become a "rock hopper" and fish places like Great Barrier and the Coromandel

Peninsula. Remember that advice about fishing the last couple of hours on an outgoing tide and using plenty of burley. Well in that case the advice is "fish your feet first" as big snapper and kingfish amble right up to your feet.

I am very fond of the odd surfcasting foray, it sometimes produces fish of staggering proportions.

Our second January 95 episode was also built around the Kaipara Harbour, a place that I had long wanted to venture onto but had never got around to.

"Kaipara Snapper Hunter" guide Peter Grooby had called up and followed the phone chat with a delivery of smoked kingfish.

"When are you coming out, Sinclair? Plenty more fish where the smoked bits come from. About time you filmed a decent show about kingfish."

It was like throwing down the gauntlet and here was a guy who knew the harbour, its endless channels and mud flats.

"Biggest harbour in the southern hemisphere", Pete said, "and one of the most treacherous if you don't know where you're going."

Two wagon loads of us and a boat turned up at the rendezvous in Helensville to the tune of driving rain.

Off we went to Pete and Trish's place for a brew while the weather coughed, spluttered and finally eased. What had initially looked disappointing was now looking like a day of promise. We launched in the 'fiver' behind the Helensville headquarters of the Kaipara fishing club and threaded our way down the mud-brown meandering channel that at some obscure point became the Kaipara Harbour. The wind had all but eased but grey columns of rain cloud dropped their bundle here and there. We hit the throttles and roared out into this vast harbour, navigable for over 100 kilometres from near Dargaville in the north to Helensville in the south. Mud flats and mangroves which, before the kauri craze, late last century and into this, would have been surrounded by magnificent forest.

Now my house and thousands of others are where most of the Kaipara kauri is buried. The old timers talk about the boatloads of fish they used to drag out of the place, and in the same breath complain about overfishing, but by today's standards Kaipara angling is still pretty darn good.

We ate up about 50 kilometres of channels and started jigging where the harbour narrows towards the entrance.

There was a discernible breeze here and a vast volume of water trying to push itself into the ocean with an outgoing tide. It forced itself into pressure waves. "This is the spot", said Pete, throttling back in the middle of nowhere, just the coloured clutter on his sounder showing that there were fish under the keel.

"Here, try this."

A Penn 45GLS and matching rod were passed my way and on the end was 300 grams of silver chrome-plated jig. The thing that really caught my attention was the 400 lb leader extending from the jig about a metre up the line. Catch my attention is an understatement,

*Mullet netted out of the surf
en route to the Kaipara.*

I was incredulous. Whenever I jig I use as light a leader as possible,
usually fluoro-carbon so that it is virtually invisible, or tie the jig
straight onto the main line.

Remember that fishing is like hunting, we are trying to fool the fish
into believing that what is presented is a natural-looking imitation.
Four hundred pound leader is like hanging up a thick obvious sign
saying "danger, danger".

Peter read my mind. "You think I'm stupid using that stuff."

I guess I raised my eyebrows a bit. "It's written all over your face.
Now watch this." Wind was whipping us across the harbour, line
snaked out at an angle of about 45 degrees. It didn't look good. I also
like to jig as close to vertical as possible so that the jig drops
perpendicular straight under the rod tip. It ensures that when you lift
the rod up and drop the tip quickly the jig flutters to the bottom
looking like a wounded bait fish. Aha, say the kingfish, and other
suitably fooled foe, it's time for a nose bag. Dinner is served and
chomp, they get a mouthful of chrome and hooks.

Pete spooled out his jig, cranked the drag up and wound like
'stink'. At this point the line was pointing straight out the stern.

"Don't look so worried", laughed the man who had begun to wind like hell.

Whack, over went the rod.

"Hah, hah, kingfish. Didn't I tell you. Hey, start winding you silly bugger."

I needed no encouragement, took a couple of cranks and whallop, something of angling note screamed off into the depths, feeling very much like a kingfish. We had another boat in attendance and two of the three anglers on her were attached to several kilos of hard work.

"Bit of all right this", yelled Ross Hunter across the waves.

Pete doesn't muck around and used his considerable bulk and a lot of drag pressure to wrestle fish to the boat.

In came the first kingfish, right to the boat and our guide leant over, grabbed the heavy leader and just hauled the fish over the side.

"Don't need to use a gaff or worry about fish going under the boat and busting off. When I get hold of that heavy leader, they're coming in."

A large ruddy-faced, tattooed gentleman smiled a crooked smile and slapped me on the back.

"What do you think of my jig system now. Even buggers like you learn something new every day."

The wind eased again and blue holes appeared in the sky. We all had a ball and although I still believe in sneaking up on fish and disguising things as much as possible, Pete's system made no difference to the Kaipara kingis, in fact life is made easy when you just drag them over the side.

"Another thing about that leader", added Pete, "is that the school sharks don't keep biting them off. We get a lot of sharks out here and if the wind would stay away I'd burley up a bronze whaler and give you some serious sport."

For the third time the wind came away and rain squalls fought to plug the blue holes that were fading in the sky.

Wind waves added to those jostling in the current and it was time to head home. We had kept a kingfish each and let a dozen or more go.

My first excursion on the Kaipara, rather than surfcasting its fringe, had proved to be superb and as we smashed our way through a short chop back to Helensville, I already had a hankering to go back. Believe it or not, it is something I am yet to do.

Back at the boat ramp the tide had gone out. We could only get the trailer a certain distance down the ramp before it was sucked into the ooze.

"This is what helps to keep people off the harbour. Unless you come in at high tide it's mud wrestling time." Mud wrestling it turned out to be with thick gluggy mud reaching to mid-thigh as we heaved and pushed our boats back onto their trailers. What a mess, but the thing I remember most is the kingfish.

Ten to 20 kilos of kingi with a voracious appetite is a sure recipe for an awesome afternoon of angling.

The week after the Kaipara we were involved in an intriguing event organised by one of the marine magazines. A chap named Mike Rose had arranged a bit of a challenge on the Waitemata Harbour. Two large, almost identical, Salthouse launches of about 50 feet were to set sail with two teams, one per boat, with the objective being to outfish, outthink and dare I say it, outcheat the other guy.

Mike told me to get a team together and he had done the same.

On 24th January we set off towards the Firth of Thames and Coromandel Peninsula. Mike Rose, with a crew that included Sean Fitzpatrick, the All Black captain and G. Sinclair with a crew that included a bunch of people out to have fun and my dive buddy for the day, Ian "Grizz" Miller.

Our skipper was a very social chap named Peter Jones who did whatever was in his power to make our day as pleasant as possible. The other guys were under the command of a chap who owned a boat called *Silver Bear*.

The day was "one out of the box", overcast but beautifully calm once we got near the tip of the Coromandel.

Each boat also had a chef on board, ours from Al & Petes Takeaways, famous for their toasted sandwiches and theirs, a very sharp gourmet chef from a fine restaurant called Ramses. At the end of the day we were to meet and based on what we had caught or otherwise captured, have a serious sort of cook-up.

We felt a little bit handicapped in the culinary department but the serious part of the challenge was the competition to see which team was the better provider.

Silver Bear and team veered off into the Firth of Thames. They had one television crew on board and we another. Unknown to us at the time, the *Silver Bear* captain was taking the competition very seriously and was telling everyone how well he knew the Hauraki Gulf and what a virtual guarantee of success that was. I get to edit all of the television footage and it is amazing what was recorded on *Silver Bear*. Added to the skipper's confidence was a longline and secret crayfish diving spot.

The old boy knew where he was going and how it was going to be done. Sean and the team were along for the ride and to dive down and gather crayfish from the secret larder. We, on the other hand, dangled a line here and there, caught a few small snapper and had a lot of laughs.

"Time for a dive", said Grizz, about lunchtime when we were tucked under the tip of the Coromandel staring longingly at Channel Island. "Looks pretty calm and those boulders where the crays usually are could be worth a look."

"Last time I dived here was a couple of weeks ago", he added, "and there were a lot of good kinigs swimming around about 20-30 kilos. Might have to go and shove a spear in one."

Grizz and I both like our spearfishing and in terms of most desirable target, kingfish are up there on the top of the list.

We thought it logical that the incredibly knowledgeable, well-prepared *Silver Bear* team would have employed the services of a diver with a speargun, just for a little insurance. But oh no, Sean and his buddy were purely there for the crays, although one of them did find a solitary scallop.

Out to Channel Island we went and what a sight, the water was calm and ink blue. "Visibility has to be better than 20 metres". I suggested to my buddy as we piled into wetsuits, turned on air and readied ourselves for a fantastic dive.

We had left from Westhaven Marina, which is downtown Auckland, and now a stone's throw away Grizz and I were angling down the face of Channel Island and onto a couple of boulders at 40 metres.

The visibility wasn't 20 metres, it was more like 30 and from quite a distance away from the first rock I could see crayfish feelers, dozens of them. The culinary delicacy was in residence and ready to be plucked. We went to work, grabbed a dozen, including a couple about 2.5 kilos, and left a few hundred wondering where their mates had gone.

With a good number of crays in the catch bag I looked up to see a dozen huge silver missiles zooming in for a close look at the crayfish, hunting intruders.

Unfortunately for them they are curious and also unfortunately their inquisitive nature dragged them too close to a couple of spearguns. I took aim at point blank range on a fish about 30 kilos, squeezed the trigger and nothing happened. My compressed air gun that had been so reliable for so long decided to get temperamental at exactly the wrong time.

"Thomp" came a sound from over my left shoulder and I turned to see Grizz attached to 20 kilos of fish. Our guns have reels of heavy nylon chord attached and once you fire a shot, if you haven't killed the fish outright, all hell can break loose. 20 kilos or more of kingfish can be a serious handful. The shot Grizz fired was good. We aim just behind the gill plates right on the yellow line, two thirds of the way up the body. Hit that zone and quite often you'll smack a vertebrae out of the way – end of story.

While Grizz fought to control the kingi the others circled around us and all I could do was stare in frustration but what a beautiful sight. Large sleek silver beasts, some nearer 40 kilos than 30, glided around then finally slipped away into the gloom.

We were on our way back to the surface, the hull of our floating home plainly visible on the surface high above. Grizz and I exchanged glances, in spite of masks covering our faces and regulators in our mouths, it was clear that both of us were acknowledging a superb dive.

On the surface our team gathered around the stern to help us with weight belts and dive tanks.

"Will you look at that", said Clint, as Grizz heaved the kingfish onto the duck board. "What a beauty. I'd like to see the other guys beat that." About then two catch bags loaded with crays also hit the duck board and our crew were briefly shell shocked.

Russell Fisk was first to break the silence.

"It must be pretty bloody good down there. You've only been gone about ten minutes. If you guys are going to have a second dive, I'm coming with you", he added, staring at the booty.

It was the best dive I've had on Channel Island and I have been there pretty regularly, for quite a long time.

Were we going to have a second dive? – too bloody right!!

"I'm going to call up the other guys and tell them to come over. It's so good that Sean and other divers won't want to miss this", I said. "I know it's a competition but it's not often you get diving this good."

So we radioed *Silver Bear* and there was no way the skipper was going to leave his productive spot with the one scallop and small snapper. We pleaded with them, told them the diving was superb and the crays everywhere. Maybe we laid it on a bit thick but the skipper, who knew better, was certainly not heading our way.

"Oh well", said Grizz, "if Russell wants to dive, we'd better go and get six more crays and have a go at another kingfish."

We fished for an hour and a half, making sure that we had an adequate surface interval before dive two, caught a few more pan-sized snapper and a couple of kahawai. The ocean remained clear and calm, Channel Island reared out of the sea and hovered above us. Hovering too were a variety of birds, gliding on silent wings, setting off in search of their own tasty morsels from the deep.

I filmed our second dive, too the underwater camera on a dive that allows viewers to share a little of the thrill which accompanies a dive in beautiful conditions. Three of us splashed onto a second favourite spot and a sea of crayfish feelers greeted us once again. A large clump of boulders covered in anemones and soft corals were the

Surfcasting the Kaipara – popular in the weekend but if you sneak down mid week you usually have the place to yourself – just a stone's throw from Auckland.

crayfish housing estate. Once again the kingfish came racing in for an inspection tour and once again, "Thomp" Grizz buried a spear in another 20 kilos of kingfish. This time the shot was not as good and after a heck of a scrap the kingi dragged itself free.

I filmed the arrival of the fish, the shot, the escape, huge fish that continued to cruise, gathering crayfish and on the way back to the surface a cloud of smaller kingfish that enveloped me in their school.

Our second dive was as spectacular as the first. All of us were elated when the gear was packed away and a course set for our culinary rendezvous.

We pulled up stern to stern so the captures could be laid out and quite frankly, we knew within seconds that we had nailed them.

As soon as they saw the tail of that kingfish sticking out of the live bait tank their faces fell.

"Hmm", said Mike Rose, "I think they caught a bigger fish than us."

"Well, where are all these crayfish you kept crowing about?" asked their skipper. Grizz just reached into the live bait tank and dragged out first one, then a second 2.5 kilo crayfish.

"Will that do you for a start, mate?" enquired my dive buddy.

"Bugger", said Sean, "we got ourselves a couple of small crays and one scallop."

A dark cloud descended on the *Silver Bear* captain, he was not a happy camper. When it came to cooking, our opposition with their gourmet chef outshone us, producing a heck of a feast with a lot of stuff they had purchased before leaving the marina. In the final analysis we had experienced a great day, felt a little disappointed that we didn't get to share a great dive with Sean, but when we stepped onto the marina and headed home, all of our team had fresh crayfish for the dinner table.

Our team was declared the winner of "The Ultimate Seafood Challenge" – an event that took place just a stone's throw from Auckland.